THIS BOOK BELONGS TO

_____

ANCIENT CIVILIZATIONS OF THE WORLD: MESOPOTAMIA, EGYPT, GREECE, AND ROME

A *Fun* Homeschooling History Curriculum For Kids!

Part of The Insightful Scholar History Curriculum Series

BY
THE INSIGHTFUL SCHOLAR

ISBN 979-8-9870786-0-0 (print)
ISBN 979-8-9870786-1-7 (ebook)
ISBN 979-8-9870786-2-4 (audio)

theinsightfulscholar.com

About This Book

The scope of this book focuses on Mesopotamia and the Mediterranean regions due to the volume of information covered. However, we explore other ancient civilizations around the world in other books.

Our reading book, workbook, and journal follow the same topics and are intended to complement each other. Students can also use the internet, library books, and videos to assist in their research.

We provide several valuable additional free resources, which you can access at theinsightfulscholar.com.

These resources include:

- Parent-Teacher Guide (includes answers to workbook questions)
- Bibliography with additional references
- Color images with citations
- Glossary
- Timeline (fill-in)

This book contains black and white line drawings of the color images provided as a free download. Many images are either photographs of actual artifacts or drawings or paintings of actual artifacts. As a result, some of these images are anatomically correct. Please consider this when choosing to purchase this product.

The target age of this book is 10 and up. However it is meant to be read and enjoyed as a family. Some of the reading material may be challenging for students. It is recommended, as with all of our educational resources, that parents be on-hand to provide support and assistance whenever necessary. Our extensive additional resources, such as the glossary, index, and audiobook version of the text are also there to help.

Table of Contents

A Note to Parents-Teachers

When you write, you are supposed to envision your audience. For me, that was easy. I pictured my daughters, who are, most likely, around the age of your children. I imagined snuggling with them on the sofa, or sharing tea and cookies around the kitchen table, and reading the stories of Alexander the Great and his horse Bucephalus or Julius Caesar, captured by pirates. These are some of the stories that inspired my deep love of history as a child. I sincerely hope your child finds a story in this book that they will remember fondly years from now.

This is also the wish of the creators of The Insightful Scholar. They have undertaken the enormous and noble task of developing a series of books for homeschoolers that is fun, academic, engaging, and substantive. They are lifelong learners who desire to champion parents everywhere to be involved in their children's education and never stop discovering. In the name of fun and engagement, this book was written in a conversational style. We wholeheartedly embrace beginning sentences with conjunctions. Shocking, I know!

This book is not just for homeschoolers. We hope it will be used by any parent wanting to give their child knowledge of and an appreciation for ancient history and provide perspective on why studying history is essential. Use it in your curriculum or as a supplement. Hand it to your kid for rainy-day reading. Share it as a family read-aloud. History has gotten a bad rap for being dry and dull. We think it deserves to be read as the fascinating, important, sometimes even hilarious subject it is!

I am a second-generation homeschooler, writer, and writing instructor. History has always held a special place in our home. I knew I had passed on my passion when my now-11-year-old was four and demanded that I read to her every library book on ancient Egypt that her small arms could carry home. We've laughed over how impossibly heavy our model of a Roman road turned out and how our Minecraft pyramid replicas went tragically wrong. We will forever cherish our history adventures, and I wish you many similar moments of connection as you read along with your child and explore the activities accompanying this book.

Happy reading!

Vida Mercer
Lead Author at The Insightful Scholar

Introduction

Hi! I'm Pavi.

And I'm Piper! We will guide you throughout this book as you explore different ancient civilizations.

We'll meet some interesting people, witness major historical events, and learn about the day-to-day lives of the people who made these civilizations some of the greatest on earth.

Along the way, we will share fun and exciting facts and help you focus on important information by summarizing each chapter's main points in the Historical Highlights section. Let's begin by finding out more about history itself!

What *is* history, really? At first glance, you might think this is a silly question. History is the study of the past: who did what and when and where it happened. That's all true! But history is also so much more.

History is a story, like a pick-your-own-adventure story. It's a lens you look through to understand where you are now, how you got here, and where you might be going in the future. History is happening now. History even *changes*. Don't believe us? Stick around and see for yourself!

Now, you may be shaking your head at this point. How can history be all of these things? Well, to answer that, let's investigate *how* we know what happened so long ago.

How Do We Know About History?

Have you ever written a letter to your grandparents or a report about your summer vacation? Do you keep a journal? I'll bet you've at least had your picture taken.

Did you know you have recorded history if you've done any of these things?

Documents or other recordings people leave behind are one of the main ways **historians**, people who study history, learn about what happened so long ago. When we examine ancient history, these "documents" might be carvings on stone pillars or marks made in clay tablets and hardened in the sun. Or they might be scrolls written in ink that somehow survived over the centuries. A thousand years from now, historians will be reading e-books and Tweets and watching TikTok to learn about what life must have been like in the early 2000s!

Herodotus, a Greek who lived almost 2,500 years ago, was called the "Father of History." He was the first person that we know of who thought that writing down big events, like battles and descriptions of different cultures, would be a good idea. He wanted to preserve these things for future generations. So, he traveled all over Europe, Asia Minor, and Northern Africa—an area roughly the size of the continental United States—to observe and record. This was in a time when a boat or a camel was "quick" transportation! Okay, he wasn't the greatest historian that ever lived. He was known to insert some of his own opinions or record things he heard as if he had actually been there. But, hey, he was really onto something! We have Herodotus to thank for much of what we know about the ancient world.

We also know about history from **archaeologists**, people who excavate sites and examine **artifacts**. An artifact is anything a person makes, but that word typically refers to something culturally or historically significant. Some artifacts discovered from ancient history include tools, pottery, art, jewelry, clothing, children's toys, and even game board pieces. Have you ever lost a flip-flop in the mud while you waded in the creek or accidentally left a toy car behind while playing in the sand? Well, you may have left an artifact for future archaeologists to wonder over! What do you think they might guess about you and your life from the artifacts they find?

Sometimes, we learn about history through **oral traditions** passed down from generation to generation. When your parents tell you the story of the day you were born or what it was like to go to school when *they* were a kid, these are oral traditions. Before writing was a thing, creating stories, songs, or poetry about your culture's most glorious moments and then teaching them to your children was the only way people had to pass on their history. Often, these stories were embellished to make them a bit more glorious than they actually were. Once writing was developed, some of these oral traditions were written down in the form of epic adventure tales complete with heroes, villains, and monsters—ancient comic books, if you will. These became some of the world's first literature!

Putting Together the Pieces

So, by understanding *how* we know about history, we can see what history really *is*. Let's investigate this.

If you like mysteries or detective stories, you may *love* to study history! History is always a puzzle with missing pieces, and sometimes *many* of those pieces are missing. Documents and artifacts are not always found complete, and even when they are, we have to figure them out. Languages need to be translated, and artifacts must be identified. Sometimes we find new puzzle pieces later and have to see where they fit in and how they contribute to the picture.

Sometimes, the puzzle pieces we *do* have paint a picture that was never entirely accurate. As mentioned earlier, oral traditions were frequently exaggerated into myth and legend. For example, monsters were added, or the triumphs of several kings were combined into the story of one. *The Epic of Gilgamesh* is a story considered to be the world's first piece of literature. It is a series of tales about a Mesopotamian king written down roughly 3,500 to 4,000 years ago, but it existed as an oral tradition long before that. In the stories, **King Gilgamesh** possessed superhero-like abilities and embarked on so many quests that he should have his own video game series. The line between reality and fantasy was more than blurred. But that didn't stop later Mesopotamian kings from associating their names with him to impress the people. This would be something like our president saying their cousin was Superman—far-fetched, to say the least, but a creative way to be popular!

Nevertheless, this lack of accuracy in oral tradition is not a bad thing. The weavers of these stories were not trying to be accurate. They were spinning a tale of how they see their place in the universe, usually *based* on actual events and real people. We can learn a lot about them by studying both the facts and the fiction.

History is also full of flawed assumptions and misconceptions that persist over time. Do you think Cleopatra was Egyptian? Most people do, yet this Queen of Egypt was descended from Greeks.

As we now understand, **Christopher Columbus** didn't "discover" America. Evidence suggests that Native people called the Americas home for at least 15,000 years before his expedition arrived! The "New World" doesn't seem all that new anymore, does it? This is an excellent illustration of how history changes. What actually happened doesn't change, but what we know about it, how we see it and feel about it, *does*.

History is about **perspective** or the way you see something. Have you ever looked through colored sunglasses? Maybe they made the world look like a brilliant amber color or a rosy pink. Well, history is both recorded and read through a lens like this. For example, Christopher Columbus thought he had landed in Asia instead of the Americas. When Europeans discovered this mistake, they wrote of Columbus's great "discovery" of the "New World." They may have had a lens that said something like: "This is a new piece of land that has been found. What an amazing discovery we have made for our benefit!" Now, think back to those sunglasses for a second. What would life be like if you didn't know you were wearing them? Would you believe the world was just that color? So, how would the story of Columbus's landing in the Caribbean be different if the Native Americans wrote it? As you can probably guess, they would have had a very different lens.

Let's bring this a little bit closer to home. Imagine that you are writing a report about a recent family vacation. By now, you know this is actually a form of recording history. It's not possible to include every detail of every minute of your holiday. Which events would you choose, and which ones would you leave out? Would you be tempted to exaggerate how brave you were on the zip line? Would you leave out the boring part where it rained all day, and you never left the cabin? How might someone's perception of your vacation change based on how you wrote it? How much of the puzzle will you give, and through what lens? Even the most objective reporters of history still have a perspective.

History is a story (It even has the word "story" in it!). When we study history, one of the most exciting questions is, *"Whose* story is this?" Many documents and artifacts from ancient civilizations tell us stories about their kings (and sometimes their queens), their military (especially the battles they won), and their wealthy and educated people. Less often do you see the stories of everyday people, women, children, or enslaved people. This leaves us to wonder what life was like for them. Unfortunately, there are far fewer puzzle pieces to show us that.

If your job was to write the future history of today, whose stories would you tell? It's tempting to say, "Everyone's!" But is that possible? Would it be more important to focus on politics or wars? Religion or education? What about climate change or social media? There is no right or wrong answer. The choice is yours! The point here is that our picture of history is always, in some way or another, incomplete. It is always someone's story and *not* someone else's.

What Are We Going to Learn in This Book?

So, now that you know how fabulous history is and how we know about it let's look ahead to what we will find in this book. As you know, this book is about ancient history. More specifically, it's about the civilizations of Mesopotamia, Egypt, Greece, and Rome (plus a few of their neighbors) during the years we refer to as ancient history.

So *when* exactly was "ancient" history? (Insert joke about your parents' childhood here.) Naturally, historians have different opinions about when this period begins and ends. For our purposes, we will start at the time tribes of humans began to gather together and form **civilizations** (around 10,000 BCE), and we will end with the fall of the Western Roman Empire (476 CE).

This looks like a good time to talk about dates. The dating system we use today is a bit like the number line that you've probably used in math. The years run both forward and backward from Year 1. Year 1 and all the years after it are in the Common Era (abbreviated CE). These are like positive numbers on the number line. Years before Year 1 run backward, like negative numbers on a number line. These years are Before the Common Era (abbreviated BCE). There is no Year 0.

So, if we are talking about dates that are BCE, the numbers count down as you approach Year 1 just like negative numbers do as you approach 0. For example, 499 BCE is closer to the present than 1499 BCE. Today, it is the year 2022 CE. This means we are two thousand twenty-two years into the Common Era. If we are going back to 10,000 BCE, that was 12,022 years ago.

Different cultures, even today, count their years in different ways. Our Year 1 was chosen by the early Christian Church to represent the year of Jesus's birth, although we don't know precisely when that was. Sometimes, in different resources, you will see years referred to as AD or BC. These stand for *"Anno Domini,"* Latin for "Year of Our Lord," which is the same as the Common Era, and "Before Christ," which is the same as Before the Common Era. The years for both systems are the same, only the names are different.

As long as we're on the topic of dates, there are a couple more abbreviations you should be familiar with. When you see a small c (c.) beside a date that means *"circa,"* Latin for "around." This means the date is an approximation. A small r (r.) next to a date indicates they are years of someone's reign.

Now, back to what we'll cover in this book! We will learn about what makes a group of people a civilization, how they rise, *and* what causes them to collapse. Then, as we look at individual societies, we'll explore several things like:

- how they came to exist,
- what made them unique,
- how they fit into their world,
- what contributions they left for future civilizations, and
- what happened to them in the end?

We'll meet some of the key players in the world at that time. We'll also learn funny, fascinating, and surprising facts about these distant cousins of ours. Like did you know that ancient Egyptians had pets? And not just cats and dogs—exotic pets like baboons and gazelles! It was even common to find mummified pets alongside their departed owners so that they could join them in the afterlife. True BFFs! Or would you believe that the ancient Romans loved board games? They had versions of dice, chess, checkers, backgammon, and tic-tac-toe. They also loved a game similar to jacks called knucklebones that was played with—you guessed it—the bones of animals. Now, how do you *not* want to know more about these people?

Why Should We Care About History Anyway?

So, besides learning how to play knucklebones, why is history important? You've probably heard that understanding past civilizations is the key to understanding our own. This is very true. Our governments, languages, laws, and cultures are some form of a hand-me-down from history. We have Mesopotamia to thank for our 24-hour day, Rome for our system of government, and Greece for magnificent sculpture! By some estimates, English-speaking people owe about 150,000 words to the Greek language. About 80% of our words have Latin bases.

Studying history also helps us foresee (and perhaps control) where our civilization is headed. First, we learn why and how societies develop, change, and sometimes crash and burn. Then, we can recognize these patterns around us and, hopefully, use our voices and efforts to take the off-ramp when we're headed toward a cliff.

Studying individual people can be just as helpful as studying entire civilizations. History is full of real-life superheroes and some pretty bad villains. But, you will also find the inspiring stories of ordinary people—like us—who lived remarkable lives. They can help us be our best selves and avoid past mistakes.

Understanding history deepens our appreciation of diversity as we study people from different cultures, races, and time periods. These were not cavemen grunting around a fire. Instead, these civilizations had a surprising amount of knowledge, wisdom, and technology. The Greek astronomer Eratosthenes had accurately calculated the circumference of the Earth over 2,200 years ago!

Knowing our history also lets us participate fully in our society because we are well-informed and educated citizens.

These are all excellent reasons to study history, but *none* of them are why *you* should care. Why? Because these reasons are a bit like telling kids they should eat vegetables because they'll appreciate it when they're older.

You should care about history because history is *your* story. It's how you got to where you are today. It's the giant 3D puzzle of the world, of which you are a piece. The people we will learn about in this book looked up at the same moon you do and wondered about many of the same questions. How did we get here? What does the future hold? What is my place in the world? History has already answered these questions for them. So, let's read their stories to understand more about the story you're writing for yourself, shall we?

CHAPTER 1

Becoming Civilized

We are on a journey to meet some ancient civilizations! The word "civilized" means "at an advanced stage of social and cultural development." Civilizations are groups of people who have reached this advanced stage. But this word can be misleading because it sounds like "uncivilized" people who lived in pre-civilization societies didn't have things like culture and technology. Nothing could be further from the truth! So, before we jump into what civilization is, let's understand how we came to have them and what came before civilizations.

Our Stone Age Ancestors

Do pictures of cavemen in leopard skins with stone axes or wooden clubs come to mind when you think of the Stone Age? If so, you're not alone. But these would be **stereotypes**. The Stone Age refers to a period of thousands of years where people worked with tools made primarily of stone. Nevertheless, these pre-civilization humans and their societies were actually quite sophisticated.

Another common Stone Age stereotype is that early humans coexisted with dinosaurs. While small mammals *were* around when giant reptiles roamed the earth, 65 million years passed between the extinction of the dinosaurs and the first humans. One caveat is that scientists now believe some types of dinosaurs survive today in the form of birds!

Historians and archaeologists divide the Stone Age into Paleolithic, Mesolithic, and Neolithic periods. **Paleolithic** (*paleo* meaning "old" and *lithic* meaning "having to do with stone") means the Old Stone Age. Scientists date some of the earliest stone tools we have found to 2,600,000 BCE! That was a really, *really* long time ago.

Sometime around 12,000 BCE, about the time the last **Ice Age** ended, humans entered the Middle Stone Age or **Mesolithic** era. This relatively short time in history was a transition period when people adapted to their changing world. For example, they developed more complex tools to deal with new challenges like clearing the rapidly growing vegetation that was popping up everywhere in the warmer climate.

The development of **agriculture** is considered the dividing line between the Mesolithic and the **Neolithic** periods or New Stone Age. When, precisely, this occurred depended on where you were in the world. In the Middle East, where people first began farming, this happened at lightning speed after the Ice Age ended. They had almost no Mesolithic period and jumped straight to being Neolithic around 10,000 to 9,000 BCE. In other areas, such as Northern Europe, Mesolithic cultures persisted for a few thousand more years. They didn't begin farming until around 4,000 BCE.

The Stone Age finally ended when someone learned that you could melt metal and fashion it into tools and weapons, ushering in the **Bronze Age** in about 3,000 BCE.

In total, the Stone Age lasted for about 2,597,000 years. This means that for 99% of our human history with technology, stone was where it was at! This says a couple of things.

First, we did pretty well for a really long time, getting by with nothing but stone tools (including surviving some pretty gnarly ice ages). Secondly, it shows the break-neck speed with which we have developed technology since.

Want a better picture of this? Imagine a football field 300 feet long. This represents our entire human history using technology, from the first stone tool until now. Only the last 36 inches of that football field is our history *since* the Stone Age. Wheels, rope, metal swords, cannons, umbrellas, bicycles, record players, cars, cell phones—every bit of technology since 3,000 BCE fits into that last 36 inches. The rest of the field? It was stone tools for us!

We will begin our story at this momentous dividing line between the Mesolithic and Neolithic periods (around 10,000 BCE), this place in time where farming makes its debut on the world stage. This critical crossroads in human history laid the foundation for civilizations. But, to understand this, we first need a better picture of what life was like *before* agriculture, so we can see how much it really changed.

From Foragers to Farmers

Let's say you're a child in the late Mesolithic era. Your family would be what all families were in the early to middle Stone Age, **hunter-gatherers**. You may live with just your own extended family: your parents, siblings, grandparents, aunts, uncles, and cousins. Or your tribe may have nearly 100 people, all distantly related in some way. But you would never live in a group much larger than that. Why? Because your way of life doesn't support massive groups of people.

As the name "hunter-gatherer" suggests, you get the food and everything else you need by hunting animals and gathering whatever is useful in the area around you. Of course, precisely what and how you hunt and gather depends on where you live. You may track deer with spears or a bow and arrows. You might trap large game, like bison, by herding them off of cliffs. Your mother may send you to collect shellfish from the mud of a nearby bay. Together, your family would forage for seeds, nuts, berries, insects, and other favorite foods of the season.

Yet, no matter where you live and what you eat, one thing remains the same—you need to move around a lot. This is because hunting and foraging quickly exhaust the resources in the area. Animals migrate and hibernate. Nuts and berries are only found at certain times of the year. Moving around to access different food sources is essential to survival. And the more people you have in your group, the faster you will use up the food in an area.

People who live in temporary settlements and frequently move to follow food sources are called **nomads**. Now, most Stone Age nomads didn't move to a brand-new place every time they moved. More likely, they traveled in a kind of circuit, having different settlements at different times of the year that they returned to again and again. Archaeologists believe this loop of seasonal settlements opened the door for farming and, eventually, cities and civilizations.

Depending on the size of the group and their location, scientists estimate that a nomadic hunter-gatherer community needed between seven and 500 square miles of land to support themselves. To put this into perspective, 500 square miles is roughly the size of the entire metropolitan area of Los Angeles, California. That's for one tribe or family group!

Imagine that one of the chores you're assigned as a nomadic child is to gather the wild cereal grains that grow by the stream next to your late-summer home. You pick them and place them in a woven basket. Before you can grind them between stones into flour, you must separate the edible grain kernel from the inedible chaff surrounding it. You spread the grains on a woven mat and beat them with **reeds** to separate the seed from the chaff. This technique is called **threshing**. Then, you carefully blow and fan away the paper-thin chaff, a process called **winnowing**. Finally, you collect the edible kernels left behind.

This grain you've gathered is essential to your family. It will feed your household for the next three days. But, no matter how careful you are, some of the grain inevitably spills onto the dirt next to your mat.

This small oversight begins what is known as the **Neolithic Revolution**, a term that Australian archaeologist, **Gordon Childe**, used to refer to the immense changes agriculture brought about. Archaeologists now think the term "revolution" is a bit strong. People did not turn from nomads into city dwellers overnight. Yet, there is no doubt that when societies began to farm, they were set on a path of gradual changes that led to the rise of civilizations.

Several months later, when your family group returns to this settlement, you notice that grain has sprouted next to your threshing and winnowing spot. Each time you visit this spot, there are more and more wild grain stalks growing. Eventually, there is so much grain here that you don't have to walk down to the stream to gather it anymore. Instead, when it is ripe, you can pick it right then. And then, you have an idea! What if you took some of your family's precious grain and planted it on purpose?

Neolithic people had the perfect combination of advancing technology and climate conditions to develop farming. As the last ice age came to a close, mild climates and abundant water increased vegetation growth. More forests, tall grasses, and thick bushes meant that people needed to develop more tools to clear their living spaces. These became the first hoes, shovels, and other farming tools of their kind.

When people began cultivating grain at one of their campsites, they stayed longer in that area to tend to it. And they *could* stay longer because the grain provided a more reliable food source. As a result, nomads who frequently traveled among many camps transitioned to become semi-nomadic, staying in fewer camps for longer.

As social groups did this, their living accommodations became more permanent. In some places, structures of mud bricks replaced tents of animal skins. Of course, you can't have a lot when you carry everything you own. But as nomads settled down, they could accumulate more possessions, so having more furniture, dishes, and even decorative items was now possible!

This period is also where we see the beginning of the domestication of animals. For instance, evidence shows that people in modern-day Syria ate wild sheep and eventually domesticated them. Raising animals near home provided families with a stable source of meat, milk, and animal skins. It also eliminated the need to wander nomadically, following herds of wild animals.

One technology used by early farmers that has stood the test of time is the **shaduf**. This ingenious device raises water out of a river and into a field or irrigation ditch. The simple design connects a long pole mounted in the middle like a seesaw, with a weight on one end and a bucket on the other. This design is so handy that it is still used in Egypt and India as it has been for thousands of years.

Shaduf

Pottery also made an appearance at this time, and that was huge! At first, pottery was baked in a plain old fire. But as people stayed in one spot and learned how to build ovens out of bricks, they also discovered that they could control the temperature of these ovens and make larger, stronger pottery that held liquids. Storing food was almost as revolutionary as growing food. Instead of grinding grain into flour and mixing it with water for porridge to eat that night, you could bake bread that would last far longer or store your grain in jars for months. This meant that in colder climates, you could feed your family through the winter, even when not a single stalk of grain was growing outside.

The more food you could store, the more stable and dependable your life became. You could live in one place now. And your parents could build a larger home to keep your fine pottery filled with grain. Your aunts and uncles could, too. In fact, land that used to only support your immediate family could now feed many more. Your family had more children. When those children grew up, they stayed and built homes of their own rather than leaving to start another tribe. Soon, you had a whole little village.

All of this took place over hundreds, even thousands of years, but you get the idea. Farming touched off a series of changes to how people lived like a spark to gunpowder, and this resulted in civilizations.

One of our best examples of a Neolithic settlement is the remains of a town called **Catal Huyuk** in modern-day Türkiye (Turkey). This important archeological site dates back to between 6,700 and 5,600 BCE, giving us a fascinating glimpse of life during the dawn of civilizations.

Catal Huyuk

In Catal Huyuk, people lived in mud brick homes that connected together. These homes had entrances on the roof where people would climb in and out with a wooden ladder. Since the houses were all crammed together, there were no streets within the village. Instead, residents simply got around by walking over their neighbors' roofs.

Each home had a hearth and oven, plus separate spaces for sleeping and working. Artifacts tell us they cultivated grains, nuts, and seeds and probably kept domesticated animals. There are also religious buildings with beautiful wall paintings. Each family's grave site was under the floor of their home, so their ancestors were always close at hand.

From Communities to Civilizations

As farming societies grew, several important things happened that would change simple villages into entire civilizations of people living in massive cities. Let's explore how and why this happened.

What Makes A Civilization?

Now, we should circle back to what civilization is. This is one of those questions like, "What is history?" that we rarely think about, but it's definitely worth doing so!

As we discussed at the beginning of the chapter, a civilization is a society that has reached an advanced stage. Still, it is more than that—much more. **Civilizations** have specific characteristics. And while archaeologists and historians don't always agree on the exact attributes, here are some important ones:

- People in civilizations live in urban areas with large population centers—in other words, cities. (Although, many people live in the country, too.)

- There are shared methods of communication like spoken and written languages, symbols, and numeric systems.
- Civilizations build monuments and create unique artistic or architectural styles to preserve their culture for future generations.
- Civilizations have **infrastructures** that serve the common good like roads, water systems, or community food storage.
- Some form of **administration** or government is used, such as laws and punishments for crimes. Additionally, kings, governors, military members, and priests fill different roles to do the administering.
- Speaking of priests—religion was a hallmark of early civilizations, giving people a shared identity and purpose.
- Class structure is another element of civilizations. People are typically divided into classes or hierarchies, usually with a king or ruler at the top and ordinary people or slaves at the bottom.
- There is **division of labor** in civilizations. People specialize in doing different jobs. This allows large populations to be supported and technology to advance.

Every time we explore a civilization in this book, we notice each element. Some civilizations tend to exhibit more of these elements than others. You will see how different societies express each element in different ways, such as in their writing or laws, but they will all have each of them in some way. Let's look at each component in more detail and how it sprang up from the humble beginnings of farming.

This is a good opportunity to talk about the difference between a culture and a civilization. The word "civilization," as we have just seen, means an advanced stage of human society that includes many different elements, part of which is their culture. "Culture" refers to the collective, or whole, way of living that is common to a particular people, including things like their language, religion, food, and family structure. Even a society that has not achieved the rank of civilization can still have a culture. These words are very similar and are often used interchangeably. Just remember that *civilization* refers to an advanced stage in human society while *culture* refers to its collective parts.

Urban Areas

In our thought experiment, where we imagined ourselves to be nomadic children, we saw how a stable food source led to settling down in one place and an increase in population. Over time, tribes became villages, which became entire cities.

The city of **Jericho** near the **Dead Sea** in the eastern Mediterranean region takes the prize for the oldest city wall. By about 8,000 BCE, Jericho boasted a colossal stone wall surrounding the settlement and at least one giant stone tower. By 7,000 BCE, they had the largest population of any city in the world—around 2,000 people! Interestingly, the spot is considered the oldest continually occupied site in the world, with over 18,000 people living there today.

Shared Communication

People living in the same civilization had shared methods of communication. Usually, this was a spoken language, but it could also be numeric systems, symbols, or even writing. This, too, was usually a product of agriculture. For many ancient civilizations, writing grew out of the practical need to keep accurate harvest calendars, food storage, and trade records.

Relief of Ramesses

One of the most well-known examples of ancient writing is Egyptian hieroglyphics. In this complex picture writing, what they mean and how they appear are not always the same. Instead, a picture might represent a sound, much like our alphabet. Or, sometimes they represent an idea or concept—simple right? Not really!

Monuments, Art, and Architecture

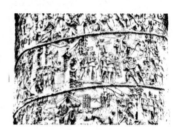

Trajen's Column

Civilizations in ancient days, just like now, looked for ways to stand out from the crowd. They wanted to preserve their greatness for future generations, inspire their citizens' and visitors' awe and respect, and keep their gods happy. Monuments and distinctive art and architectural styles were how they did this. Identity was everything!

The ancient Romans were masters of art and used it as **propaganda**, displaying images to promote their point of view in a day when not everyone could read. When Roman emperors wanted to brag about their war **conquests**, one of their favorite things to do was put up a column or an arch wrapped with carvings that told the story of their heroic victories. This was an ancient news broadcast if you will.

Infrastructure

Speaking of the Romans, they created one of the best-known and longest-lasting examples of ancient infrastructure: their roads. Rome saw the value of being able to move its large army around the empire quickly and efficiently. To do this, they built a network of roads, many of which would long outlast the kingdom itself. So if you lived in a town conquered by the Romans, one of the first things you got was upgraded roads.

These roads had several things in common with modern highways. They were made as straight and level as possible with a foundation, curbs, and sloping sides that whisked away water to drainage ditches. Many of them came with gravel pedestrian paths along the sides and grooves for cartwheels to roll in. And they worked! Soldiers could march over 20 miles a day on these wondrous roads. Infrastructure like this ensured Rome could communicate, take care of business, and defend itself.

Administration or Government

People discovered that the more they started living together in groups, the more problems seemed to pop up, and they needed some way to sort them out. Civilizations required systems of administration or government to handle everything from commanding the army to levying taxes, punishing crimes, and handling contract disputes.

One king from the Mesopotamian city of Babylon, **Hammurabi,** had a very forward-thinking solution for administering justice. In 1771 BCE, he organized laws for every possible crime or dispute. He had the laws and their appropriate punishments carved on a stone pillar in a place where everyone could see them. Some of his methods would raise eyebrows nowadays, for example, putting an architect to death if his house collapsed and killed someone. But the **Code of Hammurabi** itself was actually a significant step forward in administration for civilizations. It was the idea that everyone should know the laws and that they should be the same for everyone.

Religion

Every ancient civilization had religion in some form, although their beliefs, gods and goddesses, and ways of worshiping varied widely. Religion, then as now, gave people a way of making sense of their world. Religion could explain things people didn't understand: day and night, seasons, storms, comets, or diseases. It also provided a comforting sense of control over the unknown. Religious offerings could be made in thanks for a bountiful harvest or to secure one in the future. People felt they were in charge of their destiny by performing certain rituals to guarantee a happy eternal home. One example is the Egyptians' ritual of **embalming** and **mummifying** a dead body to preserve it for the journey to the afterlife.

Most ancient religions of these times were **polytheistic.** People worshipped more than one god. Some civilizations were **monotheistic** and worshiped only one god. Many believed that their gods specialized in various areas of life, the way we have doctors today who specialize in different parts of the body. The Greeks had gods and goddesses for everything from war (Ares) to sheep (Pan).

Class Structure

As civilizations became more complex, a hierarchy or class structure developed. Most class structures resemble a pyramid shape—a few powerful people at the very top and many people with little or no power at the bottom.

In Western society today, we see this in the wealthy, the middle class, and the poor. However, in ancient times, this pyramid often had many more tiers. For example, in Egypt, there was a single king or pharaoh; then his court, priests, scribes, and local rulers; followed by the military, skilled artisans, and supervisors; then farmers; and finally, slaves at the bottom.

Division of Labor

In a hunter-gatherer society, almost every single person, from small children to tribal elders, was involved in obtaining food. As farmers became better at their job, it took fewer of them to grow and harvest the food the community needed. Soon, only a handful of people were required to cultivate more food than the community could use. The natural result of this was something called division of labor.

If not everyone was needed to work in the fields, the people who were good at making tools worked on making more tools. The more time they devoted to that, the better they got at it. Soon, some people were well-known for their tool-making. And the farmers—who needed the tools—were more than happy to trade the food they were growing for the tools they needed. Pottery, woven fabric, home building—soon, everyone had a specialization. Finally, technology improved, and **craftsmen** and **artisans** were born!

How Civilizations Thrived and Expanded

Four elements of a civilization determined how much and for how long the society would grow and flourish. These were trade, conquest, and exploration plus innovation.

Trade

Food surpluses and finely crafted goods meant that an up-and-coming civilization had things to offer the ancient world in exchange for things it didn't have. Ancient Egypt is a prime example of this. Their fertile land, thanks to the annual flooding of the **Nile River**, gave them enough grain to store for hard times plus extra to trade. And the Nile was the gift that kept on giving because it offered an easy transportation highway to send and receive goods. Boats full of grain were dispatched to places like Lebanon and returned with much-needed wood, or **Nubia** (modern-day Sudan), in exchange for ivory. You were powerful if you had resources that other nations needed or wanted. Trade enabled Egypt to become a force to be reckoned with in the ancient world.

Conquest

War was another factor that helped determine the success or failure of a civilization. The more resources you had, the more you needed a strong fighting force to protect you from jealous neighbors. Or maybe *you* were the jealous neighbor. Early civilizations found themselves in frequent conflicts due to border disputes, control of transportation routes, access to natural resources, or simply the giant egos of their rulers.

One such emperor, the humbly-named **Sargon the Great**, ruled in Mesopotamia around 2,300 BCE. Through persistent conquest, he expanded his empire from the **Persian Gulf** to the Mediterranean Sea. Yet, even once he had consolidated all this land under his rule, he could only hold onto it by constantly putting down uprisings and fighting off outside invaders. Conflict could be a route to greatness, but it was also a lot of work.

Exploration and Innovation

A spirit of adventure and creativity was the final factor that civilizations needed to grow and survive. Societies that explored their corner of the world or developed new and better technology tended to thrive more and develop faster than their introverted neighbors who were content with yesterday's wheel. The ancient Greeks, in particular, valued thought, invention, and discovery. They were constantly coming up with new theories and ideas and applying them to solve everyday problems. Some ancient Greek inventions were:

- a portable sundial,
- an alarm clock operated by dripping water,
- an odometer that could measure distances over land, and
- a flamethrower.

Yes, ancient Greeks had flamethrowers! Need we say more?

Why Civilizations Fizzled and Fell

Civilizations don't fall or collapse for just one reason. In fact, "fall" might be another misleading word. It makes you think of a sudden and catastrophic event. In reality, most civilizations did something more like a fizzle—a campfire put out slowly by a thousand raindrops. Usually, a combination of several factors and many events gradually weakened a civilization's bonds over time. These bonds are those shared elements we learned about that hold a culture together, and as they crumbled, the civilization crumbled, too.

There are exceptions to this "fizzle rather than fall" rule. Archaeologists have found evidence of mysterious "lost civilizations" that appeared to thrive until they suddenly ceased to exist. The Maya in Central America and the settlements on Easter Island in the Pacific Ocean are two examples. Although the declines of these civilizations were sudden and left many questions, the reasons for them were no different than for other societies—it just happened a lot faster!

Problems that weaken a civilization typically come from one (or more) of three places: the environment, internally, or externally. To make things even more confusing, these problems often overlap.

Environmental Difficulties

Environmental causes of civilization collapse are the simplest to identify and understand. Drought, earthquakes, floods—all pretty devastating to ancient civilizations that depended on agriculture and built cities out of stone and mud. These problems could wreak havoc slowly, like when farmland is ruined by several years of not enough rain, or quickly, tsunami-style.

And an environmental problem often opens the door for the next type of trouble:

Internal Issues

Problems like to pop up from inside the civilization itself. Just a few examples are disease, famine, and poor leadership. Once these problems grow large enough to disrupt the elements that hold a culture together, collapse usually isn't far behind.

Let's say that your city and its surrounding fields are struck by several years of devastating drought (an environmental problem). If your city had prospered by trading extra food, this would be one of the first things to suffer since there would be no surplus food to sell or trade. Anything your city used to get by trading food, maybe wood to build buildings and spices to offer to your gods, could not be obtained anymore. No new buildings and no happy gods. Uh-oh. Religious rituals grind to a halt. So do building projects like shoring up the local infrastructure.

But then, there's an even bigger problem. Not only is there no food to trade, but food to eat is also getting low. Families begin leaving villages, searching for a home with more food and fewer people to eat it up. Pretty soon, the division of labor breaks down. The baker leaves. Oh, well. There's no grain for bread anyway. Then, the sheepherder takes their flocks to find suitable grazing elsewhere. Now, there's no meat either. Without any meat, there is no work for a butcher. So he goes, too. Your once glorious urban city is falling into disrepair *and* becoming a ghost town.

Sounds like the perfect setup for the next type of civilization-destroying problem.

Outside Aggressors

Ancient civilizations faced a constant threat of invasion. Some lived in almost unending war with their neighbors, and even those who didn't usually had to spend massive amounts of resources protecting their borders.

If a civilization was already suffering from internal problems, it was often an invader who toppled the last domino. These invasions seemed to be the final straw for the great Roman Empire. After a long decline due to increasing problems of every sort, invaders practically walked in and took over.

Eventually, all of the civilizations we will read about in this book fell victim to a combination of these problems. They were weakened by earthquakes, storms, and disease. They were fractured by incompetent rulers or breakdowns in the fabric of society. Finally, they were conquered by or absorbed into neighboring civilizations. Yet, the irony is that they all still survive. Our modern civilizations stand on the foundation that these ancient ones have laid, and their contributions to us are without number and beyond value.

Wonder While You Wander

Before we dive into our first civilization, Mesopotamia, let's look at a few of the awe-inspiring structures from the ancient world that we still marvel over today.

In 225 BCE, a man named **Philo** wrote a book called *On the Seven Wonders*. The book was a travel guide of sorts; listing the seven sites he considered *thémata* (Greek for "things to be seen") around the world at the time. His ancient must-see list included some unbelievably awesome structures, to be sure. These were modern (for their day) masterpieces of architecture, engineering, and art!

His list has remained famous ever since, even while people debate it. It doesn't include jaw-dropping achievements that were not in the Mediterranean region, like the Great Wall of China, or some pretty impressive structures built shortly after, like the Colosseum in Rome. Scholars debate whether one of his must-see sites ever existed at all. Here is Philo's list. What do you think?

1. **The Great Pyramid at Giza**
   This pyramid held the title of the tallest building in the world for more than 4,000 years until the 19th century! It is also the only one on this list that still exists today. It no longer has its blindingly-white limestone exterior or its gold cap on the top, but it is still a wonder to behold.

Great Pyramid at Giza

Hanging Gardens of Babylon

2. The Hanging Gardens of Babylon

The king of Babylon supposedly built these terraced gardens to remind his queen of the lush hillsides of her homeland. The problem? No first-hand accounts of these gardens exist. Instead, everyone seems to be writing about the beautiful gardens someone else claimed to see. So, today, scholars think this Wonder may be a mix of fact and fiction.

3. The Statue of Zeus at Olympia

You could find Zeus's temple in Olympia, the site of the ancient Olympic Games. Nearly scraping the ceiling of his temple, this 40-foot statue of Zeus, the king of the Greek gods, was decked in ivory and gold. After Christians shut down the pagan games, the statue was carted away to Constantinople and was eventually destroyed in a fire.

Statue of Zeus at Olympia

Temple of Artemis at Ephesus

4. The Temple of Artemis at Ephesus

This temple to the Greek goddess of the hunt, Artemis, consisted of marble steps leading up to a 400-foot-long terrace. This was surrounded by 127 marble columns that towered 60 feet overhead. It was deliberately set on fire in the 4th century BCE, rebuilt, partially destroyed by the invading **Ostrogoths** in 262 CE, rebuilt again, and finally torn down by a Christian mob in 401 CE.

5. The Mausoleum at Halicarnassus

Today, "mausoleum" means "a special building made to hold the dead body of an important person or the dead bodies of a family." This word comes from King Mausolus of Carnia. After he died in 353/352 BCE, his wife ordered the construction of a tomb as his final resting place. The tomb resembles a stepped pyramid on top of a temple and a hefty tower. In the 13th century, an earthquake destroyed most of it, and it was recycled as building material for a castle.

Mausoleum at Halicarnassus

6. The Colossus of Rhodes

This statue certainly lives up to its name. It was truly colossal! The towering sculpture of the sun god **Helios** was said to be 100 feet high—the tallest statue in the ancient world. Although many paintings show the statue straddling the harbor at Rhodes, most scholars now believe he stood beside it. He didn't stand for long, though. An earthquake toppled his statue after only 60 years, but his wreckage was a tourist attraction for hundreds of years after that. That is until the **Arabs** invaded and hauled it off for scrap metal.

Colossus of Rhodes

7. The Lighthouse of Alexandria

In 280 BCE, the port of Alexandria was a bustling place, so its 350-foot-tall lighthouse was both an important and impressive piece of architecture. The light stood at the top of a cylindrical tower, on top of an octagonal tower, on top of a square base. Archaeologists know this from pictures engraved on coins from the time period. Unfortunately, the actual lighthouse fell into the Mediterranean Sea thanks to multiple earthquakes.

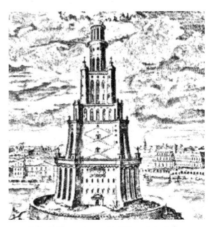

Lighthouse at Alexandria

Whether you agree with Philo or not that these seven ancient structures were the most wonderful, two things are true. First, these human creations show the exceptional intelligence, ingenuity, and technological advancement that ancient civilizations possessed, and second, it is a shame that we can only visit one of these wonders today.

Historical Highlights

Grab your journal, let's go!

We will finish up each chapter by highlighting some of the biggest takeaways. Read them over, copy them in your notebook, jot them in your journal—whatever strikes your fancy. Just know, these are the key points to remember:

- Civilizations grew out of nomadic hunter-gatherer societies mainly due to the advancement of agriculture.
- Civilizations have common elements such as communication, division of labor, infrastructure, religion, government or administration, and urban areas.
- Once established, civilizations grew and thrived due to trade, conquest, exploration, and innovation.
- Civilizations fall due to a combination of problems that fit into one or more of three categories: environmental, internal, and external.

Now, we are ready to explore our first ancient civilization, and the best place to begin is at the beginning. Civilizations started in an area known as Mesopotamia, so our next chapter takes us there in the year 5,000 BCE.

CHAPTER 2

The Sumerians

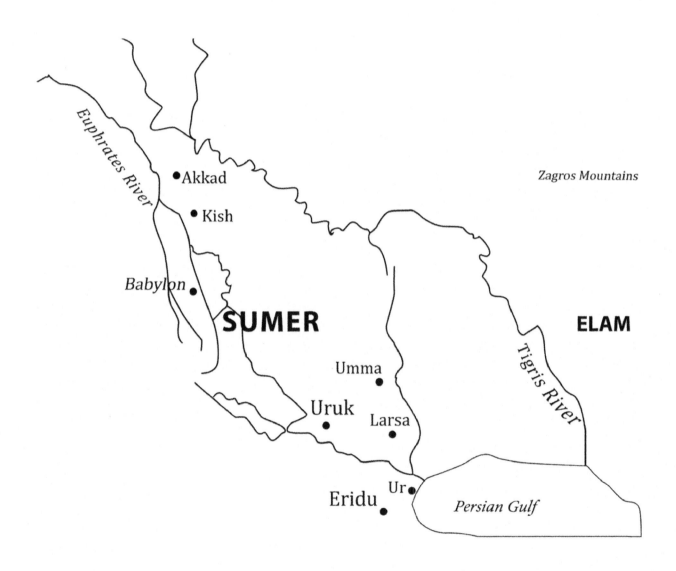

Euphrates River

● Akkad

● Kish

Babylon ●

SUMER

Umma
●

Uruk
●

Larsa
●

Zagros Mountains

Tigris River

ELAM

Ur ●

Eridu
●

Persian Gulf

Here we are in **Mesopotamia** in 5,000 BCE (just over 7,000 years ago). We should probably look around and get the lay of the land first. Let's start with the big picture and then zoom in.

If you look at a map of the Middle East in Southwestern Asia, you will see that you can draw an arch between the **Mediterranean Sea** and the Persian Gulf. This arch will begin in modern-day Türkiye (Turkey) or Lebanon and travel through Syria, Iraq, and Kuwait. This arch includes the **Tigris** and **Euphrates** rivers, which empty into the Persian Gulf. This area—literally a crescent shape—is called the **Fertile Crescent** because, in ancient times, it had a wet and fertile climate, one so favorable to agriculture that this was where farming first developed.

Now, let's take a step closer and zoom in on those vital rivers, the Tigris and Euphrates. Mesopotamia is the part of the Fertile Crescent that is in between those rivers. In fact, Mesopotamia means "between the rivers" (*meso*—between or in the middle of; *potamos*—river). Sometimes, Mesopotamia is called the **Cradle of Civilization** because it is where the first true civilizations sprang up, thanks to—as you now know—agriculture.

If *potamos* means "river" in Greek, what does hippopotamus mean? Well, literally, it means "river horse" (*hippo*—horse). So, if *hippo* is "horse," do you know what a hippodrome is? I'll give you a hint. *Dromos* means "course," like a racecourse. So, a hippodrome was an ancient performance venue for horse and chariot racing. These Greek word origins are a fantastic example of how ancient civilizations contribute to our own today! But we're getting off *dromos*. Back to Mesopotamia!

So, now, we know where we are, "between the two rivers." When we talk about Mesopotamia, we usually separate the northern and southern parts. This is because each area had a different climate, different types of land, and different resources. So civilizations developed slightly differently in the north than in the south. The northern part, or Upper Mesopotamia, was a land known as **Akkad**. We'll return to the **Akkadians** later, but they're worth mentioning now because they gave the southern part of Mesopotamia its name. The Akkadians called it **Sumer** or "land of the civilized kings," which is a pretty nice compliment if you think about it. So, our journey takes us, first, to Sumer, "between the two rivers" and close to the Persian Gulf.

The Rise Of Sumer

In Sumer during this time, the land was marshy, quite unlike the desert it is today. These wetlands full of reeds provided lots of game to hunt. The rivers also had predictable flooding cycles every year that kept the land fertile and made it easy to irrigate. This is one of the reasons civilization first developed here. Water was so easy to access that it didn't take very many people to irrigate entire fields for farming.

The **Sumerians** formed the first civilization in the world. It lasted from approximately 5000 to 1750 BCE, and, in those 3,250 years, they achieved incredible advancements in technology and culture *and* racked up a long list of world firsts! So, before diving into their timeline, let's look at some of these impressive accomplishments.

Inventions And Achievements

Sumerians were innovators in all the different areas required for a civilization: language, math, engineering, architecture, government, law, trade—the list goes on. They achieved so many important "firsts" that it's hard to choose one top accomplishment. What do you think?

Sumerians are credited with being the first to:
- build a city,
- use a wheel,
- have a calendar,
- create items with copper and bronze,
- use a formal system of mathematics,
- write literature, love songs, and lullabies (or anything at all for that matter),
- mass produce bricks with a mold and pottery with a potter's wheel,
- use a plow,
- create fabric in a factory-like textile mill,
- have schools,
- use **hydraulic** (water-powered) engineering.

And we could keep going! Experts say that the overachieving Sumerians might have been driven by what they *didn't* have. Because they lived in a land without many trees, stone, or metal, they were forced to be innovative with their resources, like clay.

Oh, but since we're going to talk about Sumer, there is one more innovation we should look at in more detail—writing.

Cuneiform—The First Writing

Historians believe that sometime between 3500 and 3300 BCE, writing evolved from a need to keep track of everyone's offerings to their local temple. This started as a form of picture writing. For example, a bull's head symbolized an animal sacrifice, and an ear of grain represented a unit of barley. Sumerians were very good at using the resources around them, so they wrote on tablets of wet clay with a pen, called a **stylus**, cut from a reed. If they needed to record something temporarily, the wet clay could be smoothed out and used again. If the writing was important, they could bake it, which would last a very long time. This was a durable way to write, but books were large, heavy, and difficult to transport until the Egyptians developed paper and ink sometime later.

As the temple authorities wrote quicker, their pictures started to look more like shapes. Finally, their writing became wedge-shaped symbols instead of images. Historians call the Sumerian form of writing **cuneiform**, which means "wedge-shaped."

Cuneiform

By about 3100 BCE, Sumerians learned that a symbol could stand for a sound rather than just an object. This marked the beginning of a true alphabet where words could be written from combinations of phonetic sounds. As a result, Sumerians could spell words and convey complex emotions or abstract thoughts, not just concrete ideas. At this point, the number of symbols they used dropped from about 1,000 symbols for things to only 600 characters for sounds.

Still, an alphabet of 600 characters is not exactly simple! Not everyone in Sumer could read and write—not even close. Early writers were the temple priests who tracked the people's offerings, and eventually, writing became a career all its own. Wealthy families could send their sons to special schools where they would train to become a **scribe**, a person whose job was to read and write for others. Scribes were used by everyone, from kings and priests to everyday people who needed a letter written or a receipt for beer. (The world's first receipt for the sale of beer comes from Mesopotamia.) Being a scribe was a highly honored position.

Much of what we know about Sumerian culture comes from tablets discovered in scribe schools. The teacher would write a lesson on one side of the tablet, and the student would practice copying it on the back. These lessons were often descriptions of everyday life, offering a unique insight into their culture.

Once the Sumerians could write anything they wanted with symbols for sounds, they decided this writing business was a pretty great thing. So, they used it! They wrote literature, hymns, poems, histories, battle accounts, spells, letters, laws, lists, recipes, business documents, and reports of daily life—pretty much any type of writing you can think of. Thanks to the Sumerians' love of writing and to the dedicated historians who learned to translate it, we know so much about the world's first civilization that might have been lost to history.

Class Structure

By the time Sumerian life reached true civilization status, their society had shifted itself into the hierarchy shape we will find in every other civilization after.

At the top of this hierarchy was the king or **lugal**. These rulers were viewed as the link between gods and goddesses and the people. If the gods favored the king, his city would prosper, and his borders would expand—an excellent motivation for a king to try to expand his territory.

Next came the priests and priestesses. They administered the day-to-day aspects of religious life by collecting and offering sacrifices, interpreting signs and omens, and presiding over religious festivals. They were also the first doctors and dentists and served as healers to the public. Since they were the literate elite, they recorded the vast amount of writing involved with religious duties.

Then came the Sumerian upper class. These were the aristocrats or wealthy members of society. They included scribes, prosperous merchants and landowners, private tutors, astrologers (who may have also been priests), and high-ranking military members.

The lower or working class did the jobs that actually kept the city running. These were your bakers, basket weavers, brick makers, home builders, farmers, fishermen, potters, and chariot drivers.

Slaves occupied the bottom tier of the social hierarchy. Slaves were:
- prisoners of war,
- kidnapped from foreign places,
- sold into slavery to pay a debt, or
- sold as punishment for a crime.

Depending on their skills, slaves might do various jobs, such as tutoring children, crafting fine jewelry, or working in the fields.

It was possible to climb the ladder of society in Sumer. Slaves could eventually purchase their freedom. Lower-class tradespeople could, through great skill, become wealthy business owners. Records show that the only woman recorded as "king" started as a tavern keeper.

Everyday Life

Let's take a look at what everyday life would be like if you were growing up in Sumer.

Early homes in this marshy part of Mesopotamia were made from reeds bundled together. By the time cities came about, most homes were made from mud bricks mixed with straw and baked or sundried. A house was a series of rooms that opened into a central courtyard. This also helped to let in light since windows were rare. Sumerians thought rooms that opened into each other were bad luck, but rooms that opened to the outdoors were good luck.

A ladder would usually lead to the roof where your family might sleep when the weather was hot. If your family was wealthy, the bedrooms might be on a second story; however, average families would have a single-story home. The courtyard was the center of your family's life. Your household—consisting of your parents, siblings, and maybe other close family members or slaves—would work, play, and eat there.

27

In your Sumerian home, you would have a reception room, bathroom, kitchen, bedroom, and a shrine where your family worshiped. The reception room is where visitors would be entertained and also sleep. Bathrooms had a drain to let waste water run out, and the kitchen had a fireplace, oven, and cooking utensils.

Sumerians ate a wide variety of foods. They hunted game in the marshes, caught fish from the rivers, and domesticated livestock for milk, meat, wool, and labor. Since cows were too valuable as work animals to eat, meat came from goats, sheep, or pigs. In addition to grain made into bread and porridge, they grew vegetables and fruit. So, if you were Sumerian, your diet would include cucumbers, lettuce, leeks, onions, figs, dates, lentils, chickpeas, beans, and more. And everyone, even children, drank a form of beer flavored with honey and dates.

Lyre

Families gathering for dinner seems to be a tradition as old as families themselves. Just like today, entertainment was often a part of the evening meal. Without TV, this usually involved singing, storytelling, or playing instruments like drums, flutes, or **lyres**.

Men and women wore full-length, short-sleeved tunics made from wool or woven from flax, a type of plant. Sumerians added many decorative touches to their wardrobe, like fringes and brightly dyed embroidery. They would accessorize with jewelry, like heavy gold earrings, bracelets, and necklaces. Men might dye and curl their long beards. For their feet, leather sandals were the norm.

Girls were taught all the skills needed to be wives and mothers, such as grinding grain, cooking, and weaving cloth. With rare exceptions, they were not taught to read or write. Despite this fact, women in Mesopotamia enjoyed almost equal rights with men. They could own and inherit property and hold jobs. Women became priestesses, entertainers, tavern keepers, beer brewers, and more. They were also the first doctors and dentists in Sumer. Women enjoyed this relative equality until the decline of the Sumerian civilization when we began to see their freedoms erode, and they were placed in a lower social class than men.

The life of a Sumerian boy would depend on his family. Boys from working-class families would spend the day helping their fathers and learning their family's trade. Wealthy families sent their boys to school where they would learn to read, write, and study mathematics, science, and history.

As a Sumerian child, you would have plenty of toys, some similar to ones you might have today. Babies had rattles to shake made from clay and filled with pellets. Girls had dolls and miniature furniture. Boys had slingshots and bows and arrows. There were small wheeled carts, model animals, carved boats, and even board games.

The fact that Sumerian families enjoyed so many material possessions, decorative items, and ways to spend their leisure time tells us a lot about their civilization. Suppose a city is barely scraping by, trying to feed its people and fend off attacks from other cities. In that case, they do not have the time or resources to develop this rich and luxurious lifestyle. Overall, Sumer was probably not a horrible place to grow up, except maybe during a couple of shaky periods, as we will soon see.

Religion

The importance of religion to the Sumerians cannot be overstated. Mesopotamians believed that gods and goddesses with human forms and personality traits controlled nature and had the power to curse or favor humankind. In fact, they believed humans were created to be co-workers with the gods, laboring for and with them to establish order in the world and care for the gods' needs. In exchange for honoring the gods, humans would be rewarded with things like bountiful harvests, rain in the dry season, and beer, which was considered a gift directly from the deities. On the other hand, if the gods were not appropriately honored, they might send natural disasters or allow evil spirits to take over.

Sumerians maintained their religion through myths and legends handed down, first through oral tradition, then committed to writing. The gods and goddesses were a favorite topic for scribes, who wrote poems, hymns, spells, and stories for and about them. One notable hymn to **Ninkasi**, the goddess of beer, accompanies a recipe for the beloved drink. The earliest discovered musical notation was also a hymn written in cuneiform around 1400 BCE. (See the Bibliography for a link to listen to it!)

The temple was at the literal and figurative center of every city. However, over time, this was not just a single building but an entire complex in the heart of the city. The temple complex included **shrines** to the gods, the priests' homes, storehouses for offerings, workshops, scribe schools, and more. The centerpiece of this complex was the **ziggurat**, a stepped-pyramid structure built for the city's main god or goddess. It would have been visible for miles in the otherwise flat landscape. Each city dedicated itself to a single deity who protected it, although they also worshiped other gods.

Unlike Egyptian pyramids, ziggurats had no internal chambers. Instead, there was a shrine on top where the god or goddess lived in the form of a statue. This statue was fed twice a day, dressed, and even taken out for walks. Cities would parade their statues around during festivals, carry them to battle, and even take them to visit the gods of neighboring towns. At least one foreign visitor was not so sure about all of this pomp and circumstance. Herodotus, the world's first historian who we met in the Introduction, once visited a Sumerian city. A priest told him that the bed on top of the ziggurat was where their god slept each night, and Herodotus later wrote, "I do not believe them."

Art and Architecture

As we learned, having a unique style of art and architecture is one of the marks of a civilization. It sets your little corner of the world apart from the rest, and Sumer was no different. They were the first to create large, imposing architectural forms like the ziggurat. Sumerians decorated with terracotta, were skilled in casting with bronze, and created complicated mosaics and elaborate wall murals. But they were, perhaps, best known for their relief carvings in stone. For their day, these carvings were surprisingly realistic.

Ziggurat

Sumerian Relief

Sumerian Time Periods

Life in the Mesopotamian region from 5000 to 1750 BCE can be divided into several general periods. Let's look at how each unfolded and led to the one after.

The Ubaid Period – 5000-4100 BCE

The Ubaid Period gets its name from a place called **Tell al-`Ubaid** in modern-day Iraq, where archaeologists first uncovered the remains of human settlements from this time. During this period, there were no great cities yet. Instead, people lived in small farming villages without walls. These early farmers irrigated their flat, marshy fields with help from the nearby rivers, and they cultivated grain crops like wheat and barley.

In archeological terms, a **tell** (sometimes spelled **tel**) means a raised mound that shows where a civilization used to be. In ancient times, buildings were typically made of mud or clay bricks. When they crumbled, people would just level off the area and build a new structure right on top of the old one. Over time, towns or cities grew into a hill shape with steep sides and a flat top. In fact, "tell" means "hill" in Arabic. When archaeologists excavate these tells, it's like peeling back the pages of history. Each new layer of rubble is a journey further back in time as you dig down. This can be an incredible way to see how a civilization developed over time and discover when certain technologies came into use!

The first temples in Mesopotamia make their appearance during the Ubaid Period. Temples were plain at first—rectangular buildings of one room with an offering table and an altar. They seemed to have been raised on a terrace, maybe to protect them from flooding.

Archaeologists believe this terrace design developed, over time, into the ziggurats we see in the same area a few thousand years later. So, as more and more families began to cluster around these temple locations, villages began to grow into small **temple cities**.

Artifacts from the Ubaid Period tell us that this was when copper tools began to replace stone ones. Later, Mesopotamians would become masters at metalworking. Archaeologists have also found significant amounts of pottery from the Ubaid Period, which tells us much about their culture. Pieces found from this period seem to have been made on a pottery wheel. Most vessels were painted in dark geometric shapes, sometimes with floral or animal designs. They often had looped handles and spouts—another historical first! What does this mean about the people who lived in these farming temple cities? Well, we can tell they were resourceful and good at using the materials around them, like clay and mud. It also seems they were good at making life easier by finding better ways of doing things. We can also tell they were creative and cared about adding decorative touches to their possessions. As we shall see, they would build on these talents in the next period.

The Uruk Period – 4100-2900 BCE

Real cities were born as the temple villages of the Ubaid Period grew and grew. This happened first in the Sumer region of Mesopotamia, with examples like **Uruk**, **Eridu**, **Kish**, and **Ur**. So which city was the very first one? We're not sure. Many experts think it was Uruk, while some say it was Eridu or Ur. Sumerian mythology says that Eridu was the first city, but that wasn't the most likely choice, as we'll see later.

Does it really matter, though? The entire Mesopotamian region grew into a bustling collection of metropolises fueled by the Tigris and Euphrates Rivers, which allowed the cities to trade efficiently with those far away. Remember, trade is one of those three essential factors that would enable a civilization to grow and flourish.

Mesopotamia was, in fact, the most urban and densely populated area of the world at that time. In around 2300 BCE, Uruk was home to about 50,000 people! That's almost the size of modern-day Carson City, Nevada. No wonder Uruk dominated the Mesopotamian region, and this period is named for it.

These were exciting times! Imagine being one of the first people to ever experience city life. Urban areas, as we learned, are another one of those fundamental necessities of a civilization, and they were a brand new thing.

Let's take a moment to ponder this occasion in history. It is the beginning of something you probably take for granted every day—what it means to be from somewhere. For tens of thousands of years, people didn't identify with a place. You came from your people. It was your ancestors that defined your group identity. This is why many ancient writings contain long lists of fathers and forefathers. "Who are you from?" would have been the question, not "Where are you from?" Then, as permanent cities formed and were given names, suddenly, it meant something to be from a place.

These early cities in Sumer grew more complex and developed their own unique cultures. These cities consisted of:
- a central temple dedicated to the worship of the local gods,
- a bustling urban area surrounding the temple,
- a defensive wall that marked the boundary between city and country life, plus
- a large area of farmland surrounding the city with many villages outside the city wall.

Sumer was not a unified nation of different cities as we think of countries today. Instead, it was a collection of independent cities that might trade or go to war, depending on the moment's needs. This type of structure is known as a city-state—a single large city with its own political, religious, and cultural identity that controls the surrounding territory.

The Uruk Period saw the rise of these city-states in Sumer along with the administrative jobs needed to run them. The most important of these jobs was the position of king or lugal (literally "big man"). But let's step back a moment.

Before *lugals* came on the scene, the temple priests were the only authority figures in the city. The rest of the people were relatively equal in status and wealth. The high priest's job was to organize community life in a way that provided for the needs of the city's gods and goddesses. This involved collecting and sacrificing offerings to the gods and managing the large areas of land owned by the temple and the people who worked that land. In return— it was hoped—the gods and goddesses would reward the people with bountiful harvests and fertile livestock.

As cities turned into city-states, there was competition for land and resources. Some "households" (more like a close community than a single family) began accumulating more land and wealth than others. A class of **aristocrats**, wealthy landowners, formed that rivaled the wealth and power of the temple. Since these wealthy households had many servants to work their land for them, the household leader or "big man" could devote his time to other things—like fighting wars. As each *lugal* sought to claim more and more land to farm, they frequently became involved in border conflicts with households from neighboring city-states.

When a *lugal* went out to fight, he would take members of his household and servants with him—a tiny personal army, if you will. But, suppose a certain *lugal* won a reputation for being particularly bold and victorious. In that case, he might be chosen to lead the entire city-state in skirmishes with neighbors.

This commander-in-chief status was temporary at first, lasting only while the city-state was at war. But as wars became more and more frequent, *lugals* retained power for longer and longer periods of time. Eventually, the word "*lugal*" took on the meaning of "king," and by about 3600 BCE the position became that of permanent head-of-state.

One way for a *lugal* to increase his power and authority was to confiscate large land areas and dedicate them to a god or goddess. This *lugal* would then oversee the land for the gods in a kind of **stewardship**. In this way, he could limit the power and influence of the temple. At the same time, he established himself as an important link between the earthly and the divine. Eventually, this link was fused. The people accepted that it was the *lugal's* job to perform the will of the gods on earth. We will see this theme again in other civilizations. Enter the Early Dynastic Period.

The Early Dynastic Period – 2900-2334 BCE

By 2900 BCE, there was a collection of city-states and kings in Sumer and north in Akkad. There were a series of floods in Mesopotamia during this period. Archaeologists and historians place at least one enormous flood at about 2900 BCE, the dividing line between the Uruk and Early Dynastic Periods. The story of a Great Flood in Sumer, called the **Eridu Genesis**, appears again and again in Mesopotamian literature. Some historians believe it is the basis for the Biblical story of Noah. After this catastrophe, several new cities were established, including Eridu. The **Sumerian King List**, a document dating from 2100 BCE, names Eridu as the city where the gods established the first kingship. This helps explain why Sumerians considered Eridu the first city, even though most historians give that honor to Uruk.

Sumerian King List

The Sumerian King List gives the Early Dynastic Period its name. A **dynasty** is a line of rulers, one after another, belonging to the same family. Sumerians believed there could only be one official kingship on earth at a time. The Sumerian King List lays out a series of kings and their home cities stretching back thousands of years, beginning with a *lugal* named **Alulim** from Eridu.

Alulim supposedly reigned for 28,800 years. He was followed by other kings who ruled for equally impossible lengths of time. This is one example of how fact meets fiction in ancient writings. Some believe its purpose was to show a long and unbroken line between the present rulers of the time and the heroes of the past. Since the Sumerian King List was written in about 2100 BCE (over 230 years *after* the Early Dynasty Period ended), it may tell us just as much about Sumerian **mythology** and how they wanted to be remembered in the world as it does about historical fact.

As we learned earlier, Mesopotamia was not united under a single king at this time—despite what the King List says. In reality, many kings on the Sumerian King List did not rule back-to-back but governed their cities simultaneously. The city-states were independent of each other, each with its own *lugal*. And they traded and warred with each other accordingly. The world's first recorded war occurred during this time (about 2700 BCE) between Sumer and their neighbor to the east, **Elam**, who, like the Akkadians, will make another appearance in this chapter.

The legendary **Gilgamesh** of **Uruk** makes an appearance on the King List. We heard about him back in the Introduction when we learned that the *Epic of Gilgamesh* was thought to be the world's first piece of written literature. Sumerians wrote several copies of this epic adventure story, beginning at around 2100 BCE—about the same time they wrote the King List. Although the story about Gilgamesh's failed quest for immortality is mythical, it was inspired by a real and influential *lugal* whose legend took on a life of its own. This adds credibility to the theory behind the purpose of the King List. If you could link your name with the likes of Gilgamesh—a demigod warrior who defeated mythical beasts—how could you go wrong?

Experts think that the first historically accurate king on the Sumerian King List was a man named **Etana** from the city of **Kish.** According to Sumerian mythology, Etana flew on the back of an eagle up to the heavens to ask the gods to grant him a son. In 2500 BCE, **Kubaba**, also of Kish, became the only female to claim a place on the list. Before she became *lugal*, Kubaba was known as a tavern keeper and brewer of beer. **Lugalzagesi** of the city of **Umma** was the final king of this period. Rather than being content with a single city-state, Lugalzagesi decided to extend his reach, conquering Kish, Ur, Uruk, and eventually all of Sumer. Since all the city-states he defeated were Sumerian, this was more of a **dominion** (an area under the control of a king) than an **empire** (multiple nations or states controlled by a single authority). But he was still the first to unite so much of Mesopotamia under a single command.

During this age of kings, technology that was first developed in the Uruk Period, like writing and wheels, became more sophisticated. Pottery became more decorative. There were children's toys, even wheeled toy carts! And there was also an exciting invention called a **cylinder seal**. As a person about town in Mesopotamia, your cylinder seal was your identification card. You would use it like a signature on official documents. Seals were, as the name suggests, cylinder-shaped and usually carved out of stone. Everyone had one, from kings to slaves, and every person's seal was different. Your seal would be engraved with your unique combination of animals, gods, geometric figures, or writing. If your seal was very nice, it would be carved backward as a mirror image. This way, the designs would appear the right way around when you rolled your seal across wet clay. They were pretty small—three to four inches tall at the most—so that you could wear your seal on a cord around your neck. This way, you had it handy whenever you needed to use it, just like an ID card.

Neo-Sumerian Seal

Akkadian Seal

Despite the occasional war, Sumerian city-states were relatively stable and prosperous places to live in the Early Dynastic Period. This prosperity was thanks to plentiful food and to the structure the organized government gave to society. As a result, trade flourished and technology advanced during this time—as it often does when times are good.

Do you remember when we mentioned the Akkadians, Sumer's northern neighbors, and how we would return to them later? Well, here they come!

The Akkadian Period – 2334-2218 BCE

The Akkadian Period and the city of Akkad begin with Sargon the Great—a man we met briefly in Chapter 1. Legend tells us that Sargon started life in the Sumerian city of Kish. His infancy, as described by a clay tablet called the *Sargon Legend,* closely resembled the Biblical story of Moses. According to this ancient cuneiform biography, Sargon's mother had to hide her infant child. So, she put him in a basket of reeds sealed with tar and set him afloat in the river. A gardener to the king of Kish found him and thus began Sargon's triumphant rise to power from humble beginnings.

Sargon grew up to be a conqueror. Eventually, he would rule all of Mesopotamia as far west as modern-day Lebanon and Türkiye (Turkey), perhaps even farther. In addition to giving himself a new name (Sargon was not his birth name, but a throne name he chose), he either built or restored the northern city of Akkad to be his home base. The Akkadian Empire was born, and this is the first time in history that we see a multi-nation empire ruled by a single conqueror.

Sargon was popular, a real man of the people. There were, now, a lot of wealthy aristocrats around. And the poorer class had formed some resentment against their power. But an ordinary person could relate to Sargon's humble start as the adopted son of a gardener.

Sargon was also a great administrative ruler. Under his reign, technology and the arts flourished. He built roads, increased trade, and appointed trusted men as governors and administrators. He even created the world's first postal system! Clay tablets would be sealed in "envelopes" of clay, marked with the recipient's name and address, and rolled with the sender's cylinder seal. There was no peeking at a letter like that. Only the person it was intended for could break the wrapper and open it. By sending secure messages on his new and efficient roads, Sargon could effectively communicate across his vast empire.

Another significant contribution Sargon left to the world was his daughter, **Enheduanna**. She was the High Priestess at the temple of Inanna in the city of Ur, and this was an important and powerful position. However, she became known to history for something else. Enheduanna is the world's first known author. She was a good writer, too, skilled at writing hymns, poems, and prayers. We know this because her name appears on the earliest documents yet discovered that are signed by their author.

Sargon ruled over the Sumerians for 56 years. Four other Akkadian emperors came after him. The Mesopotamian region thrived during this time, as it had during the Dynastic Period, thanks to the empire's safety and stability. But don't look now! Some of the other neighbors are coming.

The Gutian Period – c. 2218-2047 BCE

At this point in Mesopotamian history, there is about to be another shakeup. Records tell us that nomadic barbarians from the **Zagros Mountains** called the **Gutians** invaded and overthrew the Akkadian Empire.

The Gutians left no written records of their own, so all we know about them comes from Mesopotamian scribes. These scribes were, perhaps, not the most reliable sources of information about the Gutians. They certainly didn't have anything nice to say about them, but we know that the Gutians didn't rule this empire well. Over the next several decades, king followed king in a loose collection of rulers who were never quite able to unite the entire region. The Gutians seemed as willing to sack a city as to rule it, and they are blamed for the general death, destruction, and disorganization of the time. Cultural advances ground to a halt, and some cities, like Sargon's Akkad, seem to disappear from history entirely.

One thing does seem odd, though—how this surly band of raiders could overthrow the Akkadian Empire that had previously defeated more organized enemies. There is some archeological evidence for climate change at this time. One possibility is that the Akkadian Empire was already weakened by drought and famine, and the Gutians just conveniently waltzed in and took advantage of this.

Regardless of how they took over, the Gutian's haphazard and destructive reign lasted only a few generations before **Utu-Hegal**, king of Uruk, began rounding them up and driving them out. **Shulgi**, the king of Ur, finished this job, and Sumer was, once again, controlled by Sumerians.

The Ur III Period – 2047-1750 BCE

Shulgi not only got rid of the Gutians once and for all, but he ushered in a period known as The **Sumerian Renaissance** (also called the Ur III Period). The word renaissance means "rebirth" and is often applied to periods of time where innovations in culture, arts, and technology surge after a period of stagnation. This is a perfect description of this period in Sumer.

After ridding the land of the troublesome Gutians, Shulgi of Ur set about making everything suitable. He was a literate king and valued learning, so he reformed the scribe schools and increased literacy throughout Sumer. He set aside money for maintaining the cities, improving roads, and building new ones. He created the first roadside inns for travelers to rest at. And he stabilized the **economy** by creating a standard system of weights and measures for **commerce**.

Finally, having done all of this good for the people of Sumer, Shulgi thought it was only fitting to declare himself a god. Making someone or something a god or object of worship is called **deification**. Shulgi, always a creative man, searched for a way to solidify his god status among the people, so he chose running. Inscriptions in Shulgi's honor proclaim that in a single day, he ran 100 miles from the city of Nippur to Ur and then the 100 miles back just to preside over the religious festivals in both cities. It's interesting to note that an inscription written *later* also includes the fact that this took place during a fierce storm. Impressive, to be sure, but also suspiciously similar to those stories we've heard from our grandparents about walking five miles to school in three feet of snow. Uphill. Both ways.

No matter whether we believe that this was a fantastic feat of cardio or just a tall tale, it is a fact that Shulgi helped greatly restore Sumerian culture and stability. But, before you knew it, there was trouble with the neighbors again. Nomadic tribes called the **Amorites** were making frequent and annoying raids. And remember the **Elamites** to the east who fought with Sumer back in the world's first recorded war? Well, they were, once again, becoming a threat as well. One of Shulgi's last deeds was to construct a 155-mile-long wall to deal with this problem, but without fortifications at either end, the Amorites decided to just go around it.

Two other much weaker kings of Ur ruled after Shulgi, giving the Ur III Period its name. The Elamites finally invaded and conquered in 1750 BCE, and the Amorites established themselves in Ur and the surrounding region.

While the Sumerian civilization never returned to power from this point, their culture lived on in the societies that came after them. As we will see in the next chapter, **the Babylonian Empire** soon ruled the region, and they incorporated and added to many Sumerian innovations.

Decline and Fall

It would be easy to blame the collapse of the Sumerian civilization on the Elamite invasion, but, as we know, things are never that simple. Instead, Sumer's demise included all three elements of decline: internal, external, and environmental factors.

Internally, Sumer suffered from a string of weak rulers with only a few good ones in between *and* an agricultural society that had not learned about the dangers of overusing land. The environment also threw a curveball in the form of a severe drought around this time. The famine further weakened Sumer internally by causing mass migration to the south in search of food. Historians believe the Biblical Abraham from Ur may have been among these migrants. Combining these factors with the external problems of the Elamites and the Amorites was enough to end the Sumerian civilization. This important chapter in human history, full of so many firsts, was only rediscovered in the mid-1800s thanks to archeological excavations in Mesopotamia.

Historical Highlights

Let's recap! Here are your key points to remember about ancient Mesopotamia and the Sumerian civilization:

- Mesopotamia means "between the rivers" and refers to the area between the Tigris and Euphrates Rivers. Sumer is the southern portion of Mesopotamia.
- Mesopotamia was part of the Fertile Crescent, which got its name due to its lush climate at the time. Sometimes, this area is called The Cradle of Civilization because it's where agriculture and civilizations first developed.
- The Sumerian civilization was the first in the world and, as such, had many other notable firsts, including the first city, the first form of writing, the first calendar, the first wheel, the first use of bronze, and much, much more!
- Sumerians were an agricultural society that traded surplus grain for resources they didn't have, like wood, stone, and metal.
- The Sumer region was marshy; their most abundant local resources were reeds and mud or clay, from which they made bricks to build their cities.
- Sumerian civilization was organized into city-states independent of one another and led by a king called a lugal. These independent city-states traded and warred with other city-states as they saw fit.
- Sumerian writing was called cuneiform, meaning "wedge-shaped," which describes the marks they made in clay with a reed stylus.
- Religion was essential to Sumerian life, and they built stepped temples, known as ziggurats, to honor their gods and goddesses.
- Sumerian civilization declined and collapsed due to a combination of weak kings, the overuse of land, climate change, and outside invasions.

CHAPTER 3

The Babylonians

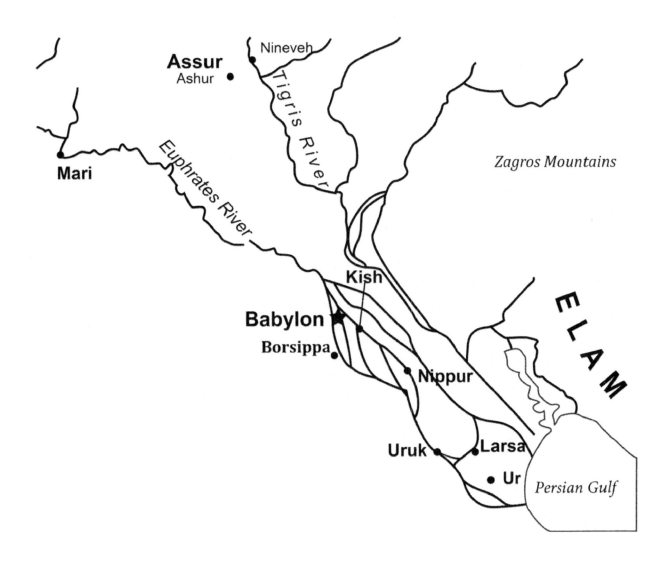

The story of the city of **Babylon** begins while the Sumerians were just entering their Akkadian Period, about 2300 BCE. And this story, too, takes place in Mesopotamia. The town of Babylon (meaning "Gate of God" or "Gate of the gods") sat on the banks of the Euphrates River and was founded by Akkadian-speaking people in what is now Iraq. Its ruins lie 59 miles south of the modern-day city of Baghdad.

Even though the Babylonian civilization lasted only about 1,700 years, it has remained the most famous ancient city in the Mesopotamian region. Most of its fame is thanks to Babylon's frequent mention in the Bible, which was never favorable.

Despite the negative press, the Babylonians had many notable and impressive achievements, particularly in mathematics, astronomy, law, and architecture. In their short shining moment in history, the Babylonians left their mark on civilizations to come, including our own. Let's see how!

The Rise of Babylon

Not much is known about the early days of this humble port city, which lay where the Euphrates runs closest to the Tigris River. Some believe Babylon was founded by Sargon the Great himself. However, most experts believe the town already existed when Sargon came into power. It's difficult to say because the oldest section of the city has been lost to archaeologists and historians under the rising water levels of the river. The ruins that survive today are from over 1,000 years after the city was founded. We know the city rose to stardom as a widely acknowledged center of culture and learning in the ancient world. Even Babylon's conquerors respected it!

It seems that Babylon began no differently than any other Sumerian city. It was influenced by a variety of cultural forces, from the northern Akkadians, whose language the residents spoke, to the nomadic Amorites, who came around Shulgi's wall.

It was around this time—when the Sumerian civilization was falling into chaos and disarray—that Babylon began to rise. In about 1894 BCE, the city became the capital of a small kingdom in southern Mesopotamia. This kingdom was ruled by an Amorite king named **Sumuabum**. Not much is known about Sumuabum, but he set the stage for some major players yet to come in world history. Before we learn about them, let's look at how Babylon crafted its own civilization from the best pieces that the Sumerians left behind.

Inventions and Achievements

Most of Babylon's contributions to learning sprung from their religion. If you were a priest, a large part of your job was trying to figure out what the gods were doing, or, more importantly, what they were about to do. Priests provided reports to the king with their predictions on the actions of the gods and recommendations on how to avoid disaster and ensure good fortune.

Priests had several ways of divining the moods of the gods. One interesting method was to examine the **entrails** of animals. Clay models of sheep's livers have been found that are marked, almost like an anatomy textbook, to show what the priests should look for. Another method, however, was much more impactful to our lives today—the study of the heavens.

Babylonians looked up and saw patterns in the sky above them. They believed that one way to know the minds of the gods was to study the celestial bodies and their cycles. So priests became astronomers, and ziggurats became some of the world's first observatories. They mapped the constellations, could tell the difference between planets and stars, *and* realized that the Earth moved around the Sun.

The Babylonian discovery that it took one year for the Earth to revolve around the Sun led them to divide the year into 12 months. They were also the first to divide a day into a 24-hour period, 12 hours for day and 12 for night. They also divided the hour into 60 minutes and the minute into 60 seconds—conventions we follow thousands of years later. This is a prime example of how ancient civilization continues to impact our own. If the Babylonians had decided to have 24 months instead, there's no telling when your birthday might be!

The Babylonian priests had to develop some pretty advanced mathematical skills to make all of these celestial calculations! For example, archaeologists found evidence that the Babylonians could track the distance Jupiter traveled over a certain period of time using geometry once thought not to have been used until the 14th century. Experts previously believed that these Mesopotamian mathematicians were limited to everyday geometric problems like figuring out the area of a field. We now know that, whether or not they were correct about the feelings of the gods, the Babylonians were leagues ahead of their time in science and math.

Art and Architecture

In addition to mathematics and astronomy, Babylonians excelled at architecture. They started with the usual elements of a Sumerian city (walls, gates, ziggurats, palaces, towers) and took them—literally and figuratively—to new heights. If you were approaching Babylon from a distance, you would first see a massive tower, almost a man-made mountain, dominating the flat horizon.

The Tower of Babel

Both Hebrew and Christian texts tell the story of the Tower of Babel. In this story, people were gathered together in a single location and spoke a single language. They reasoned that they should make bricks and build a tower reaching up to heaven. As they began to do this, God came down and, seeing their audacity, decided to confuse their language so they could not understand each other. The plan succeeded. Out of sheer communication frustration, the people abandoned the tower and separated around the world. This story is an example of an **etiology**, a narrative designed to explain the source or cause of something—in this case, different nations speaking diverse languages.

So, what does this have to do with Babylon? Historians and archaeologists believe that the Tower of Babel was, more than likely, the ziggurat of **Marduk**, the chief god of the Babylonians. Mesopotamians sometimes referred to this ziggurat as *Bab-ilu*, or "Gate of God" or "Gate of the gods." Translated to Hebrew, this becomes *Babel*, which is very similar to their word *balal*, meaning "confusion"–one possible explanation for the wordplay in the story.

Tower of Babel

The ziggurat's proper name was **Etemenanki**, and it was just one part of the massive temple complex. This complex also included the **Esagila**, the temple where Marduk's statue stood, surrounded by statues of the lesser gods and goddesses. A cuneiform tablet described Etemenanki as having seven terraced levels and rising to a staggering 91 meters (almost 300 feet) tall. That is about the height of a 30-story building! No wonder the ancient world was impressed with Babylon. This temple would have been visible for miles in the flat Mesopotamian landscape. The plans for Etemenanki have benches at the top for weary worshipers to rest. There were also chambers with a bed for Marduk himself. As we saw in Chapter 2, this was common for Sumerian ziggurats. And there would have been chambers for the chief priest or scribe, and his wife.

It is not known precisely when Etemenanki was built. Records suggest that it took a very long time and, perhaps, was never finished at all. This would make sense considering the massive size of the building, and it would also explain the unfinished tower in the Biblical story. We know that it was damaged by the time Alexander the Great conquered the city in the 300s CE. Alexander, desiring that the temple complex be restored to its former glory, ordered the ruins cleared for rebuilding. His soldiers tore the tower down. But before reconstruction could occur, Alexander died, and the project was abandoned.

The story of the Tower of Babel is far from the only reference to Babylon in scripture. The city is mentioned frequently, especially in the books of Daniel, Jeremiah, Isaiah, and The Book of Revelation. The popular story of Daniel in the Lion's Den takes place in the city of Babylon. The entire Book of Lamentations was written to express the sorrow and shame suffered due to the Babylonian's destruction of the Jewish Temple in Jerusalem.

The City Walls

As you continue to approach Babylon, eventually, the tower is not the only feature you can make out. Enormous walls begin to rise up before you.

At one point, there were three layers of walls surrounding the city. Since Babylon straddled the Euphrates, the river would have passed directly under the walls and out the other side. Many visitors to Babylon, including our friend Herodotus, wrote about these walls, and each one measured them very differently. We don't know exactly how tall or wide they were or how many miles they ran around the city. However, we do know that they had an impact on just about everyone who saw them. One account says the walls were 22 feet thick with a 10-foot wide passage between each layer. Another description puts them at more like 33 feet wide and 66 feet tall, with towers at different points even taller. Herodotus goes even further, saying they were 80 feet thick and 320 feet high. Good ol' Herodotus. Just enough facts to make you think it may be true and just enough hyperbole to make you wonder if it's not. His account is thought to be an exaggeration. Still, many agree that you could drive a chariot with four horses along the top and even turn around!

The wall itself was made of mud bricks. These bricks, dried in the sun or baked, were set with a kind of cement mixed with reeds for strength. There was, likely, a moat around the outside and possibly dozens of guard towers. However, it was not the guards in their towers that offered Babylon its solid security. That came from the sheer size of the walls themselves, which were almost impossible to scale or tunnel through.

The Ishtar Gate

As you come even closer to Babylon, you take the road destined for the city's eighth and main gate—the **Ishtar Gate**. You enter a wide alleyway where the city walls rise up on both sides of you. This high-ground advantage allows soldiers above to rain down terror on enemy armies trying to access the gate.

Ishtar Gate

As this gate comes into view, it stops you dead in your tracks. It seems like everything you have seen for days has been brown: brown rocks, brown soil, and even the bricks of the city walls and the towering ziggurat are brown. Before you, now, appears a gate of brilliant cobalt blue. It glistens in the sun like a cool, deep pool of water in a desert oasis. You draw close. The tiles are so blue and transparent that you reach out to touch them, half expecting your hand to sink into shimmering water. Instead, you touch smooth glazed tile.

The fact that these ancient people could make such a durable glazed tile of such a brilliant color that survives thousands of years later is remarkable! Experts think that the method used to make the tiles for the Ishtar Gate was a copper-glazing technique called **faience**, which was developed in Mesopotamia but perfected later in Egypt. By crushing quartz or sand with copper and other minerals and then firing it, ancient people made hard pottery with bright colors and a glassy surface. This allowed these civilizations to simulate turquoise and other rare gemstones.

The magnificent 38-foot-tall Ishtar Gate is much more than just plain blue. There are detailed patterns of white, black, yellow, orange, and beautiful muted greens. Then, rising in alternating rows, are three-dimensional **reliefs** of life-sized bulls and dragons (a lion with a serpent's head, an eagle's hind legs, and a stinger on its tail). These are contrasting yellow-orange tile that stands out against the blue background.

A *relief,* in art terminology, is a form of sculpture where the design is raised from a usually flat background. There are several different types of reliefs, and they can be found in many ancient civilizations around the world. The animals on the Ishtar Gate are examples of *low relief*, also called *bas-relief*, where the design is raised only slightly. When the design projects halfway or more from the surface, this is called *high relief,* and there is even a *middle relief* somewhere between the two. The Egyptians loved to employ the opposite of this technique with a *sunken* or *incised relief* where the image is carved instead of raised.

Processional Way

Once inside the Ishtar Gate, you find yourself in the **Processional Way**. This wide street led directly toward the temple complex and was the main route used in Babylon's important New Year's festival. This half-mile-long corridor was bordered by 50-foot-high walls of the same brilliant blue tiles. But here, snarling lions march obediently along, trimmed with a motif of delicate flowers. Lions were the symbol of the goddess Ishtar, the Babylonian name for the Sumerian goddess of love and war, **Inanna**. Tiles along the bottom of these walls were inscribed with prayers from the king to the god Marduk.

Anyone coming to the Ishtar Gate would have thought Babylon a fearsome and powerful place, which is precisely what the king who built it intended. **King Nebuchadnezzar**, who we will learn more about shortly, dedicated the gate with a plaque reading:

> "I [Nebuchadnezzar] laid the foundation of the gates down to the ground water level and had them built out of pure blue stone. Upon the walls in the inner room of the gate are bulls and dragons and thus I magnificently adorned them with luxurious splendour for all mankind to behold in awe."

Indeed, that is exactly what mankind has done. When the ruins of the Ishtar Gate were discovered, they were reconstructed at the Pergamon Museum in Berlin, Germany, where people behold them in awe to this day.

The Hanging Gardens

Once you move through the Processional Way, you *might* have found your way to Babylon's legendary Hanging Gardens, perhaps in part of the palace complex. In Chapter 1, we learned that these gardens were on Philo's list of the Seven Wonders of the World. It seems that Babylon's impressive walls and magnificent Ishtar Gate were considered for the list as well but, ultimately, dropped in favor of other wonders. This is ironic since we have evidence that the walls and gate actually existed. Unfortunately, the same is not so for the mysterious gardens.

So what were these gardens about, and why did they hang? Several second-hand accounts speak of wondrous terraced gardens—similar to the terraced ziggurats of Sumer and Babylon—overflowing with exotic trees and flowers. From a distance, this would have looked like the gardens were hanging in the air. These gardens would have required sophisticated irrigation technology to move and lift the water that the plants needed. But that is not why people doubt that the gardens existed in Babylon.

Hanging Gardens

The story goes that King Nebuchadnezzar had the gardens built as a gift for his foreign wife, **Amytis**, who, in the flat arid landscape of Mesopotamia, missed her lush mountain home. Although this is a romantic story, there are some suspiciously missing pieces.

Chief among the problems is the fact that no written accounts from Nebuchadnezzar's time mention the gardens. And Nebuchadnezzar loved to write about *everything* he was building in the city, lest anyone forget that he did. Even Herodotus, who oohs and aahs over the walls, gates, and ziggurats, says nothing about hanging gardens. And if Herodotus doesn't mention it. Well, you know. That's just a bit weird, isn't it? Also, no strong archeological evidence for the gardens has been found in Babylon.

However, there are some clues about where all this garden talk may have originated. Scholars believe it may be just a big mix up and that the gardens existed in a different city altogether. There is both written and archeological evidence of gardens, similar to the description of the hanging gardens, in the Mesopotamian city of **Nineveh**. Nineveh was even called "old Babylon" at times, making the connection a bit more suspicious.

Where these gardens were located or even if they existed at all may, at this point, remain a mystery. However, this serves as an important example of how what we claim to "know" about history changes over time or how something as innocent as a city's nickname can lead to giant misunderstandings about what really happened.

Religion

Like so many other aspects of Babylonian civilization, their religion was an extension of the Sumerian religion. In addition to paying tribute to a **pantheon** of traditional gods and goddesses, Babylon had a chief god for whom the major ziggurat was built. This was **Marduk**, god of, among other things, justice and agriculture.

Until this point in Mesopotamian history, the goddess of love and war, Inanna, held the top spot as the main goddess, while Marduk started as a minor regional god associated with farmers. (We met Enheduanna, one of Inanna's priestesses and the world's first named author, in the city of Ur.) Once Babylon became a force to be reckoned with, Marduk received a major promotion—although Inanna continued to be worshiped by many. As Babylon extended its power and influence, so did Marduk.

Marduk was elevated to Babylon's supreme deity, expanding his significance. The mythology of the time calls him the creator of the heavens and earth. Originally, Marduk, patron god of farmers, had been **iconized**, or shown in physical form, with a spade in his hand. Marduk 2.0, the chief god of Babylon, continues to hold his spade, but he also holds a serpent that resembles a dragon and is dressed in royal robes. Marduk's role as protector and provider for the people made him so important that the people of Babylonia were practically monotheistic for a time. He was often referred to as Bel, meaning "Lord," because people thought his real name was too holy to pronounce.

Marduk's annual festival to ring in the new year was called **Akitu**. It lasted more than a week. Since a Babylonian new year marked the sowing of the barley, this would have happened in March or April, a month that, for them, was called **Nisannu**. The Akitu festival was a holiday for the entire city and the kingdom of Babylonia, and everyone celebrated! Let's imagine, for a moment, that you are a child living in Babylon at this time.

Today is 8 Nisannu—the most exciting day of the year! Four days ago, the high priest officially opened the festival. You and your family visited the temple of the new year, outside the city to the north, to hear the annual reading of the *Enuma Elish*. This poem tells how Marduk defeated chaos to bring the earth into existence and order. You stood quietly, hanging on every word of that solemn occasion. But today is when the real excitement happens!

For the past several days, statues of other gods have been arriving from other cities to honor Marduk. They are cleaned and dressed in new clothes. Your family leaves home early, hoping to get a good view of the festivities. As you pass through the streets, you see the magnificent statues lined up to pay tribute to Marduk. How wondrous that all the other gods and goddesses come to honor the god of *your* home city!

The streets, which have been widened just for this event, are already getting crowded. People are singing traditional hymns along the way. You hear your favorite one and join in! In it, the gods are questioned about why they are not in their temples. One part of the crowd sings this part. The gods respond that they must go to be with Marduk. Another part of the crowd sings this answer.

The crowd is very thick when you reach the **Esagila**, Marduk's temple at the city's center. Here, you stand, shifting from one sandaled foot to the other as the sun grows warmer. Your family listens attentively as the priests read the gods' proclamations about the year to come. They always foretell blessing, fortune, and favor. The crowd cheers and you breathe a sigh of relief. Then, it's time to move on to the *really* exciting part!

The gods are now paraded around the entire city. They will end by exiting the Ishtar Gate and boarding boats that will take them up the Euphrates River to the temple of the new year. Your family intends to see this from the perfect vantage point.

After a long walk, your family reaches the enormous city wall and, with anticipation, you climb the steps to the top. The sheer size of the wall and its height are dizzying, but you press forward to the edge. As you wait for the procession to begin, you jostle for space in a prime spot. Your father has to hold you up so you can see over the **ramparts**. The sight of the city stretched out before you, rising out of the flat landscape, is incredible. How lucky you feel to live in Babylon—the greatest of all cities!

Finally, you hear commotion below, and the shimmering blue Ishtar Gates swing slowly open. Marduk is coming! A flash of gold in the hot Mesopotamian sun catches your eye, and you see him—Marduk's golden statue arrayed like a king with stars on his robes. In one hand, he holds his traditional spade, a symbol of his power over the harvest. In the other hand, he carries the serpent-dragon. You hold your breath, understanding the importance of this moment for your city and the success of the year to come. You watch until the statues are all boarded onto boats. At the temple of the new year, the king will receive Marduk's final blessing, "If you will take due care of my majesty and you will protect my people, the year now beginning will be a year of plenty for Babylon!" The new year has officially begun!

Akitu is still celebrated today by Assyrians in present-day Iraq and elsewhere around the world. Their celebration is more commonly called **Kha b'Nissan** or The First of April. As part of these celebrations, people still share poems about creation, have parades and processions, and rejoice in the renewal of spring. This year, 2022, is the year 6772 on the Assyrian calendar.

Babylonian Time Periods

Now that we've taken a brief tour of the city of Babylon and its wonders, it's time to stroll through the different time periods of the Babylonian Empire to see how it all came together.

The Early Years — c. 2300–1792 BCE

Babylon started as a simple Sumerian port town along the Euphrates Rivers sometime during the Akkadian Period. No source references the existence of Babylon as a city before 2200 BCE. Around the time the Sumerian civilization was disintegrating, a king with Amorite origins named **Sumuabum** conquered the area around Babylon to create a small kingdom. There is not much more to say than this about Babylon's humble beginnings. That is until **Hammurabi** came on the scene in 1792 BCE.

The Empire of Babylonia — 1792–1750 BCE

Hammurabi was a man with a vision. He took Babylon from a modest city-state to the capital of the Empire of Babylonia, drastically increasing its wealth, power, and influence. He also left the world his namesake **legal code** that inspired many civilizations after his. But, first, where did Hammurabi come from?

Born in Babylon around 1810 BCE, Hammurabi was already destined for greatness. He was the son of **Sin-Muballit**, the fifth king in the dynasty of Amorite kings that ruled Babylon. In 1792 BCE, Hammurabi took the throne as number six.

At this time, Babylon was a stable but small kingdom that included—in addition to Babylon itself—the cities of **Kish**, **Sippar**, and **Borsippa**. Hammurabi spent his early years in power working to improve the area he already governed. He continued the public works projects his father had begun, building temples, improving irrigation, and beautifying his cities. He was known by the nickname *bani matim* or "builder of the land" thanks to his building projects, many of which he personally supervised. And it would seem that his efforts were quite sincere. Many letters and documents speak of Hammurabi's genuine desire to improve the lives of his people.

Perhaps, the most significant way Hammurabi impacted the lives of Babylonians was through his code of laws. You see, Hammurabi was dealing with a society that was evolving. Instead of one unified people worshiping one accepted set of gods, Babylon was becoming more and more **cosmopolitan**. Babylonians may have come from any number of different nations or nomadic tribes. As a result, people living right next door to one another might have different beliefs about the will of the gods, standards of right and wrong, and ways of exacting justice. These differing ideals were becoming a problem. Families were seeking private revenge for wrongs. Feuds were developing between different ethnic groups. Legal matters were generally not handled in an orderly and consistent manner.

To solve this problem, in 1771 BCE, Hammurabi wrote 282 laws (actually, they were more like rules or consequences for specific sets of circumstances) and had them carved onto a 7-foot tall pillar of black stone called a **monolith**. The laws were organized into sections based on topics like slavery, commerce, marriage, debt, and inheritance. At the top of the pillar, a relief carving shows Hammurabi receiving the laws directly from the sun god—further proof that they came with authority that should not be questioned. This pillar was then displayed in a public place so everyone could see and read the laws governing them.

Code of Hammurabi (Top)   Code of Hammurabi (Front)

As we saw in Chapter 1, some of these punishments might seem a tad harsh to us today. For example, if a son struck his father, his hands would be cut off. If someone knocked out the teeth of a peer, his own teeth would be knocked out. This is literally where we get the expression, "an eye for an eye."

However, cruel paybacks aside, the Code of Hammurabi was an important stepping stone for law and order in several ways. The code stressed that it was important for everyone in a society to be subject to the same laws and the same punishments for breaking them *and* that the people should know what those laws and punishments are. The code also contained ideas about using evidence to prove crimes, protecting the weak from oppression, and how the law should act to preserve the stability of a society.

Hammurabi enjoyed a stable and prosperous reign in his little kingdom with his well-managed administration and generous infrastructure. Of course, there were the usual troubles with rival city-states, but relative peace was maintained through alliances with friendly ones. That is until all of this was interrupted by the city-state of Elam. In 1765 BCE, the Elamites conspired to start a war between Babylon and a neighboring kingdom called **Larsa**. Elam may have hoped this would give them more control over the river trading routes. Whatever the reason, Elam would be sorry.

Hammurabi caught wind of this plan, and what happened next would rocket the small kingdom of Babylon to become the dominating Empire of Babylonia. Hammurabi allied with Larsa and quickly crushed Elam, but he didn't stop there. He promptly broke off his friendship with Larsa and took it over, as well. Then, in 1761 BCE, he continued north through Mesopotamia to the city-state of **Mari**.

After Mesopotamian kings conquered a city, they would typically restore and integrate it into their kingdom. However, for reasons we don't entirely understand today, Hammurabi chose to destroy Mari instead. Scholars speculate that the reason could have been as simple as Mari's wealth and power, which rivaled that of Babylon. Hammurabi may have wanted his capital city to be the greatest. At any rate, by 1775 BCE, Hammurabi controlled all of Mesopotamia. The Empire of Babylonia had begun.

Fully controlling the vital trading routes of the Tigris and Euphrates Rivers secured Babylon's power and further increased its wealth. Through his skillful management, genuine regard for his people, and shrewd military conquests, Hammurabi had achieved a vast and stable empire. There was just one problem, one that many capable emperors throughout history have shared. Hammurabi was a little too hands-on.

Hammurabi was an incredible manager but did not like to **delegate**. He was directly involved in so many projects and decisions around his empire that he failed to create a **bureaucracy** capable of managing without him. Around 1750 BCE, the empire began to unravel. Hammurabi suffered from old age and illness and was compelled to pass the throne to his son. Babylon was about to undergo a tumultuous period of transition and rule by several foreign conquerors.

The Occupation Years — c. 1750—627 BCE

Babylonian kings after Hammurabi were unable to maintain his large and cohesive empire. Babylon shrank back to a lowly kingdom and was barely hanging on by its fingernails when invaders from the northwest, called the **Hittites,** easily sacked the city in 1595 BCE. This event is generally recognized as the dividing line between Old Babylonia and Middle Babylonia.

Next came the **Kassites**, who took Babylon from the Hittites and temporarily renamed the city **Karanduniash**. Scholars are unclear on what that name means, but it didn't stick, and neither did the Kassites. About 1225 BCE, King **Tukulti-Ninurta I** from the northern kingdom of the **Assyrians** (which had once been part of Babylonia) came down and sacked Babylon. Tukulti-Ninurta plundered Babylon's temples and storehouses and carried the statue of Marduk back to his capital of **Ashur**—a major insult in ancient times.

The Assyrians took more than Marduk, however. They took a large portion of the city's population captive, including the king, and left an Assyrian ruler in his place to rebuild. A series of different kings ruled Babylon next with equally different results. Although power was generally in the hands of the Assyrians, the Babylonians restored Marduk to his temple, and the city's reputation as an excellent center for learning and culture continued to grow, that is, until **Sennacherib**.

Sennacherib came to the Assyrian throne in 705 BCE. He was the son of **Sargon II**, and there seems to have been no love lost between the two. Instead of following the Assyrian custom of taking his son to battle, Sargon II left him in charge of administrative affairs like building his new capital city. Upon becoming king of Assyria, Sennacherib abandoned his father's half-completed capital city and moved the capital to Nineveh. It is here, under his rule that some experts believe the Hanging Gardens may have indeed existed.

Sargon II didn't do his son's reputation any favors either. It seems he spoke poorly of him to regional rulers and government officials. So, when Sennacherib ascended the throne, people saw him as a weak and untested ruler. Meanwhile, down south, Babylonians crowned a new king. They were living their lives, secure in the belief that the son of Sargon II would not be a problem. However, Sennacherib did not like to be underestimated.

The first army he sent to Babylon, led by his commander-in-chief, was defeated, causing Sennacherib himself to go down and put the upstart city in its place. The Assyrian king then turned his attention to other projects, but he was constantly being drawn back to Babylon for one reason or another. The trusted administrator Sennacherib had left in charge turned out to be weak and ineffective. Sennacherib had to travel to Babylon again to put down more revolts and left his son in charge this time. Next, the Elamites invaded and kidnapped his son, holding him hostage and causing a full-scale war that Sennacherib lost. This cost him control of Babylon for a little while. When that Elamite king died, Sennacherib, who was having none of this, struck Babylon again and regained control.

Now, he was done messing around. Babylon had caused him more problems during his reign than it was worth, and he was determined that it wouldn't cause him any more. Sennacherib razed Babylon to the ground. He dug canals to flood the city and carried off Marduk again. Now, he thought, Babylon would stay conquered.

This fit of rage, however, would wind up being a massive miscalculation. We should remember that the Assyrians, who were once Babylonians, worshiped many of the same gods that the Babylonians did, even if they called them by different names. This disrespect of Marduk was a little too much for Sennacherib's sons, who are believed to have assassinated him for the insult. Clearly, Sennacherib had crossed a line.

Sennacherib's son, **Esarhaddon**, took the Assyrian throne in 681 BCE and rebuilt and restored Babylon. In 668 BCE, Esarhaddon was succeeded by his son, **Ashurbanipal**, who would be the last of the great Assyrian kings. When he died in 627 BCE, the Assyrian Empire fell apart, turning a page in the history of the city of Babylon and of Mesopotamia as a whole.

It is worth pausing here to note one of Ashurbanipal's most outstanding achievements. In the Assyrian capital of Nineveh, he constructed an enormous library and collected over 30,000 clay tablets to fill it. Among the works found inside were the *Enuma Elish* and the *Epic of Gilgamesh*. Until the discovery of this library in the 1800s, many believed the Bible was the oldest written work. Even Ashurbanipal, a man of learning, thought the library was his most important accomplishment. He was right. This collection is considered one of the most important archeological discoveries ever made.

The Neo-Babylonian Empire — 626–539 BCE

After the Assyrians, a tribe called the **Chaldeans** under king **Nabopolassar** took over Babylon. The first recorded mention of Nabopolassar's son refers to him working as a laborer to restore the temple of Marduk in Babylon—this was Nebuchadnezzar II. He took his throne name from an earlier Babylonian king, Nebuchadnezzar I, who had once recovered the stolen statue of Marduk from the Elamites. Nebuchadnezzar's people would credit his devotion to Marduk, the god who made order out of chaos, for Babylon's later success.

As you've already seen, it is almost impossible to talk about Babylon without discussing Nebuchadnezzar II. He was an ambitious fellow when he came to the throne in 605/604 BCE. He had two major items on his bucket list: 1. to expand the Babylonian empire, and 2. to make Babylon the greatest city the world had ever seen. He did both.

This period of time is referred to as Babylon's Golden Age or the Neo-Babylonian Empire (*neo* meaning "new"). It is characterized by flourishing art, architecture, science, and learning. Nebuchadnezzar expanded the city to a whopping three square miles. It was the largest city in the world at that time. He built no less than three palaces in Babylon alone. And he embarked on other ambitious building and beautifying projects, like the Ishtar Gate, the Processional Way, and the ziggurat for Marduk.

Jews Morning the Exile in Babylon

Where did Nebuchadnezzar get the cash (well, gold and gems and other fancy things), not to mention the manpower, to accomplish all of this? Why from the nations he plundered in pursuit of his world domination goal, of course.

In 598/597 BCE, Nebuchadnezzar stormed the city of Jerusalem in Judah for the first time. He looted their temple, took thousands of Jews captive—exceptionally skilled artists and craftsmen—and installed a puppet king who would pay tribute to him. In 589 BCE, when the puppet king decided to take sides with Egypt, Nebuchadnezzar came roaring back. Only, this time, he didn't just pillage the temple. After an 18-month siege, the Babylonians destroyed Jerusalem and its temple. They carted thousands more Jews away to Babylon for 50 years of exile. It's easy to see why the Bible speaks so poorly of Nebuchadnezzar II and Babylon.

Interestingly, no one had a mediocre opinion of Babylon in its Golden Age. While the Bible tells of its great wickedness, every other ancient writer speaks of the city with awe and wonder. Whether one loved Babylon or hated it, everyone had an opinion, and the city inspired a kind of respect or reverential fear the world over.

Decline and Fall

The Neo-Babylonian Empire continued to play a powerful and key role in the region after the death of Nebuchadnezzar II. However, in 539 BCE, the city fell to the **Persian** king **Cyrus the Great** during the **Battle of Opis**. As the story goes, since the Persians could not surmount the massive walls, they laid siege to the city instead. Remember how the Euphrates River flowed directly under the walls—in one side of the city and out the other? While the Babylonians were busy celebrating a religious festival, the clever Persians devised a plan to divert the river's course. This allowed them to literally walk in—through the now empty space under the wall where the river used to flow—and take over, ending the age of the Chaldean kings.

Babylon continued to be a great center of art and learning under Persian rule. The Persians even made the city their administrative capital for a time. They also liberated the exiled Jews, many of whom returned to Jerusalem. Some, however, remained to create their own thriving Jewish community in the Babylon area.

After 200 years, **Alexander the Great** conquered Babylon, and even he fell under its spell. He planned to rebuild the city to its height of glory and make it his capital. But, when he unexpectedly died there in 323 BCE, his generals fought so hard for control of the city that the residents fled. Within a few hundred years, Babylon was completely deserted and never revived. Eventually, it was lost to the desert sands until the 1800s, when interest in Biblical studies drew archaeologists to the area.

Historical Highlights

Warm up your brain! It's time to recap the important points to remember about the Babylonian civilization:

- Babylon was located in Mesopotamia on the Euphrates River, which—as the city grew—ran right under its walls and through the city's center.
- The Babylonian civilization grew out of the Sumerian and Akkadian civilizations and had similar forms of writing, customs, art and architecture, gods and goddesses, and more.
- Babylon was known throughout the ancient world as a great center of culture and learning. At its height, it was the largest city in the world and (except in the Bible) was frequently written about with awe and wonder.
- The Babylonians pioneered advancements in math and astronomy and gave us our 12-month year, 24-hour day, and 60-minute hour.
- King Hammurabi and his code of laws established several influential ideas about justice. Two that stand out are that everyone should be subject to the same rules and punishments and that evidence should be required to prove guilt.
- King Nebuchadnezzar II brought Babylon into its Golden Age with many ambitious building projects like expanding the city walls, the Ishtar Gate, the Processional Way, and the seven-tiered ziggurat for Marduk (suspected to be the Tower of Babel).
- King Nebuchadnezzar II was also responsible for destroying the Jewish Temple in Jerusalem and exiling thousands of Jews to Babylon.
- Evidence has never been found for the existence of the legendary Hanging Gardens of Babylon, but it is possible these gardens were actually in the Assyrian capital of Nineveh.
- Babylon was captured and occupied by several different nations over the years. Finally, it fell, once and for all, to the Persian king, Cyrus the Great, who diverted the Euphrates River so he could march his army under the city walls.

CHAPTER 4

Egyptian Civilizations

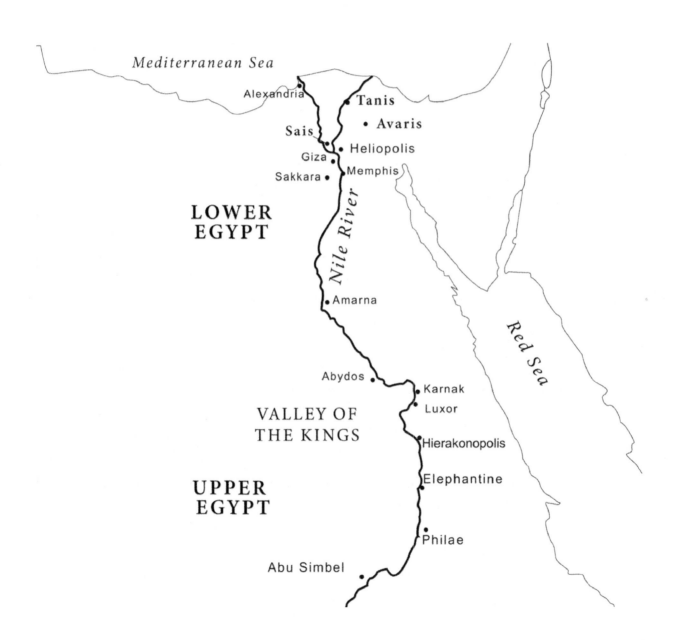

When we think about ancient civilizations, Egypt is usually the first one that comes to mind. Ancient Egypt is known for its pyramids filled with fantastic treasures, sphinxes, and mummies. This civilization has inspired endless books, movies, TV shows, and even entire hotels built to look like the Great Pyramid. We are so fascinated by Egypt that a whole field of study is devoted to it—it's called Egyptology. But why? Why are we so in love with the culture and achievements of the Egyptians? And how much of what we think we know about Egypt is fact versus fiction? Well, we should look closer and find out!

In (sort of) modern times, Egypt became all the rage thanks, in large part, to the French Emperor **Napoleon Bonaparte**. In 1798, he led his army into Egypt with two goals in mind. First, he could use Egypt to take control of the trade routes with India. That would really stick it to France's enemy, the British, something that made Napoleon very happy. Secondly, he wanted to collect scientific and historical information about ancient Egypt because the French suspected that the Egyptians were a civilization that rivaled the greatness of ancient Greece and Rome. We could spend the rest of this book on what happened next. So, let us just say that Napoleon's military campaign failed spectacularly, but his archaeological campaign set a flame burning in Europe to know and understand *everything* about ancient Egypt. **Egyptology** was born.

The Egyptian civilization began around the same time as the Sumerian civilization, about 5000 BCE, but it lasted much longer. It outlasted the Babylonians, too. For over 5600 years, Egypt survived famine, invasions, and even rule by the Roman Empire. Through all of this, the Egyptians maintained their culture, religion, and what it meant to be Egyptian until about 640 CE. At this point, Egypt was captured by the Arabs and converted to the religion of **Islam**, ending their long run as one of the great ancient civilizations.

Speaking of ancient Sumer and Babylon, they were distant neighbors of Egypt and often interacted through trade and war. Let's zoom out now from Mesopotamia so we can reorient ourselves and see precisely where Egypt is.

Looking down at the Mediterranean Sea, we see the Fertile Crescent with the Tigris and Euphrates Rivers to the east. Let's focus our attention, now, on the northeastern part of Africa—right in the corner where the Mediterranean almost touches the long, narrow Red Sea. This is Egypt. At its height, ancient Egypt stretched from modern-day Syria, down the eastern coast of the Mediterranean, and as far south as modern-day Sudan.

One thing you may notice right away is that Egypt shares a prominent feature with Sumer and Babylon, a giant river. This is no coincidence. Rivers of this sort were vital to the early stages of agriculture and civilization. The Nile River is (by some measurements) the longest river in the world. It runs for over 4,000 miles; from south of the equator in central Africa, it flows northward to the Mediterranean Sea.

Before we move on, it would be helpful to get a bit more acquainted with the Nile River. First, we should notice that the Nile runs from south to north. This is important because it is a common misconception that rivers always run from north to south. Rivers run downhill because of gravity, and "downhill" can be in any compass direction: north, south, east, or west. We will also talk a lot about the **Nile River Valley**, which refers to the fertile strip of land on either side of the river where crops could flourish. And we should know where to find the **Nile Delta**. A delta occurs when the flow of a river slows as it approaches a sea or ocean. This causes the sand or silt the water carries to be deposited and splits the river's single stream into a fan of smaller streams as it empties into the larger body of water. This fan shape resembles the triangle-shaped Greek letter delta, thus its name. The Nile Delta, then, is found where the Nile empties into the Mediterranean Sea, and it is easily visible in satellite photos as a lush green triangle in the desert.

The Rise of Egypt

Like Mesopotamia, Egyptian civilization began as a collection of independent city-states along a river that was eventually unified into a kingdom. For 3000 years, Egypt was the leading civilization in the ancient world, and its geography had a lot to do with that.

The Nile River was absolutely essential to Egyptian civilization. It sustained their agriculture, which fed the Egyptians and gave them a surplus of food to trade with other societies. It gave them an easy transportation route around their kingdom and allowed them to move the massive stones needed for their monuments. It inspired technologies like ship-building, at which the Egyptians became masters. And it was the basis for their culture, calendar, religion, art, and literature.

The deserts also played a part in the rise of Egypt. The Nile River Valley was like a giant **oasis** protected by deserts to the west, south, and east. Few invaders were intrepid and prepared enough to cross them. In this protected environment, nurtured by the Nile, Egyptians were able to carve out their identity and establish their nation as a giant among civilizations of the time.

It wasn't a smooth climb to the heights of civilization by any means! Yet, what the Egyptians accomplished along the way is astonishing, to say the least. So, before we look at Egypt's timeline of events, let's step into this fascinating civilization and see what it would have been like to live in ancient Egypt.

Religion

Their religion was one of Egyptian society's most fascinating and complex aspects. They were polytheistic, worshiping many gods and goddesses. Egyptians were expected to observe their religious principles daily to please the gods they believed were all around them—in the Nile, the reeds, and the sky. Although some accuse the Egyptians of being obsessed with death, we shall see that the opposite was actually true. Egyptians valued harmony, thankfulness, gratitude, and recognition of all the wonderful things the gods had given them. They believed there was no better place on Earth to live than right where they were. They loved life so much, in fact, that they went to great lengths to ensure transition to the afterlife beyond. They envisioned the afterlife as a more perfect mirror-image of life on Earth. Death was merely the crossing over to this beautiful, eternal life.

Chaos Versus Order

Like the Mesopotamians, the Egyptians' religion was based on a **dichotomy** of chaos and order. However, unlike the Mesopotamians, the Egyptians did not believe people needed to co-labor with the gods to create order. Instead, they believed that the gods had already done this and that it was their job to express thankfulness and live in harmony with that order—a somewhat optimistic thought process.

The Creation Story

Amun Ram Statue

Atum, also known as **Ra**, was the god of the sun and the creator of the universe. (Later, Atum would be virtually replaced by **Amun,** or **Amun-Ra,** the patron god of the city of Thebes. Amun was symbolized by a ram or ram-headed man.)

According to myth, when Atum came on the scene, there was nothing but the chaos of swirling water. He brought order, causing the Earth to rise from the waves as a hill known as a ***ben-ben***. The top stone of a pyramid and the top of an **obelisk** are symbols of a *ben-ben*. Atum became so popular that, at one point, king **Akhenaten** banned polytheism and created Egypt's first **monotheistic** religion devoted to him. This single-minded devotion, however, did not last, and the Egyptians returned to their polytheistic ways.

After creating the earth and bringing order out of chaos, Atum, or Ra, also created humans and other gods. Two of the most important, **Osiris** and his wife **Isis**, were given the task of ruling over Egypt. Osiris, the god of agriculture and rebirth, is shown with green skin in Egyptian paintings, symbolizing new growth. Isis would, at one point, grow in popularity like Atum to something resembling monotheism, where other gods were said to be just aspects of her. Together, they were two of the most important Egyptian deities.

However, In Egyptian mythology, the rule of Osiris and Isis would not be a happily-ever-after story. Osiris's younger brother **Set**, overcome with jealousy, killed Osiris and cast his body into the Nile. After a long journey fraught with challenges, Isis was able to retrieve Osiris's body and bring him back to a form of life. However, now, Osiris would be the king of the dead. We will meet him again in a bit when we look at the Egyptian's beliefs about what happens in the afterlife.

Meanwhile, the god **Horus**, the son of Osiris and Isis, would seek out his evil Uncle Set and banish him to the desert, restoring order. Horus would be the god associated with the king of Egypt. He is often shown with a falcon head, wearing the crown of the king. The king was not just chosen *by* the gods but considered to be their embodiment on earth and the intermediary between the gods and the people. The king would, like Horus, maintain harmony and order in Egypt, and the people were to follow his lead.

Osiris, Horus and Isis

The Soul and Afterlife

To the Egyptians, each person's soul had nine distinct parts. The two parts that we need to know about are the **Khat**, or the physical body, and the **Ka**, or "double-form," which we think of as a spirit. The Egyptians believed the Khat was essential to the success of the Ka. If your Khat was destroyed, your Ka might get lost and not find its way to paradise. This is why the Egyptians took great pains to preserve, or **mummify**, a person's Khat. Alternatively, if something terrible happened to your Khat, your Ka could inhabit a statue of you. This is why we see statues of the king or other mummified people placed alongside their bodies in a tomb . . . just in case.

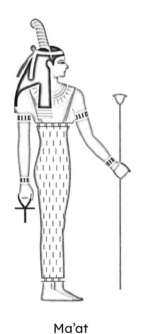

Ma'at

Paradise, for the Egyptians, was called the **Field of Reeds**. Here, you, or rather your Ka, would live forever in an idealized version of your earthly life. You would find your home and any family members or pets that had gone before you. There would be no pain, loss, or sadness—only an endless string of the happiest moments imaginable. All of this for having lived your life in harmony with **Ma'at**.

Ma'at was both the goddess of harmony and justice *and* a key value in Egyptian society. She was depicted as a woman with a white ostrich feather on her head. Ma'at was order. Ma'at was what Horus and the king-as-god were supposed to embody, leading the people by example.

So to reach the Field of Reeds, you must pass the Ma'at test. This was done in a place known as the **Hall of Truth** and involved an ominous piece of equipment called the **Scales of Justice**. If this sounds like the climax of a superhero movie, we assure you it is just as fantastic and twice as suspenseful. But let's take a quick detour to understand how your Ka gets to the Hall of Truth.

Egyptian Funeral Practices

As a young king, your journey to the Hall of Truth would begin with your everyday life. You would work hard to live a harmonious and orderly life that would please the gods, especially Ma'at. You would value justice, try to live gratefully, and lead your people to do the same.

Much of your life would be spent preparing for your journey to your eternal home. You would need a tomb to house your Khat. These tombs for kings started out as simple structures made of mud bricks called **mastabas**. Later, kings would create the tombs we call pyramids. After that, tombs were hidden in secret caves in an attempt to foil the tomb raiders trying to steal the treasure inside.

No, matter what kind of tomb was in style when you were king, it would be built while you were alive so that you could supervise the construction. Then, after it was done, you would fill it with the many things you would need in the afterlife: food, clothes, furniture, jewelry, and even games. Oh, and don't forget the statues. Statues were very important. You might have statues of servants and soldiers to wait on and protect you. And you would definitely need at least one statue of yourself so that your Ka could recognize its earthly home if something happened to your body.

Even though we are focusing on the funeral practices for a king, it is essential to know that the Field of Reeds, tombs, and grave goods were for everyone. Eternal life was not only for the king; it was important that each person in Egypt be buried with the best they could afford. Even pets received the best mummification and burial their owners could give. After all, it was believed that if you were cheap about the burial of a loved one, they would know and return to haunt you for it!

One artifact that everyone, rich or poor, wanted in their tomb was **Shabti dolls**. Everyone in Egypt was obliged to perform work for the king when called upon—building temples or roads and such. Since the afterlife was just an extension of your earthly life, it was thought that you would also be called upon to serve Osiris at times. But if you would rather enjoy paradise with, say, some figs and a good book under a shady palm, you would need to send a worker in your place—just like you would have on earth. Thus, Shabti dolls.

Each doll could do one day's labor a year for you. So, of course, the more dolls you were buried with, the more leisure time you would have in the afterlife. Kings would have one doll for each day of the year, made of precious stones or metal and in their own likeness. Ordinary people might only have a few mass-produced wooden Shabti dolls.

Living a good life and preparing your tomb were all you could do while alive. Once you died, the priests would take over for the next *extremely critical* step of the process, preserving your body for eternity. The mummification process could take 40 to 70 days for the most expensive treatment, such as the king would receive, and it was not for the faint of heart!

First, the body would be washed and laid on a slanted table so all the blood could drain out. After that, the brain and other internal organs, except the heart, would be removed. The heart would be needed later, once the departed person arrived in the Hall of Truth. Four organs received special treatment. These were placed in **canopic jars**. This set of four jars had lids decorated to look like each of Horus's four sons. The human-headed jar was **Imsety** and held the liver. The baboon-headed jar was **Hapi** and held the lungs. The jackal-headed jar was **Duamutef** and held the stomach. Finally, the falcon-headed jar was **Qebehsenuef** and held the intestines.

| Hapi | Duamutef | Qebehsenuef | Imsety |

Canopic Jars

Next, the body would be packed with salts inside and out to dry it and prevent decay. After 40 or more days, the body was removed from the salts and coated with tree resin to seal it. Finally, the body was wrapped in yards and yards of linen. If you unwrapped the bandages, some would stretch for almost a mile! Magic amulets were placed inside the linen wrappings, and people who could afford them would have a funeral mask placed over their faces. The mask would be painted to look like themselves and might be embedded with beautiful gems.

Last of all, the mummy—now ready for the afterlife—would be placed inside a casket called a **sarcophagus**, which might also be crafted to look like the person inside.

There could be, in fact, several layers of sarcophagi. When King Tutankhamen's untouched tomb was discovered in 1891, he was buried in three sarcophagi nested inside each other. The outer two were made of wood and covered in gold and jewels, and the inner sarcophagus was solid gold.

Sarcophagus

At last, it was time for the funeral procession. Everything about the Egyptian burial process was a symbolic echo of the story of Osiris and Isis, and the procession was no exception. As the sarcophagus was carried to the waiting tomb, professional mourners who were always women (to mimic the role of Isis mourning for Osiris) wailed loudly, inspiring others to join in and grieve for the dead. This mourning would be heard in the Hall of Truth.

When the sarcophagus reached its final resting place, the priest or son of the dead would perform a ceremony called, *"The Opening of the Mouth."* This was the most crucial part of the burial process and involved touching various tools on different parts of the body, either on the sarcophagus or a statue of the deceased. This would, in a sense, awaken the body to be able to breathe, see, eat, move, and function in the afterlife. Finally, the tomb was sealed, and it was time for the mourners to feast!

But while the mourners were ending their funeral duties, the soul of the dead was just beginning the perilous journey to the Hall of Truth. This is where you would find out if all these preparations would admit you to eternal happiness or whether it was all for nothing.

The Hall of Truth and Judgment

Upon awakening in your tomb, you would naturally be a bit confused and disoriented. But, then, you would discover your **Pyramid Texts** (c. 2400-2300 BCE). These writings on the walls of Egyptian royal tombs are considered the oldest religious writings in the world. They are one of the best ways for historians to learn about the kings buried there. They describe their great accomplishments and even show us insights into their personalities. They also help us understand the Egyptians' religious beliefs because the Pyramid Texts are a guidebook, helping the Ka find its way to the Hall of Truth.

After Pyramid Texts, **Coffin Texts** (c. 2134-2040 BCE)—spells, maps, and other religious writings that were engraved onto the coffin itself—were used to help the soul avoid trouble on its way. Both royal and non-royal wealthy Egyptians could have Coffin Texts. And both the Pyramid and the Coffin Texts inspired the later *Book of the Dead* (c. 1550-1070 BCE). *The Book of the Dead* is literally translated as *The Book of Coming Forth by Day.* Like the Pyramid Texts and Coffin Texts, these writings, written on a scroll, were a series of spells and instructions for overcoming challenges and reaching the Field of Reeds. More copies are still being discovered in tombs today.

Some people refer to *The Book of the Dead* as the Egyptian Bible, but it is not. This book did not provide religious instruction for the living. It was written only to help the deceased. Also, this book was not the same for everyone. It was personalized. A scribe would write spells specifically for an individual based on how they had lived their life, what they would need to know in the afterlife, and, of course, their budget. The more you could afford, the more spells you could have in your *Book of the Dead* to assist you.

So, you would awake in your tomb, find your written instructions, and be on your way. Not only that, you would have a travel companion. **Anubis**, a god depicted as a man with the head of a black jackal, is one of the oldest and most recognizable figures from ancient Egypt. He is the god of mummification, burials, and the protector of lost souls. Priests sometimes wore a jackal mask in his honor during rituals, and it was Anubis who would guide you as you *finally* arrived in the Hall of Truth.

Here, you would find Osiris himself. There would be a complicated ceremony and a confession you needed to make. Hopefully, your *Book of the Dead* had given you precisely the right things to say because this was the moment of truth. Would you move on to the Field of Reeds or not? This was where the Scales of Justice, Ma'at's white ostrich feather, and your heart, which was left inside you for this reason, came into the story. If you had lived a life true to the principles of harmony and justice, your heart would weigh less than the feather, and you could proceed to your eternal happy home. If not, the heart would drop to the floor to be eaten by **Amut**, a beast

Anubis

that was part crocodile, lion, and hippopotamus. Your soul would, then, simply cease to exist—the worst fate imaginable to the Egyptians.

Weighing of the Heart Scene

Government and Administration

Pharaoh or King?

During most of its history, ancient Egypt was ruled by kings who were the mediators between the gods and the people. The king's job was to dispense justice and maintain the principles of *ma'at*, keeping his kingdom in harmony and order. The king ruled by decree, passed laws, built temples to honor the gods, and owned the majority of the land, which the people farmed in exchange for a portion of the crops.

Now, we use the term **pharaoh** as a generic word for the kings of Egypt, but this was not a title they used for themselves until late in Egyptian history. *Pharaoh* comes from the Egyptian word for "great house" and refers to the palace or home of the kings. Over time, this term became synonymous with the person who lived there, and it wasn't until about 900 BCE that this was a common term of respect for the king.

Cartouche

Kings had five names, four given at their coronation and the fifth, their name from birth. It was not common for a king to use all five names. Usually, they used their fourth and fifth. In the 4th Dynasty, kings and queens began to wear rings engraved with their fourth and fifth names outlined by an oval. This design is called a **cartouche**.

The "birth names" Egyptians used were not their real names either, just nicknames. To Egyptians, names held magical properties. They believed that if you knew a person's true name, you could control them. For that reason, a person's real name was kept secret for their entire life.

During the king's life, he was often associated with the god Horus, who had banished Set and the forces of chaos from the land of Egypt. After his death, the king became associated with Horus's father, Osiris, the first "king" of Egypt. To symbolize this, the king is often shown in art holding Osiris's symbols, the **crook and the flail**. The crook was a staff used for herding sheep, and the flail was used for herding goats and threshing grain. Together, these symbolized the king's role in guiding the people and ensuring agricultural bounty.

Crook and Flail

Viziers and Nomarchs

Next to that of the king, the most powerful position in Egypt was the **vizier**. The *vizier* was a trusted advisor to the king. In addition, the vizier served as administrator or manager of the government and its day-to-day operations. He oversaw the agencies that managed all aspects of daily life like the government's military, judicial, agricultural, architectural, and religious branches. Sometimes there would be two *viziers*, one for the north and one for the south.

Nomarchs were like regional governors, dispensing the king's will at the local level. During some periods of Egyptian history, Nomarchs ruled their territories like mini kings when the central government was weak or absent altogether. These regions or provinces were called **nomes**. Once a year, the king would travel to each nome in an event called the *Shemsu Hor*, or "Following of Horus." This served two purposes. First, it gave the people a visual taste of the power and presence of their ruler. Second, the king and his officials would personally assess the wealth of each *nome* and decide how much taxes each one would pay. These taxes were collected in the form of crops and used by the central government to trade with other nations.

Innovations and Achievements

The Egyptians were inventors, no doubt. You can look at the pyramids and see that they had some quite original accomplishments. Building the pyramids required many other advancements in knowledge and technology, like how to use ramps and levers, geometry, and even knowledge of astronomy. (Certain temples and pyramids are aligned with different celestial bodies.) The Egyptians were skilled for their time in medicine and dentistry. They invented many sports and games, which they were very fond of. They were also the first to use a 365-day calendar.

The Egyptians were also improvers. They knew how to take the best things from the civilizations around them and make them better or retrofit them for their own uses. For example, the Egyptians borrowed and improved the wheel from the **Hyksos**. They perfected the art of glazing tiles in beautiful colors, called faience, which they used on everything from game boards to Shabti dolls. The Egyptians also borrowed a lot from the Mesopotamians. They improved their agricultural and irrigation techniques. And they improved beer to a drink so close to the modern version that the Egyptians are sometimes given credit for inventing it.

However, despite the technology, recipes, and techniques that the Egyptians borrowed, they had a style all their own. From hair and makeup to art and architecture—ancient Egypt had a unique and recognizable flair, and we don't see that anywhere better than in their writing.

Hieroglyphics

Egyptians were not the first to invent writing. As we saw in Mesopotamia, that distinction belongs to the Sumerians. But the Egyptians did develop their own beautiful writing system. In fact, their system was their own invention. It was not a repurposed version of cuneiform. Instead, Egyptians created the picture-writing we know as **hieroglyphics.**

Thoth

Hieroglyphics were developed before Egypt was unified under a single king, prior to 3100 BCE. In the Egyptian religion, writing was given to humans by the god **Thoth**. Thoth is depicted as a scribe with the head of an ibis, a common bird of the Nile.

The first writings were probably for record-keeping purposes, much like in Sumer. But we also see very early writings in tombs, called Offering Lists, which describe who is buried there, what they had done in their lives, and what offerings people should leave for them.

This picture writing is not as easy to translate as you might think. For much of Egyptian history, there were around 1,000 hieroglyphic symbols. This rose to as many as 5,000 symbols toward the end of its use. They were typically read from right to left and top to bottom, but that was not always the case. (Hint: The animal and people figures in hieroglyphic writing always face the beginning of the line.) Additionally, there were no punctuation marks or spaces between the words.

The hieroglyphic writing system was a combination of three types of images. **Logograms** capture the essence of a word. **Phonograms** (like alphabet letters) stand for a spoken sound. **Ideograms** represent an idea or concept. One example of this would be if a friend sent you a text that says, "Lunch 🍕😋." "Lunch" is written in phonograms. You must understand the sounds the letters stand for in order to interpret the word. The pizza emoji is a logogram. It literally stands for pizza. The smiley emoji with its tongue out is an ideogram that conveys a sense of "yummy" or "scrumptious." Even still, you would need to know the context and the timing of the text to interpret its full meaning. It could be, "I had pizza for lunch. Yum!" or "I'm going to have pizza for lunch. I can't wait!" or "I *really* hope the cafeteria has pizza today," or even "Do you want to grab pizza with me today?" This is what historians were up against when they tried to translate hieroglyphics.

Fortunately, the code was cracked in the 1820s thanks, in part, to Napoleon Bonaparte. One day, in the city of **el-Rashid** (translated as Rosetta), one of Napoleon's engineers, **Pierre Bouchard**, noticed a stone covered with inscriptions. This stone was part of a wall being demolished to clear the way for a new French fort, but it caught Bouchard's eye, and he saved it. What a good thing for history that he did! The significance of the stone, later called the **Rosetta Stone**, is that it had the same message engraved in three different languages: hieroglyphics, **demotic** (a later Egyptian writing system), and Greek. At the time, people knew how to read Greek, so the race was on to translate the hieroglyphics. It took years, but eventually, a British scholar by the name of **Thomas Young** figured out that the cartouches were the names of kings and queens and which direction the writing was meant to be read. Finally, a French scholar named **Jean-François Champollion** discovered that the writing was a mixture of logograms, phonograms, and ideograms and could fully translate the hieroglyphics.

Hieroglyphic writing has been found on all types of writing surfaces and was used for various purposes. Still, it is a highly artistic and labor-intensive format and was primarily reserved for carving in stone on monuments, temples, and tombs. The Egyptians developed quicker and easier forms of writing for everyday purposes or for lengthy literature. In the Early Dynastic Period, Egyptians developed a system called **hieratic writing**, a simplified form of the hieroglyphic pictures. This is the form we find most frequently written on paper with ink.

One of the Egyptians' greatest inventions was paper. They used the stems of a **papyrus** plant to make this early writing medium. It was less durable but more convenient and easier to transport than carved stone or mud bricks. Papyrus grew wild in the Nile, but the Egyptians eventually cultivated it for paper manufacturing. The reeds referred to in the Field of Reeds are actually papyrus plants, and the Books of the Dead were written on papyrus paper. Scrolls or rolls of this paper, which could be quickly and easily written on with brushes and ink, were later adopted for use by the Greeks and Romans.

Later, hieratic writing was replaced mainly by a script called demotic writing, one of the three writings carved onto the Rosetta Stone. For a while, all three forms—hieroglyphic, hieratic, and demotic—were used at the same time for different purposes.

H = Hieroglyphic; C = Hieratic; D = Demotic

Art and Architecture

Surprisingly, even as we admire the beauty of Egyptian art, the Egyptians would not have considered it art at all, at least not in the way we do. Everything, to the Egyptians, was for a practical purpose. Statues were homes for gods and spirits. Paintings and carvings gave instructions to the soul for the afterlife. Amulets warded off evil spirits. Nothing was made *just* to be pleasant to look at. This practicality was one of the reasons for the standardization of art in Egypt. That is not to say that Egyptians were not concerned with beauty. Beauty and **symmetry** were very important to the Egyptians because they were consistent with the need to maintain *ma'at*. This was reflected in the precise and orderly nature of their art. Again, it was not done just for the sake of beauty itself but to stay in tune with their religious values.

Egyptians went to a lot of trouble to create their standard artistic style. So it is no accident that drawings, carvings, and sculptures of gods, people, and animals made hundreds of years apart look like they could have been done by the same artist.

Egyptian artists and craftsmen used a technique called **frontalism**. In this style, the artist is more concerned with representing each individual part of the body in its ideal form rather than worrying about how the figure as a whole will look in the end. This is why almost all Egyptian figures have their arms and legs to the side, torsos and shoulders facing the front, head to the side, and eyes to the front. Egyptian artists also used a grid pattern when sketching to create all their figures with the same proportions and in one of a few formal positions. These techniques give Egyptian art its distinctive and formal style, immediately recognizable to us today.

Egyptian architecture took a wide variety of forms in the temples, tombs, administrative buildings, and palaces they created. However, the most well-known form of Egyptian architecture is the pyramid, and the best examples of the pyramid are those at **Giza**.

The Pyramids and Sphinx at Giza

Giza is a **plateau** that sat just across the Nile from the ancient capital of **Memphis**. This was the site chosen by three kings from Egypt's Old Kingdom, **Khufu**, **Khafre**, and **Menkaure**, to build their pyramids. Khufu's father, **Sneferu**, had been the first king to create a true pyramid rather than a mastaba or stepped pyramid. Khufu took this to the next level by making the tallest man-made structure in the world, that is until the Eiffel Tower was completed in 1889.

Khufu's Great Pyramid was constructed from over 2 million sandstone, limestone, and granite blocks. Some stones weigh as much as 60 tons. That's about as many as 12 average-sized African elephants. These stones needed to be quarried, transported, and then lifted and assembled into place, one at a time, to create the only surviving Wonder of the World. Altogether, the Great Pyramid weighs about as much as 16 Empire State Buildings!

Precisely how the Egyptians accomplished this heavy work is still a mystery. Ramps, levers, rollers, and perhaps even hydraulics (using the force of water) are the leading theories. It would be an impressive feat even with today's technology. We do know that the pyramids were not built by slave labor—a popular myth. Skilled and unskilled laborers were employed to work on the pyramids. They lived in temporary cities built around the worksite. This was one way that the government kept people employed during the times of the year when the Nile flooded and it was impossible to work in the fields. It is believed that slaves may have been used to quarry the stones; however, workers were free Egyptians who were compensated, well-treated, and promised favor in the afterlife for their services.

When the Giant Pyramid was finished, it looked very different than it does today. Now, we see the rough-cut sandstone blocks that would not have been visible then. At that time, we would have seen a smooth surface of gleaming white limestone. The **capstone**, which symbolized the *ben-ben* or first hill of earth that emerged from the swirling waters of chaos, was covered in gold. The sight that this must have presented to visitors to ancient Egypt—rising out of the flat desert and shining in the sun—is incredible to imagine. Sadly, the white limestone facing fell away and was used as construction material for other buildings.

Khufu's son, Khafre, was responsible for the second largest pyramid at Giza. Although visiting today, you might think Khafre's pyramid is the biggest. Due to the loss of the capstone and outer facing, Khufu's pyramid has shrunk slightly from its former height of 481.4 feet. This and the fact that Khafre's pyramid sits on slightly higher ground makes the son's tomb appear taller than dad's today. Menkaure's tomb, smaller still than the other two, round out the three large pyramids of Giza.

Of course, the Egyptians would not have used feet to measure their buildings. They had a unit of measurement called a cubit, which became the standard in the ancient world all the way through medieval times. A **cubit** was approximately 18 inches and based on the length of a man's arm from his elbow to his fingertips—a handy reference tool.

The Giza site included a great complex of buildings, including much smaller pyramids and mastaba tombs of high-ranking officials and construction supervisors. A monument to the workers who built the pyramids was also discovered, along with the ruins of the villages where they lived. In those days, the pyramids at Giza were a center of bustling activity, with temples and priests to manage the offerings devoted worshippers brought. However, next to the three largest pyramids, one object stood out above all others—the **Great Sphinx**.

Great Sphinx with Pyramid of Khafre in Background

The Great Sphinx is one of the world's largest statues. Carved from a single piece of limestone, it stands 66 feet tall and 240 feet long and was likely painted when it was new. The statue shows a lion in a lying or **recumbent** position with the head of a human. This isn't just any human either. We know the Sphinx depicts a royal person since it is wearing a *nemes*, the striped headcloth worn by kings. Scholars debate when the Great Sphinx was carved and which king it honors. Most experts think it depicts Khafre, especially since it lies in front of his pyramid. Some believe the statue is much older and that Khafre built his pyramid behind the Sphinx. We may never know for certain which king we are gazing at when we look at the Great Sphinx, lying guard.

The Lighthouse at Alexandria

Lighthouse at Alexandria

The Great Pyramid was not the only Wonder of the ancient world in Egypt. The **Lighthouse at Alexandria** also makes the list.

The city of **Alexandria** was founded late in Egypt's history, about 331 BCE, by Alexander the Great. It became Egypt's capital until it was overtaken by the Arabs in 642 CE. Alexandria was different from previous capital cities of Egypt because it was not centrally located. Instead, it lay on the western edge of the Nile Delta, just where it empties into the Mediterranean. Here at the intersection of the great sea and the great river, Egypt greeted the world.

The city had two natural harbors, which made it a bustling trading port. In addition, Alexandria drew tourists from far and wide to see the tomb of Alexander the Great, the city's world-famous library, and even the lighthouse itself. To guide this tremendous traffic of ships, the Egyptians constructed the tower and light on the island of **Pharos**. The 23-story tall lighthouse would come to be known by this name as well.

The base of the tower was square or rectangular, followed by a second octagonal section with a circular tower at the top. It is described in multiple sources as made of white marble, which certainly helped it to stand out visually. Still, we don't know whether it always had a light at the top or if that came later. Roman imperial coins show the lighthouse with no visible light. However, some later Arab accounts mention a bronze mirror that helped reflect the light, or sun during the day, far out to sea.

The Pharos was eventually destroyed by a series of earthquakes. Its ruins still lie below the surface off the coast of modern-day Alexandria. Interestingly, so do the wrecks of over 40 ancient ships, which makes one question how effective the Pharos actually was. We'll never know how many wrecks there might have been if the great Lighthouse of Alexandria had never been built.

Class Structure

As we learned in Chapter 1, having a class structure or hierarchy is one of the trademarks of civilization. The Egyptians were no exception to this. They had not only literal pyramids made of stone but social ones as well. At the very top of this hierarchy, the *ben-ben* of Egyptians was the king. Number two in Egyptian society was the *vizier*, with the priests' class close behind. In fact, the *vizier* often was a priest. This was followed by people with specialized skills, such as scribes and doctors, then management positions, like military leaders or government officials. Next came skilled artisans and soldiers, then unskilled laborers and farmers. Finally, servants and slaves rounded out the bottom tier.

Only about four out of every 1,000 Egyptians were literate, so being a scribe was a rare and honored profession. The ability to read and write was considered a gift from the god Thoth. Particularly bright young boys, whose parents could afford to do without their help in the family business, might be sent to scribe school in a temple. There, a boy would study for years the hundreds of hieroglyphics necessary to work as a scribe. If he persevered, he would be guaranteed a good job in the government or priesthood and an honored position in society. Although, probably, some Egyptian businesswomen or daughters of scribes could read and write, records of only five female scribes have been found.

Despite the lack of female scribes, women enjoyed a high social status. They were better treated in Egyptian society than in any other ancient civilization. Women were considered equals with men in many aspects of Egyptian life. A woman could buy and sell property; take legal action in court, including seeking a divorce; work outside the home; and inherit property or leave her belongings to anyone she chose after death. This was all quite different from how women lived in other civilizations around the Mediterranean at that time.

Slavery was not common in Egypt. Most slaves were captured from foreign countries during war or had sold themselves into slavery to pay a debt. Slaves often did skilled work. If a slave knew how to make pottery, weave fabric, or build boats, they could work in those industries and eventually buy their freedom. Household slaves were considered members of the family and sometimes married into it. In these ways, slaves often found their way into free Egyptian society.

Everyday Life

The majority of Egyptians fell into the class of unskilled laborers or farmers. The entire family would work in the field together: plowing, planting, watering, and harvesting. March through June was a busy time when ripe crops needed to be harvested and irrigation canals repaired before the Nile began to overflow its banks. Then, during the summer months, when the fields lay underwater, the family could devote itself to rest—or maybe to other projects the king needed doing. Ready to build a pyramid, anyone?

Food and drink were very similar to what was on the table in Mesopotamia. Wheat and barley were grown to make bread and beer, drunk by everyone at every meal. Grain was crushed into coarse flour on grinding stones, and the worn teeth of Egyptian mummies tell us that quite a lot of sand and ground stone made its way into their bread. Garden vegetables consisted of foods we know today, like lettuce, onions, melons, celery, and herbs. Dates, figs, grapes, and honey provided sweet treats. Some meat and fish were eaten, but without refrigeration, they would have to be fresh or salted and dried like jerky. Crops were grown for textiles as well. Papyrus was cultivated for making paper, boats, woven mats, and sandals. Flax was grown and woven into fabric.

Since wood was very scarce in Egypt, most homes were made of mud bricks. Sometimes the mud was mixed with straw to make the bricks stronger. Then, it was packed into molds to shape it and baked in the sun. The average Egyptian house was about 850 square feet, the size of an average American two-bedroom apartment. Like Mesopotamians, Egyptians often cooked, ate, and even slept on the roof to take advantage of the cooler air. More affluent families might have a limestone bathroom in their home or even a garden with a fish pond.

Bastet

Egyptians loved pets, and almost every family had one, especially cats, which the Egyptians worshiped in the form of the goddess **Bastet**. Bastet was the goddess of the home, women's health, and childbirth, so a pet cat was thought to bestow blessings on the house and ward off evil spirits. As a result, hundreds of mummified cats have been found. Egyptians had other pets, too. Dogs and monkeys were also popular choices. Monkeys, trained to pick figs and other fruit, are featured frequently in Egyptian art.

The Egyptians considered personal appearance to be very important. Wigs, jewelry, and perfume were worn by anyone who could afford them. Makeup was worn by everyone from the king to slaves, male and female alike. You may notice in Egyptian art that everyone seems to be wearing eyeliner. This makeup served the same purpose as the black grease paint football players wear—it helped reduce glare from the sun.

Cosmetic Container

Some of ancient Egypt's most beautiful stone, glass, and ceramic artifacts were containers for makeup and perfume.

One fact that may seem strange to people today is that clothes were more optional than makeup. Children up to the age of puberty rarely wore clothes. Adults would wear tunics or wraps made of flax linen, sometimes covering the entire torso and legs and other times only as a skirt. People often went barefoot but sometimes wore sandals made from leather or woven from reeds.

Speaking of children, boys and girls, beginning at about age four, would spend their days helping their families with work. Boys who were not selected to attend scribe school, which were most of them, would help their fathers and household servants (or slaves) with the family trade. Young girls would learn to run a household, cooking, weaving, and tending the garden.

Adulthood came early by today's standards. Girls would marry at around 13 and boys at about 18. One aspect of Egyptian life that was *not* equal between the sexes was that women were only allowed one husband, but men could have multiple wives if they could afford them. Despite this, most Egyptian couples were **monogamous** (one husband and one wife) except the king. It was not unusual for him to have many wives. Some of them he might marry for political reasons to ensure good trade relationships with other nations.

The brief Egyptian childhood, however, did not mean that Egyptians didn't like to have fun. Quite the contrary! Children had a wide variety of toys. Balls and ball games were very popular. Kids had dolls, puppets, model animals, toy horses and chariots, and toy weapons of all sorts. Adults enjoyed games and sports as well. People of all ages watched and participated in wrestling, racing, swimming, and boating. Hunting was popular, too. But big game hunting, like for hippopotamuses or lions, was reserved only for the king and whomever he chose to invite.

The most favorite pastime for Egyptians might have been board games. Everyone *loved* board games. One of their most popular games, which looked a lot like backgammon, was called **senet**. Scholars still aren't sure exactly what the rules of the game were, but they know it was popular! Multiple *senet* sets have been discovered in the tombs of kings—ready for them to play in the afterlife. Even Egyptian paintings depict the royal family enjoying a game night, much like modern families.

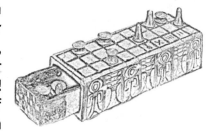

Senet Gaming Board

Historical Highlights

Wow! There is a lot to learn about Egypt, so much, in fact, that we've put the Egyptian time periods in the next chapter! For now, let's recap the most important tidbits to remember about the ancient Egyptian civilization in general:

- Egypt is located in northeastern Africa, bordered by the Mediterranean Sea and the Red Sea and dissected by the Nile River.
- The Nile River was the center of life, culture, and religion for the Egyptians. They depended on its annual flooding cycle to raise food and provide transportation and everything else they needed.
- The Egyptian religion was based on the concept of chaos versus order. Order was called *ma'at*, worshiped as a goddess, and was the Egyptians' main guiding virtue.
- The Egyptians worshiped a pantheon of gods and goddesses. Chief among these were various forms of the sun god, Ra (or Amun), and Osiris, the god of the underworld.
- The afterlife was extremely important to the Egyptians, inspiring funeral practices such as mummification and building tombs and pyramids filled with grave goods.
- Egypt contributed two major works of architecture to the list of Seven Wonders of the Ancient World: the Great Pyramid at Giza and the Lighthouse at Alexandria. The Great Pyramid is the only Wonder on the list that still survives.
- One of Egypt's best-known cultural contributions was hieroglyphic writing, a combination of logograms, phonograms, and ideograms. These were deciphered for the first time in modern history after the discovery of the Rosetta Stone.

CHAPTER 5

Egyptian Time Periods

Egypt had *many* dynasties, and we organize them into several different time periods. This helps us study and understand everything that happened during this remarkable civilization's time on Earth. However, Egypt did not have a nice, neat arc of rise, rule, and fall. Instead, their timeline was more like waves with three distinct periods, called kingdoms. During the kingdom periods, the Egyptians flourished. These kingdoms are separated from each other by intermediate periods, which were times of instability. Some additional pre- and post- periods are also thrown in for good measure. If this seems like a lot, it is. But don't worry. The periods actually help us break down this vast civilization into bite-sized chunks. So, let's dig in!

The Predynastic Period — c. 5000–3100 BCE

Before we get to 5000 BCE, let's rewind even further to about 15,000 years ago. This is around the beginning of the Mesolithic Period and just after the last ice age. At this time, nomads hunted and gathered food and supplies in the area that would later be known as Egypt. To the west, the region that is now the **Sahara Desert** was a **savannah**. Here, people lived a more settled lifestyle, grazing their herds on the open grasslands. But around 5000 BCE, a climate shift caused the Sahara region to dry out very quickly. So these people moved east to the Nile River Valley, where they formed a different way of life, becoming farmers instead of herders.

The switch to agriculture was possible thanks to the predictable flooding of the Nile River. Our friend Herodotus said, "Egypt is the gift of the Nile." However, the Nile was also a gift to the Egyptians. Each year, melting snow and heavy rain in the mountains would cause the Nile further downstream to overflow its banks. The overflow would cover the Nile River Valley with nutrient-rich mud *and* fill the irrigation canals that the clever new farmers dug to make watering crops easy. We saw this same practice in Sumer, where they used the regular flooding of a river for agriculture. Egyptians even used the same shaduf technology for lifting water and filling irrigation ditches that the Sumerians did. And there are even more similarities. These earliest Egyptians grew wheat and barley that they made into bread and beer; kept cattle, sheep, and goats; and lived in reed huts. Now, where have we heard that before?

In the last 1500 years of the Predynastic Period, the Egyptians, whose fertile fields produced more grain than they needed, traded with other civilizations. Among their favorite trading partners were the Mesopotamians and the **Nubians** further south in present-day Sudan.

Artifacts show that these cultures influenced the Egyptians. Many items familiar to us from Mesopotamia have been found. Gradually, baked brick homes with courtyards replaced reed huts. Copper made its way into tools and jewelry. Pottery became more decorative *and* complex, with handles and spouts. By the end of the Predynastic period, you even find the use of cylinder seals.

Egyptians would soon develop a complex religion that touches every aspect of life and life after death. Some think this, too, took early inspiration from the Mesopotamians because of the chaos-order dichotomy. But in the Predynastic Period, nearly the only sign of religion was the practice of burying the dead with food and personal possessions—the very infancy of their future belief system.

During this period, the groups who called Egypt home grew and changed from hunter-gatherers to farming communities to larger tribes. There was no single, unified kingdom of Egypt. However, before we talk about how Egypt did become a nation ruled by one king, we should get ourselves clear on one confusing point of geography.

When we look at a map, north is at the top or upper part of the page, and south is at the bottom or lower part. Toward the end of the Predynastic Period, the tribes along the Nile organized themselves into two major groups. The Lower Egyptians were a group ruled by the Red Crown King. He wore—you guessed it—a red crown. And then there were the Upper Egyptians led by the White Crown King, who, yes, had a white crown. Anyway, back to the tricky geography bit. Because the Nile was the center of life, "upper" meant "up the river," while "lower" meant "down the river." So, because the Nile flows from south to north, when we speak of **Lower Egypt**, that place is actually higher up (north) on the map but "lower" on the Nile. You'll find it close to the delta. Likewise, you will find **Upper Egypt** lower down (south) on your map but "up" in terms of the direction of the river. This feels upside-down to us north-is-up folks, but it made perfect sense to the Egyptians.

At any rate, by around 3100 BCE, both the Red Crown King and the White Crown King wanted to rule the whole of Upper and Lower Egypt as rulers are **wont** to do. After much sailing up and down the Nile to fight each other (or is it down and up?), the White Crown King, named King Narmer, was victorious. Egypt was now a single nation with a single ruler. To symbolize this merger, King Narmer placed the red crown over his white crown. This double crown, called a **Pschent,** was worn by the rulers of Egypt for long afterward to show their dominion over the entire land.

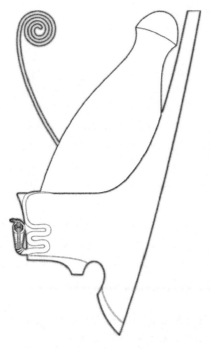

Pschent

The Early Dynastic Period — c. 3100–2686 BCE

The unification of Upper and Lower Egypt under a single king marks the beginning of the Early Dynastic Period. The Egyptians made several kings lists to record their rulers, similar to the Sumerian King List. However, they are all partial lists, or only pieces of the lists survive. Additionally, they were made well after the Early Dynastic Period, so we're not sure how accurate they are. Despite these archeological challenges, it has been established that **Menes** (c 3150 BCE) was the first official king of a unified Upper and Lower Egypt.

But hold on. Didn't we just find out two paragraphs ago that Narmer first wore the double red and white crown? Well, yes. Archaeologists believe that Menes and Narmer may have been the same person. No one knows for sure. In fact, it is also debated whether the Upper and Lower Kingdoms were unified peacefully or through war. However, carvings of King Narmer's (aka Menes) victory seem to indicate that it wasn't peaceful.

King Narmar Palette

Whether through conflict or negotiation by Narmer, Menes, or Narmer/Menes—historians agree that the important point is that Upper and Lower Egypt became unified. This first king (We shall call him Menes from this point.) founded the first Egyptian dynasty and the city of **Memphis**, Egypt's first capital. Memphis is located in Lower Egypt at the dividing point between the Nile Delta and the beginning of the Nile River Valley. In its early days, Egyptians called Memphis **Inbu-Hedj**, meaning "white walls," because the mud brick buildings were painted a brilliant white that gleamed for miles in the sun. Memphis remained the Egyptian capital until about the Eighth or Ninth Dynasty.

The First Dynasty

During the **First Dynasty** (c. 3150—c. 2890 BCE) of Egypt, their civilization became recognizable to us and what we think of as "Egyptian." People were moving, more and more, to urban areas. A calendar, writing, math, and astronomy were firmly established. Kings were organizing larger building projects, and religion was becoming more sophisticated. During this time, Egyptians began to use a type of tomb called a **mastaba**. It consisted of a rectangular monument of clay bricks built over an underground passage that led to the burial chamber. The mastaba is the predecessor of the pyramid.

Menes' queen, **Neithhotep**, might have been Egypt's first female ruler, taking over for a time after his death. A series of eight somewhat effective rulers in Menes's family inherited the throne, one after another, until 2890 BCE. **King Qa'a**, who had not properly chosen a family member to rule after him, died at this time. He had either no sons or, perhaps, multiple sons who fought over the throne. At any rate, the tug-of-war for the double crown was ended by a prince from a different family named **Hotepsekhemwy**, who, then, began Egypt's Second Dynasty.

The Second Dynasty

Our understanding of Egypt's **Second Dynasty** (c. 2890—c. 2670 BCE) is quite foggy. There is very little clear, consistent, and **contemporaneous** archeological evidence for who ruled, what happened, and why. However, there are a few things we know.

First, there were some kings. Hotepsekhemwy was the first. There could have been about six more. Some of those, though, might have been kings from the First Dynasty who were just called something different, so we're not sure.

Second, this was a period of turmoil. Again, we're not sure why, but it seems Upper and Lower Egypt spent much of this time fighting each other and were possibly divided again for a while. Egypt also expanded its territory south into Nubia.

Third, despite all of this fighting and uncertainty, Egyptian culture continued to develop. Experts believe that, perhaps, the most certain thing we can say about the Second Dynasty is that it was a bridge between the First Dynasty, where Egypt was unified, and the Old Kingdom, where Egypt truly came into its own. So let's head there now!

The Old Kingdom — c. 2686–2181 BCE

The Old Kingdom of Egypt spans about 500 years and includes Dynasties Three through Six. This was the first major period of prosperity in Egypt, and it is known as Egypt's Golden Age and the Age of the Pyramids. During this time, the kings continued to have their capital city at Memphis; however, they looked for other locations to place their tombs.

During the Fourth Dynasty of the Old Kingdom, King **Khufu** (known by the Greeks as **Cheops**) built what would become the only surviving "Wonder" of the ancient world—The Great Pyramid at Giza. Not just any civilization could build a structure like this. It required enormous manpower, resources, and organization, not to mention advanced knowledge of math and engineering. This is one reason why ambitious building projects such as this took place during times of great stability and prosperity.

During the Old Kingdom, Egypt was run by a large and efficient central government that employed many civil servants to oversee the administration. In addition, there was a large army to protect the kingdom. Religion was also becoming highly structured, and priests were growing in power. This was another development that would lead to the building of giant tombs. The more complicated and important funeral rituals became, the more kings needed a special place to spend eternity.

The Third Dynasty

The most notable king from the **Third Dynasty** (c. 2670-2613 BCE) was named **Djoser**, but the real star of his reign was his architect. As Djoser considered the large number of items he hoped to need in the afterlife, it was clear that a regular old *mastaba* would not do. Enter **Imhotep**.

Imhotep

Imhotep (c. 2667-2600 BCE) is an excellent example of mobility within a class structure. Knowing your place in society and being content with it was considered good form. This was in keeping with the harmony and order of *ma'at*. However, Egyptians did love a good rags-to-riches story, and Imhotep was one. He rose from a commoner to the very top of Egyptian society—*vizier* to the king. He was a skilled physician, a poet, a mathematician, and much more. His titles included Seal Bearer of the King of Lower Egypt, First after the King of Upper Egypt, Sculptor and Vase Maker in Chief, and more! And as if all that was not enough, Imhotep was eventually **deified** and worshiped by the Egyptians as the god of medicine. But let's get back to how Imhotep helped Djoser with his afterlife problem.

Imhotep may have begun his career as a temple priest. He rose through the ranks to high priest thanks to his talents in various areas helpful to the king. When it came time for Djoser to consider his royal tomb, Imhotep was in the perfect position to advise him about what the gods would like to see, and his vision was grand.

Instead of a rectangular, mud-brick *mastaba*, Imhotep proposed a series of square mastabas stacked on each other—reaching toward heaven, if you will. This tomb would not just house Djoser's body but also statues to receive the eternal offerings his people would surely bring *and* all the other items he would need for, well, forever.

Maybe one of Imhotep's titles should have been "Overly Enthusiastic Architect to the King" because he didn't stop there. Why have just a tomb when you can have a tomb *complex*? Temples to the gods standing next to the tomb were in order. And, of course, priests would be needed to handle all of the offerings that would be coming, so we must have homes for them. Oh, and since we're going to build this tomb 204 feet tall, mud bricks will not cut it. We're going to have to construct it out of stone.

The result was the first **stepped pyramid** (similar to a ziggurat) at **Saqqara** near Memphis. But if you think Imhotep went wild, wait until you see how Khufu of the Fourth Dynasty broke the tomb-construction bank!

Stepped Pyramid at Saqqara

The Fourth Dynasty

The Fourth Dynasty begins with two intriguing kings, **Sneferu** (c. 2613-2589 BCE), a wise and well-loved ruler, and his son, Khufu (2589-2566 BCE).

Egypt's Golden Age really began to shine under Sneferu. He was a clever military commander and a wise administrator, and he created a strong central government. Records tell us that his people loved and respected him. All of this weaved a stable, prosperous society that would set the stage for his son's lavish spending on the Great Pyramid. But before we get to Khufu, we should take a quick look at Sneferu's pyramids. Yes, that's pyramids—plural.

Sneferu built three pyramids, actually. The first one is in a place called **Meidum**. It is considered Egypt's first *true* pyramid with sloping sides; however, it was given the nickname "the collapsed pyramid" because it did so. Not to be deterred, Sneferu started his second pyramid at **Dahshur**. This one has a nickname, too—"the bent pyramid." And so it is. Architects began making the sloping sides at too steep an angle, realized it mid-way through, and tried to correct the error.

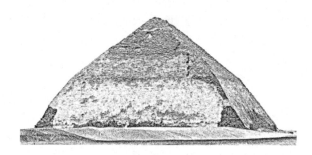

Bent Pyramid

Sneferu, unhappy with its bent-ness, simply began a third pyramid, also in Dahshur. This one earned the happy nickname "the red pyramid" for its colored limestone and was *finally* the first successful true pyramid in Egypt.

When Sneferu's son Khufu came to the throne, he inherited a wealthy and happy land. However, Herodotus criticized him much later for bringing "every kind of evil" upon Egypt by building the Great Pyramid for his glory at the cost of anyone and everything. Herodotus also appears to have started the rumor that the pyramids were built by slaves. I'm not sure why Herodotus disapproved of Khufu so strongly, but Khufu's people didn't seem to agree. Khufu was well-liked and maintained Egypt's prosperity through lucrative trade agreements and successful military campaigns. He did, indeed, devote about 20 years to the monumental (literally) construction project of the Great Pyramid at Giza, but this did not affect Egyptian society negatively.

When Khufu's Khat went to live for eternity in his Great Pyramid (at least until it was looted), his son **Djedefre** (2566-2558 BCE) took the throne. *His* most notable decision was to use the title "Son of Ra." This might sound like a pretty awesome title, but it was really a demotion for the king. Remember that until this point, the king was seen as the literal manifestation of Ra on earth. So making yourself not Ra but Ra's son was undoubtedly a step down. The effects of this would ripple through history because it decreased the king's authority and increased the power of the priests, who became the middle point between the people and Ra.

The Fifth Dynasty

The last kings of the Fourth Dynasty were plagued by problems with succession to the throne and dwindling resources for their enormous pyramids. Some were, sadly, unable to finish their pyramids before they died. Once we reach the **Fifth Dynasty,** the role of king is in serious trouble. The people now worshiped the sun god directly. So kings, trying to stay relevant, built temples to Ra instead of being Ra.

But not **Djedkare Isesi** (2414-2375 BCE). This king saw a civilization heading into decline, and instead of building a temple to Ra, he overhauled the government and priesthood. He was trying to create a more stable economy, but, ironically, one of his methods would help speed up the Old Kingdom's decline. To lower the costs of the massive central bureaucracy at Memphis, Djedkare Isesi put more power in the hands of the *nomarchs.* But unfortunately, this **decentralization** took even more control away from the king.

During the Fifth Dynasty, Egyptians started another noteworthy custom. Djedkare's son, **Unas** (2375-2345 BCE), was the first to have **Pyramid Texts** painted inside his tomb. As we learned, these writings have been critical to our understanding of ancient Egyptians and their religion. They appear throughout the pyramids of the Fifth and Sixth Dynasty rulers at Saqqara.

The Sixth Dynasty

The **Sixth Dynasty** of Egypt saw the collapse of this glorious unified civilization that had existed for the past 500 years. The first king, **Teti** (2345-2333 BCE), was murdered by his bodyguard—a crime that historians believe no one would have dared to commit a short time before. During this time, *nomarchs* were creating more elaborate burial chambers than kings were, more evidence of the growing power of the *nomes.*

Almost the last ruler of the Old Kingdom, **Pepi II** (2278-2184 BCE), put the proverbial nail in the coffin of unified Egypt. His greatest mistake was ruling too long—94 years by some accounts! Pepi II outlasted all of his heirs. So, chaos ensued when he died with no clear successor to take the throne.

It didn't help that a horrible drought struck around this time, bringing famine to the land. Without a strong central government to handle things, each *nome* adopted an "everyone for themselves" attitude and split.

The First Intermediate Period — c. 2181–2055 BCE

The **First Intermediate Period** is a span of about 125 years when much of Egypt is silent to us. No great monuments were built, records were not well kept and sometimes not kept at all, and art was of poorer quality. This has caused some to label this period Egypt's "dark age" and describe it as chaos and **anarchy**. But we now have a different understanding of this time. Historians no longer see the First Intermediate Period as a complete cultural void. You probably would only have thought so if you were Egyptian nobility at that time. Instead, it was a transition to another way of life—a period of change.

The decentralization of government meant the decentralization of wealth as well. Some compare this period to the **Industrial Revolution,** where items once considered luxuries became available to regular people. Mass production of goods came into use. Previously, only the most elite members of society could have superior tombs and Pyramid Texts. Now, a middle class arose where almost everyone could have nice things, even if they were of lesser quality.

The Seventh and Eighth Dynasties

The Seventh and Eighth Dynasties were little more than a rapid series of kings. These kings seemed to rule more out of tradition and lack of a new system of government than out of real authority. The regional rulers were the ones with real power. We do not even know the names of many of the kings, and, while they continued to rule from Memphis, they probably only had control over the local people there.

The Ninth and Tenth Dynasties

Records were still fragmented and confusing about who ruled and when during the Ninth and Tenth Dynasties. However, we do know that the kings of Memphis moved their capital south (up the Nile) to a more central location, **Herakleopolis**.

A different family began ruling in the southern city of **Thebes**. They eventually declared themselves the rightful rulers of Egypt and challenged the Herakleopolis rulers for power. Around 2055 BCE, **Mentuhotep II** from Thebes conquered Herakleopolis and united Egypt again. He was considered a second Menes for this feat and thus began the Eleventh Dynasty and the Middle Kingdom.

The Middle Kingdom — c. 2055–1786 BCE

The nickname scholars gave to the **Middle Kingdom of Egypt** is the "Classical Age." This age was the height of Egyptian culture, art, and literature, and it was not just a new copy of the Old Kingdom. So even though Mentuhotep II had united Upper and Lower Egypt once more, this was not your grand-pharaoh's kingdom.

The powerful and wealthy *nomes* that marked the end of the Old Kingdom remained in place. *Nomarchs* were more like mini-kings, and the ability to move up in society increased. This regional power is reflected by the diversity in the art, architecture, and literature of the Middle Kingdom. Artistic styles were very uniform during the Old Kingdom when the king and the central government held all authority. There was one style, and it was the one favored by the king of the day. During the Middle Kingdom, we see a variety of artistic influences that reflect the diversity of the different provinces.

The Eleventh Dynasty

The Middle Kingdom was ancient Egypt's second significant period of prosperity. Experts disagree on exactly when the Middle Kingdom should start and stop. After all, these periods were arbitrarily created long after these people lived just to help us study Egypt's long history. The Egyptians did not think of their history in this way. Some begin the Middle Kingdom in the middle of the Eleventh Dynasty, some at the beginning of the Twelfth. Most everyone agrees that without the **reunification** of Upper and Lower Egypt that happened in the Eleventh Dynasty, we would never have had the prosperity of the Twelfth. Whenever you choose to place it, Mentuhotep II and his dynasty paved the way for what was to come.

The Twelfth Dynasty

Amenemhat I (c. 1991-1962 BCE) begins the Twelfth Dynasty and Egypt's second period of tremendous wealth and stability. One of his actions was moving the capital from Thebes to **Itj-tawy** in Lower Egypt near Memphis. Amenemhat had been vizier to Mentuhotep IV. When he came to the throne, he brought a new idea to ensure that power would transfer smoothly to the next person he chose. He made his chosen heir **co-regent**, helping him rule while he was still alive. This strategy worked well. His successors did the same thing, and his dynasty ruled a strong and united Egypt for over 200 years.

During the Twelfth Dynasty, Egypt conquered **Lower Nubia**, a land rich in gold, ivory, and other precious resources. Kings began building pyramids again, although now they were more reasonably sized. Authentic literature was written, and art began to show scenes of everyday people living their everyday lives. Egypt started trading with nations as far north as Syria and **Palestine**. And Arab nomads called **Bedouins**, who had made their way into Egypt during the First Intermediate Period, were shown the door. The Middle Kingdom was at its height of grandeur.

Before this period, Egyptian art was **idealized**. Kings and queens were always depicted as strong, beautiful, and young. In the Middle Kingdom, we see the artistic touches of **realism** creep in. We can see age lines and other details that try to capture people as they were, not as perfect versions of themselves.

Amun Temple

One example of Classical Egyptian architecture from the Twelfth Dynasty is the **Temple of Amun** at Thebes (modern-day **Karnak**).

Amun was another name for Atum or Ra, the sun god. For temple-goers, the experience was a walk through Egypt's creation story. Thebes was chosen as the location because it was thought to be where Amun stood on the first hill of the earth (*ben-ben*) to begin the work of creation. In keeping with this story, the temple was surrounded by man-made sacred pools symbolizing the swirling waters of chaos. This temple was begun during the Middle Kingdom, but each ruler afterward added to it through the centuries. Today the temple complex sprawls across more than 200 acres, and it is said that three Notre Dame Cathedrals could fit in the main temple alone.

The Thirteenth Dynasty

In the Thirteenth Dynasty, we can see the slow slide of decline that has become familiar. There were about 70 kings who ruled in the span of 100 years, some of them for mere months at a time.

Decentralization was happening again, too. Even though the *nomarchs* had not completely disappeared, their power was limited during the Middle Kingdom. But, now, we see private tombs and monuments growing in splendor again. And the government is handing out so many titles that important officials are like Starbucks—one on every street corner.

Toward the end of the Thirteenth Dynasty, Egypt lost control of Lower Nubia. Then came the Hyksos.

The Second Intermediate Period — c. 1786–1567 BCE

The Hyksos were a people originally from the Palestine area who settled in Lower Egypt around the eastern edge of the Nile Delta sometime around the Thirteenth or Fourteenth

Dynasty. They brought new technology to Egypt—horses and chariots, the compound bow, and better metal weapons. But they also brought instability and, eventually, foreign rule. This period came to be known as the **Second Intermediate Period**.

The Fourteenth through Sixteenth Dynasties

Sometime during the Thirteenth Dynasty, Egyptian Kings moved their capital back south to Thebes. This move coincided with more Hyksos arriving in the northern city of **Avaris**. Egyptians later described them as cruel invaders and conquerors. However, historical records show that they were more likely traders who gradually increased in number until they took over politically and militarily. The Hyksos seemed to have admired Egyptian culture and religion and adopted a lot of it as their own. The lists of kings show foreign names for the Fourteenth through Sixteenth Dynasties. In fact, the Egyptians' name for the Hyksos, *heqa-khase*, is translated as "Rulers of Foreign Lands."

The Second Intermediate Period was not a time of chaos and despair under the thumb of strange kings. But it *was* disorganized and a quiet time for culture and technology. Hieroglyphic script was replaced mainly by hieratic, and art was, again, of poorer quality. Hyksos ruled the north from Avaris. Egyptian kings held onto Middle Egypt from Thebes. Nubians regained their territory in the south. A tentative peace and mutual respect were established. These separate states even traded with one another. But all that would be disrupted right about the Seventeenth Dynasty because of some nasty business about a hippopotamus.

The Seventeenth Dynasty

Who knows, the Hyksos and Egyptians may have lived side by side in peace to this day if it weren't for those noisy hippos. You know how it is when the neighbor's dog won't stop barking? Well, **King Apepi** of the Hyksos apparently sent a message to **King Ta'O** (c. 1580 BCE) of the Egyptians saying something like, "Do away with the hippopotamus pool which is on the east of the city, for they prevent me sleeping day and night." Well, King Ta'O seems to have taken this as a challenge.

War followed, and although it took three different kings to do it, the Hyksos were driven out. The Seventeenth Dynasty consisted of these three Egyptian kings—Ta'O, his son, **Kamose**, and his brother, **Ahmose**. They successfully routed the Hyksos from Egypt and restored their kingdom.

The New Kingdom — c. 1567–1085 BCE

Reunified once more, Egypt entered its third and final period of prosperity, the **New Kingdom**. Thanks to the abundance of records from this time, we know a lot about this period of Egyptian history. It was when the term "pharaoh" became the honorific title for kings. Many of the famous pharaohs we recognize from Bible stories, history class, and pop culture references come from this age.

The New Kingdom had several defining characteristics. There was an increasing devotion to the worship of the sun-god Amun or Amun-Ra. Egypt reached what some would consider empire status for the first and only time. There were some incredible and interesting female pharaohs. And there was an entirely new way of ensuring your Khat rested for all eternity.

New Kingdom pharaohs had figured out that pyramids were essentially giant flashing signs saying, "Pillage here!" Remember that if one's mummy, statues, and grave goods were robbed or destroyed, this could significantly impact your Ka's enjoyment of the afterlife in the Field of Reeds. So, New Kingdom pharaohs began hiding their tombs deep underground in the **Valley of the Kings**. There is also a **Valley of the Queens**. Both sit just across the Nile from the city of Thebes and the Temple of Amun (present-day **Luxor** and Karnak). However, this strategy still didn't work, and many tombs were robbed *during* the New Kingdom. Greek travelers report being able to tour some of the open and looted tombs in the 1st century CE.

The Eighteenth Dynasty

The first pharaoh of the Eighteenth Dynasty, **Ahmose I** (c. 1570-1544 BCE), was determined that neither the Hyksos nor anyone else would come traipsing into Egypt again. So he expanded Egypt's borders to create a buffer zone. As a result, Egypt retook the land of Nubia, then inhabited by the Kingdom of **Kush**. He also chased the Hyksos as far north as Syria. By controlling land beyond the borders of Egypt, Ahmose brought stability back to the Egyptians and gave Egypt its first claim to the word "empire."

This dynasty also saw a resurgence of trade with other nations, especially across the Mediterranean with lands like **Phoenicia** and **Crete**. Egypt was becoming more prosperous, but not all of these riches went to the central government. Instead, the cult of Amun-Ra was raking in the offerings and slowly increasing the wealth and power of the priests.

Amenhotep I (c. 1541-1520 BCE), son of Ahmose I, began the tradition of burial in the Valley of the Kings. This tradition would be followed by every New Kingdom pharaoh afterward except one. *The Book of the Dead* also reached its final form under his reign.

Hatshepsut (1479-1458 BCE) became the first female pharaoh to rule with all of the authority of a male pharaoh. Early statues show her in female form. Later, she was depicted as male, beard and all, reinforcing her power as divinely appointed pharaoh. She seems to have been a good ruler. She maintained peace with Nubia and encouraged trade. No king before or after, except Ramesses the Great, would undertake more building projects. Many later kings would try to claim her beautiful buildings as their own. This was possible because her successor tried to have her erased from history. He ordered the removal of her name and image from public places—an early version of **cancel culture**. To the Egyptians, this was far worse than just erasing someone from public memory since destroying one's name and image had implications in the afterlife.

Amenhotep IV (1353-1336 BCE) and his queen, **Nefertiti** (c. 1370-1336 BCE), were an Eighteenth Dynasty power couple. For the first five years of his reign, Amenhotep followed the traditions of his fathers, worshiped the gods (mostly Amun), and everything was fine. However, in his fifth year, something dramatic happened.

Whether for political reasons or true religious zeal, Amenhotep suddenly stopped worshiping the sun god Amun, started worshiping the sun god Aten, and caused quite a commotion by doing everything different in Egypt for the next twelve years.

Now, you might be asking, "Wait, they're both the sun gods? Then aren't they the same? Plus, what about the sun god, Ra?" And the answer to all of this is yes and also, no. The sun was worshiped in a variety of different aspects. Ra was the daytime sun. Horus was considered the sun at sunrise. Amun was the sun while in the underworld. Aten was the actual physical sun in the sky. So, they were the same but different, and these differences mattered to the Egyptians.

Amenhotep not only declared that Amun was no longer the main god but also said that Aten was the *only* god the Egyptians should worship—essentially creating a monotheistic religion. To further solidify this decision, he made many other changes, too. He changed his name to **Akenaten**, meaning "of great use to Aten." He built a new city dedicated to Aten's worship, called **Amarna,** moving the capital away from the traditional capital at Thebes. And he closed the temples to other gods, a move that devastated the Egyptian economy, which relied heavily on those temples, their land, and the crops they produced. Needless to say, all of this change did not sit well with the Egyptians.

Aside from Akhenaten's **heresy**, he was also known for his wife. Nefertiti was arguably the most powerful woman in Egypt after Hatshepsut. Some say she was co-regent with her husband, ruling while he was busy creating his new religion and capital city. Her name means "the beautiful one has come," and she was known for her great beauty and the loving family she shared with Akenaten. We can tell from the poetry he wrote about her that she was greatly loved. They had six daughters, and many carvings depict the family spending time together in play and worship.

While **Akhenaten** did not have a son with Nefertiti, he did have one with a minor wife. This son, **Tutankhaten** (meaning "living image of Aten"), is someone you will recognize. When Akhenaten died, Tutankhaten saw that his father's attempts at reforming the Egyptian religion were failures. He promptly reopened the temples, moved the capital to Memphis, and resumed the old ways. Also, he ditched his name, honoring Aten by changing the ending to honor Amun instead. This was the legendary Tutankhamun (King Tut) (r. 1336-c.1327 BCE).

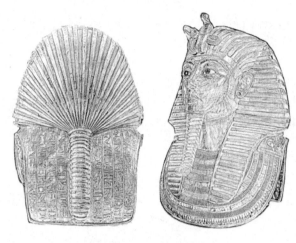

King Tut's Gold Mask

We have all seen what Tutankhamun looks like, whether we know it or not. This is because his tomb is the only one that has been found still untouched in the Valley of Kings, complete with grave goods, just as it was left over 3,000 years before. Its discovery in 1922 revolutionized what we know about ancient Egypt and sparked much of our modern-day obsession with the culture. Tutankhamun's gold death mask is instantly recognizable around the world and synonymous with what we think of Egyptian pharaohs.

The Nineteenth Dynasty

The Nineteenth and Twentieth Dynasties are sometimes referred to as The **Ramesside Period** due to the many pharaohs who took the name Ramesses (also spelled Ramses). There were eleven, to be exact. Ramesses II, also known as **Ramesses the Great** (r. 1279-1213 BCE), deserves a closer look.

Ramesses II was given the 19th-century nickname "the Great" thanks to his extra-long reign—the second longest in Egyptian history—and his many building projects. The sheer number of temples, statues, and other buildings he commissioned is a testament to the fact that Egypt was stable and prosperous during his time.

Ramesses II Battle Carving

Ramesses the Great loved statues of himself and carvings showing him in battle. One famous relief shows Ramesses firing arrows at the Hittites from his speeding chariot in **The Battle of Kadesh.**

Both sides claimed they won this battle; however, as is usually true when two sides claim a victory, neither one really did. The result of this battle was a momentous historical stepping-stone—it gave us the first recorded peace treaty. In 1258 BCE, the Egyptians and Hittites documented their agreement to end hostilities in The **Peace Treaty of Kadesh.**

Ramesses the Great also built a new capital city for himself near the Nile Delta called **Pi-Ramesses** (or Per-Ramesses), which means "House of Ramesses." Descriptions and artifacts show that this city matched a king named "the Great." The city housed over

300,000 people. It covered six square miles and was built on a series of hills so that the city was transformed into a collection of luxurious islands when the Nile overflowed its banks.

The Twentieth Dynasty

Ramesses III (1186-1155 BCE) of the Twentieth Dynasty was the last strong pharaoh of the New Kingdom. During this time, Egypt was invaded for the third time by a mysterious group called simply the **Sea Peoples**. Their nationality is unknown, but they had a reputation for raiding and pillaging the Mediterranean coast. The Sea Peoples acted on their own behalf but also became **mercenaries**, paid fighters, for other nations attacking Egypt, like the Hittites and the Libyans. Ramesses III was victorious against them, but the cost of victory came high in both lives and resources.

These wars against invaders had interfered with trade and depleted the storehouses of Egypt. Eventually, this problem snowballed into the first recorded **labor strike** in history. The royal tomb builders were repeatedly not getting paid their grain rations on time, which was far more serious than just empty bellies. It was a failure of the pharaoh to maintain *ma'at*. They refused to work until they were fully paid—a bold move considering that they, too, were not upholding the principles of *ma'at* by doing this. It worked, however, and they received what was owed to them. But this was a sign of times to come and of the ever-weakening New Kingdom.

Rule by the High Priests

Several weak kings followed. By the end of the New Kingdom, the priests of Amun were gaining more power while the pharaoh's authority was shrinking. Every New Kingdom pharaoh had contributed to the temple at Thebes, and by this point, it employed over 80,000 priests. The richest among these had more land and wealth than the pharaoh himself.

Eventually, the priests wielded so much influence in Thebes that they took over this region entirely. Egypt was, again, divided with the pharaoh ruling a limited kingdom from Pi-Ramesses. This ushered in the Third Intermediate Period.

The Third Intermediate Period — c. 1085–664 BCE

The Twenty-First through Twenty-Fifth Dynasties

The pharaohs of the Twenty-First Dynasty made the city of **Tanis**, in the eastern Nile Delta, their capital. Conveniently, they built it with pieces of the ruins from then-abandoned Pi-Ramesses. Rule was divided fairly equally between the secular pharaohs of Tanis in the north and the religious, or priestly, rulers of Thebes in the south. In reality, the priests consulted Amun on every little decision, making this god the true king of Thebes.

Top members of Libya's military had inserted themselves so thoroughly into high society in Tanis that they were in power by the Twenty-Second Dynasty. The pharaohs for the next two dynasties would be Libyan.

By the end of the Twenty-Second Dynasty, Egypt was fractured by civil war. Various leaders of different origins declared themselves ruler or king in Tanis, Thebes, Herakleopolis, Memphis, and Hermopolis. This was all not very *ma'at* of them. Finally, all this chaos and internal distraction allowed the Nubians from the south to invade. They ruled a unified Egypt for the Twenty-Fourth and Twenty-Fifth Dynasties.

But this was really just the beginning of foreign rulers for Egypt. The invaders just kept coming. Next, the Assyrians, led by Esarhaddon and his son Ashurbanipal, who we saw back in Babylon, invaded in 666 BCE.

The Late Period — c. 664–332 BCE

The Twenty-Sixth through Thirtieth Dynasties

Some scholars start the Late Period of Egypt when the Nubians took over. The hallmark of this period was invasion and rule by foreign leaders. Yet despite this series of takeovers, Egypt was still Egypt because the people were allowed to maintain their culture and religion. Moreover, some conquerors, like the Persians, admired Egyptian culture so much that it saw a revival under their rule.

In 666 BCE, when the Assyrians swept in, they did not have enough resources to leave a large army and maintain their hold on Egypt. In their place, the Assyrians installed a Libyan prince from the Egyptian city of **Sais** as a **vassal** king. This family, however, decided it would be better to just rule Egypt for themselves and skip reporting to Assyria. They began the Twenty-Sixth Dynasty—called the **Saite Dynasty**—while Assyria was busy with other problems.

From the Twenty-Seventh through Thirtieth Dynasties, Persians ruled Egypt. **Cambyses II** (525-522 BCE) invaded in 525 BCE, officially ending the Egyptians' **autonomous** rule. Persia would dominate the position of pharaoh for the next 300 years despite a few upstart rebellions that tried to throw them off here and there. Demotic script began to appear, as did other evidence of an Egyptian-Greek blend of artistic styles.

The Late Period ends with the arrival of **Alexander the Great** of **Macedon** (a part of Greece) in 332 BCE. Alexander had a reasonably easy time conquering Egypt since they were sick of being ruled by the Persians by then. The Macedonian or Hellenistic Period begins here. It is so named because the ancient Greek word for "Greece" was *Hellas*. Alexander spread Hellenistic culture far and wide in the Mediterranean region. A new and final chapter in Egyptian history was ready to unfold.

Decline and Fall

Greek Egypt

Alexander the Great was only in Egypt for a short time before heading off to conquer elsewhere. Still, he was busy while there. Founding the city of Alexandria (What else would he call it?), he left plans for the city with his Macedonian administrators, whose job was to build it. To legitimize himself as the pharaoh of Egypt, he also made a dangerous desert crossing to an oasis called **Siwa**. Here, a priest declared him the son of **Ammon** (the Libyan version of Amun). The Greeks identified this god with their chief god, **Zeus**, calling him Zeus-Ammon. It is remarkably fitting since the Greek word for "sand" is *ammos*. So basically, they were calling him "Sandy Zeus."

Alexander's title, "son of god," reinforced his right to rule. In addition, he pleased the Egyptian people by sacrificing to their gods and respecting their traditions. Then, off he went on more world-domination campaigns where, as we learned, he died unexpectedly in Babylon. Chaos ensued after his death, and Alexander's vast empire was divided between four of his generals. Of these, **Ptolemy** took the Egyptian portion along with Alexander's body back to Alexandria for burial.

And so begins the **Ptolemaic Dynasty**—about 300 years of Greek rule in Egypt. These Greek pharaohs never really assimilated themselves into Egyptian culture any more than was absolutely necessary to rule. They ruled from the highly Greek city of Alexandria. They spoke Greek. They maintained Greek culture. And they married Greeks. To preserve their heritage, it was common in the Ptolemaic Dynasty for brothers to marry sisters or uncles to marry nieces. It maintained their ethnicity, but it was less than ideal genetically and promoted fierce jealousy and in-fighting for power within families.

The legendary **Cleopatra VII** was the last ruler from this line. In fact, she was the last pharaoh of Egypt. She was the only Ptolemaic pharaoh to learn the Egyptian language (as well as several others) or attempt to know and understand the Egyptian people.

This effort to govern wisely served Cleopatra well. She was known as a shrewd and independent leader and negotiator. She ruffled feathers in her court by daring to speak with foreign diplomats without a translator or consulting her advisors. She was a swift and intelligent decision-maker, guiding Egypt through rough times. Time and again, she navigated extremely difficult and complicated threats to her life and throne from foreign forces and her own siblings. And through all this, she maintained Egypt for her people, even as Rome began dominating the rest of the Mediterranean world.

Cleopatra's later years were a series of romantic and political maneuvers that kept Egypt both independent from and in favor with the tumultuous Roman Republic. Although she has gone down in history for captivating the hearts of two of the world's most powerful men at the time, **Julius Caesar** and **Mark Antony**, her most significant achievements were political and strategic.

Unfortunately, however, Cleopatra did not have Octavian (soon to be Emperor Augustus) charmed when he came to power in Rome. After losing to the Roman army in the **Battle of Actium**, she died, at age 39, by a self-inflicted snake bite rather than be paraded through the streets of Rome as a captive. In 30 BCE, Egypt became a province in the new **Roman Empire**.

Roman Egypt

The following 700 years are called the Roman Egypt years. This name holds even after the Roman Empire split and Egypt became a part of the new **Byzantine Empire**. During this period, the Roman emperor appointed a governor to manage the Egyptian territory, and legions of Roman soldiers were stationed there to keep the peace. However, Egyptian culture was left relatively intact. Temples and priests continued operating and society functioned much as it had before.

This doesn't mean everything was the same, though, and it doesn't mean there were no problems. There were a series of revolts and uprisings that required putting down by Rome. Rome also charged Egypt an enormous amount of taxes, which they took in the form of grain. They also imposed a new social structure on the Egyptians that favored "Hellenized" people or those with Greek heritage.

The Final Take-Over

Egypt, to this point, had been ruled by not only Egyptians but also Hyksos, Libyans, Assyrians, Nubians, Greeks, Romans, and more. Yet during all of this, Egypt had still held onto its Egyptian-ness because it managed to maintain its culture and religion.

In 639 CE, the **Arabs** conquered Egypt. It was a dividing line in Egypt's history, deeper than any we have seen before. Here, we begin to see a society that moves away from the culture and religion of ancient Egypt and toward a **Muslim** culture and the religion of Islam.

As with every other civilization in this book, the final conquest was not the only reason ancient Egypt declined and fell. There were many. Everything from a lack of iron in the area for better weapons to Egypt's reliance on the Nile and their entrenchment in the old ways of doing things played a part. But, as long as Egyptians held onto a sense of who they were, their civilization continued to bounce back time and time again.

But you don't have to be an enormous powerhouse like Egypt to make a huge contribution. So, now, we will turn to three smaller Mediterranean civilizations that made outstanding achievements in the ancient world: the Minoans, the Mycenaeans, and the Phoenicians.

Historical Highlights

My goodness, that's a lot of dynasties! Don't worry about remembering every single king. Here are some highlights to focus on:

- Egyptians came to the Nile River Valley because their grassland homes to the west were turning to desert. Here, they started farming.
- In the Predynastic Period, Egyptians formed two separate kingdoms, one in Upper Egypt (the south) and one in Lower Egypt (the north). King Narmer (or Menes) united these two kingdoms into one.
- Most of Egypt's history is divided into three periods when Egypt was strong and prospered, the Old, Middle, and New Kingdoms. These periods are separated by two Intermediate Periods, when Egypt experienced decline.
- The Old Kingdom was Egypt's Golden Age. This was when most pyramids were built, including the Great Pyramid at Giza—the only surviving Wonder of the Ancient World.
- During the Middle Kingdom, the government became more decentralized, regional rulers and priests gained power, a middle class formed, and the temple complex for Amun in Thebes was begun.
- The New Kingdom had many famous pharaohs and queens, like Tutankhamun, Nefertiti, and Ramesses the Great. Their tombs were hidden in the Valley of Kings, but tomb raiders found them anyway.
- Kings, or pharaohs, ruled Egypt for about 3,000 years in a series of about 30 dynasties. Some were Egyptian, and some were foreign rulers.
- Alexander the Great conquered Egypt, founding the city of Alexandria. This was where the other Egyptian Wonder of the Ancient World—the Lighthouse of Alexandria sat.

- Cleopatra VII was the last pharaoh of Egypt. Though she was of Greek descent, she tried to rule the Egyptian people wisely. Her reign ended when the Roman Empire took over their Egyptian territory.
- Egypt's culture and religion withstood lengthy rules by both Greek and Roman civilizations. They were eventually conquered by the Arabs and **assimilated** into Muslim culture.

CHAPTER 6

Other Mediterranean Civilizations

Whew! We traveled a long way—from the land "between two rivers" to the deserts beyond the Nile—and encountered some of the giants of ancient civilizations. But we would be missing so much if we didn't pause to look at some of the smaller, but just as interesting, civilizations of the time.

This chapter will explore three of these peoples: the Minoans, the Mycenaeans, and the Phoenicians. They may not have built wonders of the world or commanded vast empires, but their contributions have been critical to us today and to the powerhouses of the ancient world like Egypt and Greece. In fact, those more well-known civilizations might never have achieved their glory without these smaller, hard-working guys.

These civilizations were bridge-builders, figuratively speaking. They bridged gaps in time between tribal groups and major empires. They bridged distances, often sitting at the crossroads between warring neighbors or lucrative trade routes. And they bridged cultural divides, connecting distant peoples by trading goods or sharing technology.

Let's take a look at the highlights of these three civilizations and see how, where, and when they fit into the puzzle of the ancient world. We'll start with the Minoans.

The Minoans

Who Were They?

About 7000 to 6000 BCE, a dark-haired group of people arrived on the island of **Crete** from **Asia Minor**. They became the **Minoans,** a small but influential Mediterranean people who traded with giants of their time, like Egypt, and set the stage for later civilizations in their area, like Greece. Notably, they are considered the first "high" civilization in Europe, meaning they developed fine craftsmanship, art, and writing. They are sometimes called **Cretans** after their island home.

In modern times, we refer to these people as Minoans because of their legendary **King Minos,** who was immortalized in **Homer's** Greek epic poem, *The Odyssey*. This story began in Greek oral tradition and relates the myth of **Odysseus**, a general in the **Trojan War**, and his 10-year journey to return home. Along the way, Odysseus encounters a variety of challenges and tricky situations. One of the characters he meets is King Minos. Most of Homer's account is fictionalized; however, there is evidence for a historical King Minos or perhaps even a dynasty by that name.

According to Greek mythology, King Minos of Crete was the son of the god **Zeus** and **Europa**, the daughter of the king of Tyre in Phoenicia. Zeus courted Europa while in the form of a bull and carried her off on his back across the sea to Crete. Later, they had a son—King Minos.

When King Minos grew older, he prayed to the god of the sea, Poseidon, asking for a bull, which he promised to sacrifice. But when Poseidon granted his request, King Minos did not keep his word and refused to sacrifice the beautiful animal. As punishment, **Poseidon** caused Minos's wife to fall in love with the bull, and together, they had a son—a fierce monster with the head of a bull and the body of a man. The myth of the **Minotaur** was born.

Minotaur

Under his palace, King Minos built a maze called a **labyrinth** and chained the Minotaur in the center of it. To feed it, King Minos forced the Greek city of **Athens** (which had angered him for other reasons) to send seven young men and seven young women every few years to fill the beast's stomach. (We must remember this is a Greek myth, not a Minoan one.)

Theseus was the prince of Athens. One year, when the Minotaur was getting a bit hungry, Theseus decided enough was enough. He boarded the ship to Crete as one of the seven men destined to be dinner. At the palace, Theseus caught the eye of Minos's daughter, the princess **Ariadne**. She secretly made sure that Theseus entered the labyrinth with a sword and a ball of thread. But this was not for Theseus to knit a sweater. He unwound the thread as he wandered the twisted passages of the labyrinth and, once he found the Minotaur, slew him and followed the thread back to the entrance where he escaped.

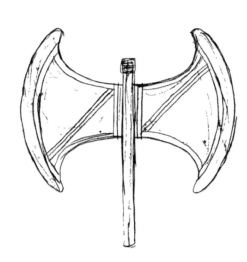
Double-Headed Axe

Although this is a Greek story and clearly fictional, elements of truth about the Minoans can be found. This could be an allegory for how the early Greeks threw off the domination of the Minoans. The importance of the bull to Minoan religion and culture is explained. And the remains of Minoan palaces show entrances on all four sides, leading to twisted passageways. These were, perhaps, the inspiration for the labyrinth.

One tool or weapon that was distinctively Minoan was the double-headed ax. This object is seen repeatedly in Minoan art, usually wielded by a goddess or female figure. Several gold double axes have been found, far too thin and soft to be of actual use. These were **votive objects** used by the Minoans for religious symbols or rituals—not for war or chopping wood.

Where Did They Live?

As we know from the real estate business, location is everything, and the Minoans had a good one, at least for a while. The island of Crete is located about 99 miles off the coast of mainland Greece, just where the **Aegean Sea** meets the Mediterranean. It is the largest of the Greek Aegean Islands.

Crete is also a reasonable sailing distance from Egypt, with whom the Minoans traded, and it was, conveniently, a stopping point along Phoenician trade routes. We'll learn about them later in this chapter.

When Did They Live?

Linear A

The Minoans entered the Bronze Age at about 2600 BCE, possibly a bit earlier. However, their early days are mysterious to us because they used a form of writing, now called **Linear A**, that has never been interpreted. (If you like a mystery, here is one waiting to be solved!)

By 2000 BCE, the Minoans were becoming prosperous and accumulating enough olive oil and other goods to trade with other nations. This began the Palace Period when they constructed large palace complexes, including buildings for administration, religious offerings, storehouses, and other activities of city life.

Their civilization reached its peak about 1600 BCE, and, thanks to a combination of natural disasters and the invading Mycenaeans, their cities were abandoned by 1200 BCE. Crete would sit silently in the Mediterranean for hundreds of years until the Greeks later colonized it.

How Did They Rise?

Like many other ancient civilizations, the Minoans reached a tipping point where they had things to offer the world. They had accumulated surplus goods such as wool, olive oil, honey, corn, and wine. They refined their craftsmanship by carving ivory, gold, and silver and making thin finely-painted pottery. They also had the transportation to trade. Living on an island had made the Minoans expert sea-goers. Their trade with the Egyptians, Phoenicians, Mycenaeans, and others propelled them into prosperity.

We don't know much about the Minoans from their written record. Contact with the Egyptians had given the Minoans their earliest form of writing—a version of hieroglyphics. This was replaced by Linear A, which, as we mentioned, has not been deciphered to this day. Then, around 1400 BCE, the Mycenaeans modified Linear A to create Linear B, which the Minoans adopted. Most examples of Linear B, made on clay tablets or sometimes vases, are administrative records no literature or poetry. But they do provide insight into the trade and commerce of the Minoans.

What Were They About?

Art

The Minoans had distinctive artistic styles that made their work recognizable throughout history. In addition to their works in metal and ivory and their signature double-headed ax, they were famous for their pottery, ceramics, stoneware, and **frescoes**.

Their pottery was admired for being quite thin and delicate. It came in a variety of motifs. The most popular was floral or marine. Marine animals were, not surprisingly, a favorite subject of Minoan artists, and their vases depicting octopi were exceptionally striking.

The Minoans also manufactured **amphorae**. An amphora was a tall pottery jar with two vertical handles. Their name comes from the Greek for "carried on both sides." They were the primary way to transport and store olive oil, wine, and other foodstuffs in the ancient world—the shipping containers of their day.

Amphorae

Once they became mass-produced, they were **ubiquitous**, a fancy word for "everywhere you look." The Romans used them. So did the Greeks, the Phoenicians, and others. Shipwrecks in the Mediterranean are still being discovered thousands of years later loaded with amphorae. Sometimes the contents are still identifiable.

Frescoes, or large wall paintings, decorated the palaces of Crete. These were made by applying the colors onto the lime plaster while the wall was still wet, which absorbed the **pigment**. They often show religious rituals, processions, or sports. For example, one now famous fresco shows us the Minoan sport (or perhaps religious tradition) of "bull leaping"— one participant grasps the bull, literally, by the horns as another somersaults over its back!

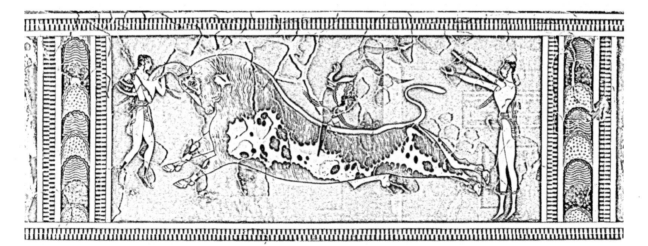

Bull-Leaping fresco

Another stunning fresco from the palace at Knossos continues the marine animal theme, showcasing beautiful blue dolphins swimming with other colorful fish.

Religion

Snake goddess

Bulls were obviously important to the Minoans. Even the Greeks noticed that. They are featured in frescoes, pottery, and sculptures. Although their exact role is unclear, bulls were a part of the Minoan's religious life. Enormous stone bull horns, called Horns of Consecration, have been found on some of their buildings.

The Minoan religion was largely **matriarchal** (led by women). The themes of nature, fertility, and rebirth were meaningful to them and would have resonated with their everyday lives. They worshiped goddesses who oversaw animals, crops, and the home. Statuettes of goddesses have been found holding snakes—another common theme in Minoan art.

Palaces

The height of the Minoan civilization was characterized by the construction of palaces across the island. These were not just homes for the city leader. They were the hub for all aspects of Minoan life. Agricultural, commercial, administrative, and religious activities took place there.

Of all the palaces on Crete, the most famous is **Knossos**. This is the name of the massive palace complex and the city surrounding it. It was the home of King Minos and the palace visited by Odysseus and Theseus in Greek mythology.

Knossos was indeed a complex—1200 rooms surrounding a central courtyard that included spaces for religious services, the king and queen, storerooms, and public audiences. The entrance passageways are so twisted and confusing that it is easy to see how the legend of the labyrinth was started. Everything about the palace is distinctly Minoan, from the life-sized frescoes to the rows of stone bull horns on the roof to its hall of double axes.

Why Did They Fall?

By now, you will not be surprised to discover that the fall of the Minoans was due to a variety of factors—some caused by nature and some by other civilizations.

This area of the world was particularly prone to earthquakes, and there is evidence that palaces were destroyed and rebuilt at least once. Also, being an island with limited resources, overuse of the land and deforestation were likely factors too.

The Minoans also had a tenuous relationship with the Mycenaeans, who we will learn about next. They lived on mainland Greece and, arriving at the civilization scene somewhat later than the Minoans, the Mycenaeans borrowed from Minoan culture and artistic styles. They made good trading partners for a time. But as the Minoans were declining, the Mycenaeans were rising. There is evidence that, eventually, the Mycenaeans invaded and took over the unfortified island of Crete, calling it their own for a time.

Finally, a volcano on the nearby island of **Thera** (now **Santorini**) erupted cataclysmically sometime between 1650 and 1550 BCE. This had devastating consequences for the entire area and caused a tsunami that definitely affected the island of Crete. Many think this was the final straw for the Minoan civilization.

The Mycenaeans

Who Were They?

The story of the **Mycenaeans** is like the prologue to the story of the ancient Greeks. The Mycenaean culture will contribute a lot to the Greeks who come later. And the Greeks will, in turn, influence art, science, literature, philosophy, and so much more around the world.

Although they influenced so much, very little is known about the Mycenaeans themselves. They left few written records, and the ones we do find are business records. But they left a legacy recorded in Greek mythology, just like the Minoans.

According to Greek legend, the city of **Mycenae** was founded by **Perseus**, son of the god Zeus, who commanded the one-eyed giants, **Cyclopes**, to build its walls with stones no human could lift. (Walls made from giant stones are called "cyclopean walls" thanks to this myth.)

Cyclops

Death Mask of Agamemnon

Like Knossos, Mycenae was home to a legendary king featured in the writings of the Greek poet Homer—**King Agamemnon**. In Homer's epic story, *The Iliad*, King Agamemnon of Mycenae led an expedition against the city of **Troy**, beginning the Trojan War. A gold mask found in Mycenae and nicknamed "the death mask of Agamemnon" was crafted far too early to match up with any possible timeline for the Trojan War. But it does give us an incredible look at the craftsmanship of the Mycenaeans.

Trojan Horse

The Trojan War is the story of a conflict between the ancient cities of Mycenae and Troy. Homer recorded this story in his epic poems, *The Iliad* and *The Odyssey*. Although these fictional accounts feature gods fighting alongside men, terrible monsters, and magical events—there is some archeological evidence for an actual conflict that could have inspired them.

The famous story of the **Trojan Horse** tells of a trick used by the Mycenaean army to sneak their soldiers inside the walled city of Troy.

As the story goes, the Mycenaeans (and other Greek city-states who had joined them) had trouble defeating the Trojans. So, they built a giant wooden horse and hid their soldiers inside. They placed the horse outside the city gates and then—to be very convincing—sailed their ships away as if they were giving up. Just to ensure the plan worked, they left a man behind to tell the Trojans that the Greeks had left them a very nice present and that they should bring it inside. The plan worked. The unsuspecting Trojans brought the horse into the city, and, while they were partying to celebrate their gift and their victory, the Greeks snuck out of the horse and defeated the Trojans.

Where Did They Live?

Whether or not the Mycenaeans first started in Mycenae or some other place, they developed their civilization on what is today mainland Greece. Eventually, they controlled most of that **peninsula** and many islands in the Aegean Sea, including Crete, after they had defeated the weakened Minoans.

Other cities the Mycenaeans established would remain occupied even after their downfall and later be rebuilt as Greek city-states. These include **Mycenae**, **Thebes**, **Athens**, and others. Unlike the Minoans, the Mycenaeans fortified their cities or at least portions of them—as we know from the Greek myth about cyclopean walls. For this reason, their settlements are often referred to as **citadels**—fortifications on a hill or high ground.

When Did They Live?

The Mycenaeans arrived fashionably late to the Bronze Age, between about 1900 and 1100 BCE. They were hugely influenced by the Minoans, who rose slightly before them. By about 1450 BCE, they had taken over as the dominant civilization in the Aegean Sea.

Unfortunately, though, they didn't spend very long at the top. Between 1230 and 1100 BCE, the Mycenaeans were part of what scholars call the **Bronze Age Collapse**. This was when many civilizations around the Mediterranean and throughout the Middle East declined, collapsed, or vanished due to a combination of factors. Natural disasters, climate change, internal divisions and class struggles, a breakdown in trade, and those pesky Sea People have all been blamed. Whatever the reasons, this was a difficult age for everyone. The Mycenaeans might have lasted longer if they had come around at a different time.

How Did They Rise?

The Mycenaeans built their civilization by borrowing different aspects of the Minoan civilization and adapting them to their purposes.

They learned to make pottery on a wheel like the Minoans but gradually changed their decorative style to more geometric patterns or scenes of daily life. This became the dominant pottery style in the Mediterranean.

They took the Minoans' writing style, Linear A, and created **Linear B**, which we have been able to decipher. This script is read from left to right, and symbols represent syllables, either a vowel or consonant-vowel combo. Linear B is the first written form of Greek.

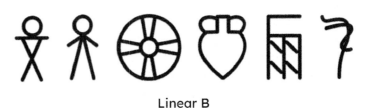

Linear B

The Mycenaeans borrowed from Minoan architecture, creating palace complexes around central courtyards called **megarons**. Of course, they also added their legendary walls and fortifications to their cities, a detail that the Minoans might have been wise to borrow from *them*.

Slowly, the Mycenaeans replaced the Minoans as the powerhouses of the Aegean Sea. They took over much of the trade with lands like Canaan and Egypt, but they also raided, looted, and participated in piracy. Eventually, they even took over the Minoans, expanding their territory to include the island of Crete.

What Were They About?

Pre-Greek Religion

The Mycenaeans are seen as the beginning of Greek culture. Nowhere is this more evident than in their religion, which they also adapted from their frenemies, the Minoans. Their earth goddesses and sky gods eventually evolved into the Greek pantheon of Zeus and his extended family. Their oral tradition of myths and legends was passed down to become the basis for Greek literature, like the epic tales of Homer. Their megarons would become the blueprint for Greek temples, which they would build on the sites of Mycenaean citadels.

But considering everything the Mycenaeans borrowed from the Minoans, it does make you wonder. Would it be fair to say the beginning of the Greek civilization was, in fact, the Minoans?

Architectural Advancements

Lion's Gate at Mycenae

With their cyclopean walls and megarons, the Mycenaeans have gone down in history for their architectural advancements. One amazing example that remains for us to see today is the **Lion's Gate** at Mycenae. The **lintel** across the top of the city entrance weighs approximately 20 tons (about the same as 14 average cars). Above the lintel sit the two carved lionesses who give the gate its name. They stand on either side of a Minoan-style column that tapers toward the bottom. The lions' heads, which may have been bronze, are missing now, yet it's easy to see why the ancient Greeks thought that giants must have lifted these stones into place.

Grave Circles and Shaft Tombs

Much of what we know about the Mycenaeans is thanks to artifacts discovered in their tombs, like the Mask of Agamemnon. It is clear from the jewelry, gold masks, valuable swords and daggers, and other wealth deposited there that burial was an important religious ritual for them. They constructed **shaft tombs**, trenches dug straight into the ground with a burial site at the end. These shafts were organized into **grave circles**, one or more circular areas separately walled within the city. Two grave circles have been discovered in Mycenae.

Why Did They Fall?

We don't know the precise reasons why the Mycenaeans fell. We have lots of guesses, though. There is evidence of a series of fires at Mycenaean citadels between 1200 and 1100 BCE. These could have been caused by internal battles, outside invaders, or natural disasters. Likely, there was a combination of causes, similar to those destroying other civilizations during the Bronze Age Collapse.

One possible explanation was the arrival of a group called the **Dorians**. These low-technology tribes might have contributed to the Mycenaean downfall as "invaders," or they might have coincidently appeared at this time. We don't know for sure. However, the Dorians were the first of what we call the ancient Greeks.

The period between when the Mycenaeans abandoned their citadels (1200 to 1100 BCE) and when the ancient Greeks began to rebuild on those sites (about 800 BCE) is sometimes called the **Greek Dark Age** due to a lack of written records from this time.

The Phoenicians

Who Were They?

Phoenicians were brave, seafaring traders who dominated the Mediterranean and connected the known world with their complex system of trading routes. They were also manufacturers and innovators. Some of their products were so prized that many larger civilizations left them alone simply so that they would not disrupt the supply of goods that the Phoenicians made.

The Phoenicians were also responsible for an invention *we* rely on today, every day. I'll give you a hint. You're reading it right now. They invented the first true alphabet, which was the basis for our own.

Phoenicians did not call themselves Phoenicians. In fact, they really didn't call themselves anything at all. They were a collection of city-states that shared a language, religion, and culture but had no central government. People thought of themselves as being from their city, not from Phoenicia. The term "Phoenician" comes from the Greek word *Phoinikes*, meaning "purple." Yes, the Greeks called them "the Purple People," a good example of how nicknames stick. We'll see why shortly. First, let's look at where this fearless and clever people lived.

Where Did They Live?

Do you remember King Akhenaten in Egypt, who decided to buck the system and try to create a monotheistic religion for the god Aten? Well, if you recall, he also built himself a new capital called Amarna. Archaeologists found an entire cache of clay tablets there that came to be known as the **Amarna Letters**. These were correspondence between different nations that talked about gifts rulers were giving each other, who was marrying who, and complaints about how Egypt was ignoring their vassal states. But, among these were letters from Phoenician rulers who referenced the land of **Canaan**. This is where Phoenician city-states lay.

Canaan was a region along the eastern coast of the Mediterranean Sea, sometimes called the **Levant**. The Phoenicians lived in the northern part of Canaan, in what is now Lebanon and portions of modern-day Israel and Syria. So Phoenicians were Canaanites, but not all Canaanites were Phoenicians. Their major cities were **Tyre** and **Sidon**. Their religious center of **Byblos** is also important to notice, so we'll look at these cities in a moment.

In addition to their home base in Canaan, the Phoenicians had a vast network of trading posts—colonies, if you will—around the Mediterranean Sea. In this way, they created stepping stones around Africa, Europe, and Asia from which they could conduct their **transit trade**.

The most influential of these colonies was the city of **Carthage** in North Africa. Eventually, Carthage would grow to be an empire of its own, the Carthaginian Empire. And it would go down in history for its rivalry with Rome during the infamous **Punic Wars** (*Punicus* is the Latinized form of the Greek *Phoenix*).

When Did They Live?

Like other civilizations, the history of the Phoenicians goes back long before their height of power. Sidon was founded about 4000 BCE. There was trade between Egypt and Byblos shortly after that. Yet, the Phoenicians weren't mega-traders, colonizers, and manufacturing giants until about 1500 BCE. Their golden years stretched until about 332 BCE. We will primarily focus on this period.

In 332 BCE, mainland Phoenicia in Canaan was conquered by the Greeks led by Alexander the Great; however, many of their colonies lived on for a while. By then, some were city-states in their own right and continued to flourish under their own control. Carthage, founded by the city of Tyre in 814 BCE, is the best example of this. The Carthaginians were not entirely defeated by Rome until the end of the Third Punic War, about 146 BCE. Eventually, the Roman Empire snagged up what remained of the Phoenician outposts.

If you think the year 332 BCE sounds familiar, that's because you've heard it before. This was the same year Alexander the Great invaded Egypt. It was a very busy year for Alex—a seven-month siege of Tyre *and* becoming pharaoh-god of Egypt!

How Did They Rise?

Geography and natural resources allowed the Phoenicians to become masters of the sea. They lived along the coast and were hemmed in by mountains to the east. When they needed to move from place to place, the sea was the easiest way. They also liked the security of the islets just off the coast and sometimes placed their cities directly on them. This, too, made ship-going necessary.

Fortunately, the Phoenicians had everything they needed to make a sailing lifestyle work for them. While great civilizations, like Mesopotamia and Egypt, had to do without large trees and weave boats out of reeds or use small planks, the Phoenicians had a ready supply of large cedar trees. The cedars of Lebanon were coveted throughout the ancient world and are even referenced in the Bible. They not only enabled the Phoenicians to make big, sturdy vessels, but these trees gave them something valuable to trade with other nations. Egyptian sarcophagi were often made with cedar trees from Lebanon.

With their easy access to the sea and fine ships, the Phoenicians were naturally inclined to strike out into the world via water routes. Over time, they perfected the arts of sailing, navigating, and shipbuilding and then applied those skills to trading. In this way, the Phoenicians became Mediterranean powerhouses, small yet mighty. The major civilizations absolutely depended on them and the goods they brought, even though the Phoenicians never became a large civilization themselves.

What Were They About?

The Alphabet

The Phoenicians exported many essential goods, but none have stood the test of time quite like their written language. Before 1000 BCE, the Phoenicians used Mesopotamian cuneiform to write their language, which was very close to Hebrew. At some point, the Phoenicians took simplified versions of Egyptian hieroglyphics and created the first true alphabet—22 symbols, written from right to left, representing consonant sounds. Combining these sounds, the Phoenicians could write any word without requiring hundreds or thousands of symbols to represent different concepts.

There were no symbols for vowels in the Phoenician alphabet. However, this is not a major problem. We often abbreviate words today by leaving out the vowels and can still read them just fine. To see some examples, just check out some customized license plates next time you're riding down the highway. Eventually, the Greeks adopted this alphabet and added symbols for vowels. That was, then, taken by the Romans and Latinized. Voila! You have the basis for our own alphabet today. You can even see the resemblance in some of the symbols.

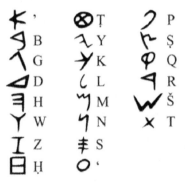

Phoenician Alphabet

Speaking of writing, did you know the name for the Bible comes from the Phoenicians? Byblos, you'll recall, was an important religious city for the Phoenicians. They considered it the oldest of all cities, founded by their god, El, at the beginning of time. It was, in fact, a prosperous trading city by around 3000 BCE and is a candidate for "oldest city in the world" because it has been inhabited continuously for 7000 years! Anyway, one item traded through Byblos that the Greeks treasured was papyrus from Egypt. The Greeks associated paper with this city so much that they adopted its name as their word for "book"—*biblos*. From this word, we get the title "Bible."

Purple Dye

The Phoenicians did not just trade their local timber and foreign goods. They were also craftsmen, skilled in making decorative items like carved ivory, blown glass, and sculpted metal bowls. But one **commodity** they manufactured was more sought after than all the others, purple dye. And this is how the Phoenicians got their colorful name—the Purple People—from the Greeks.

According to Phoenician mythology, the dye was discovered when the patron god of Tyre, **Melqart**, was walking along the beach with his dog. When the dog chewed on the washed-up shell of a **murex**, Melqart noticed the dog's mouth was stained purple. Melqart's wife asked for a garment made in that color, and the reddish-purple dye was born.

Murex

Sometimes called Tyrian purple, the dye was not easy to make. First, the shellfish, which lived in deep water, were baited and trapped. Then, the shells were crushed and left in the sun for three days. Salt was added, and the mixture boiled down. Can you imagine the smell? No wonder the workshops at Sidon were over eight miles from the city!

It took 10,000 tiny, stinky murexes to make about a gram of dye. That's about the mass of a paperclip or a piece of gum. The pile of shells left at Sidon is as tall as a 13-story building. So, of course, with all this work involved, the dye didn't come cheap. But it wasn't worth its weight in gold; it was worth more! In 301 CE, a Roman emperor records that a pound of the dye cost him three pounds of gold. That's almost $60,000 today.

The color was unique, long-lasting, and expensive. Because of this, only the wealthiest people could get it. Roman emperors even controlled its use, forbidding foreigners from buying it and reserving it for elite people to wear on the most special occasions. Even today, we associate purple with royalty because of the Phoenicians.

Trading

Phoenicians were the long-haul truckers of their day. Their bulky, square-sailed cargo vessels, which could carry as much as 450 tons of goods, often sailed in fleets of 50 ships and were guarded by the Phoenicians' warships. They also had a third, smaller type of ship for local trips or fishing excursions known for its horse-head prow.

As their trade routes expanded, so did the Phoenicians' need for permanent trading posts. These stops around the Mediterranean, about a day's sail from one another, eventually grew into entire colonies. Here, traders would acquire local goods to trade elsewhere and drop off raw materials obtained from other destinations to be manufactured into fine, finished pieces.

Phoenician traders were everywhere. They served the eastern empires of the Persians and Babylonians. They are considered the only mariners from the Mediterranean to dare venture into the Atlantic in those days. They sailed down the west coast of Africa and wandered as far north as Britain and Ireland. Herodotus claimed that they **circumnavigated** the entire continent of Africa on behalf of the Egyptians. But you know how reliable Herodotus was. This story has its doubters.

Phoenician Trading Ship

A Phoenician ship might leave from Tyre with cedar logs, purple dye, and fine glass and stop in the Greek islands of Cyprus, Rhodes, and Crete to collect more goods. From there, they may head down to Egypt for papyrus and then cross the northern coast of Africa, stopping at their main colony of Carthage. Next, they would strike out into the Atlantic and down the coast of Africa to modern-day Senegal, where they could trade for gold. Then, they would turn north, as far as Ireland, to trade for the tin that Mediterranean civilizations needed so badly for their alloys. On the way back south, they would stop in Spain for iron, which they bought with their African gold. Then, back in the Mediterranean, they would drop off more gold at their colony in Sardinia, where it would be crafted into beautiful decorative pieces, which they could sell for much more than the raw gold alone.

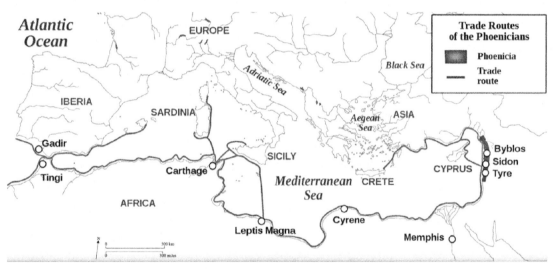

Phoenician Trade Routes

In this way, the Phoenicians were invaluable middlemen to the other ancient civilizations. No civilization had all the resources they needed and wanted in their area, but they all had things they were willing to trade. The Phoenicians made these connections possible *and* dispersed culture, language, and art in the process.

Why Did They Fall?

Well, everything was going quite well for Phoenicia, really, until Alexander the Great. Even as he began his march south from Macedonia in 333 BCE, conquering all the way, things looked like they were going to be okay. The cities of Sidon and Byblos had acknowledged Alexander's greatness with many gifts, and Alexander had left them intact.

Tyre thought they would do the same thing and sent an **envoy** to meet him along the way with gifts just as lovely as those Sidon sent. Alexander accepted them, and everything looked good. But then, Alexander had one request.

You see, the new city of Tyre was built on one of those islets just off the coast that the Phoenicians loved. They were easy to fortify and defend. This is where Tyre's entire navy was stationed. Alexander let it be known that he wanted to sacrifice to the god of Tyre, Melqart, in the new city. (Melqart was the equivalent of the Greek demigod **Hercules**.) The Phoenicians, suspecting this was just a ploy to occupy the city and take over their defenses, offered for Alexander to sacrifice in the old city on the mainland instead. Alexander, unused to hearing the word "no," would not be deterred. He sent **emissaries** to Tyre demanding its immediate surrender. When the Tyrians killed them, Alexander knew he would not be doing this the easy way.

Tyre was exceptionally well protected on an island with a powerful navy and massive walls that had withstood sieges in the past. Alexander knew all of this. His motto must have been, "Go big or go back to Macedonia," because, after consulting with his generals, he decided that the best tactic would be to unmake it an island. Alexander began constructing a giant **causeway** with rubble from the old city to bridge the half-mile gap and link Tyre with the mainland. This way, he could just drive his massive siege weaponry out there directly to the city walls.

Tyre is no longer an island thanks to the effort of Alexander the Great and his army. Aerial photos show it's now a peninsula with the original island connected to the mainland by Alexander's causeway.

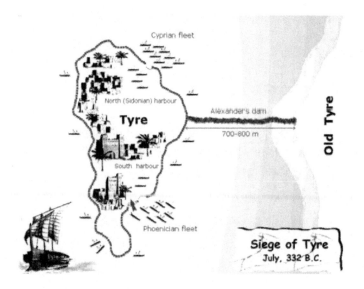

110

Alexander pounded away at the city from his causeway and ships from January to July. The Tyrians put up a valiant defense, often winning the battle but, ultimately, losing the war. At long last, Alexander offered his sacrifice to Melqart (Hercules). Four hundred of his men had been killed, and, in return, Alexander slew 8,000 Tyrians and sold 30,000 more into slavery. Then, he was off to Egypt!

After this, the Phoenicians were ruled by the Macedonians and, later, by the Romans. Although some of their colonies like Carthage persisted for a time, by the first century CE, most of their native culture had vanished.

Historical Highlights

Minoans and Mycenaeans and Phoenicians, oh, my! Let's review the really important takeaways from our visit to these small but influential Mediterranean civilizations:

- The Minoans built their civilization on the island of Crete. They are sometimes called Cretans after their island or Minoans after their legendary King Minos.
- The palace of King Minos at Knossos shows us the Minoans' art and architectural styles, including life-sized frescoes, bull and marine animal themes, and the double-headed ax. The palace is also the site of Greek mythology's legendary labyrinth and Minotaur.
- The Minoans were taken down by a variety of causes such as earthquakes, land overuse, and invasion by the Mycenaeans.
- The Mycenaeans rose to power on mainland Greece, borrowing and adapting much of their culture from the Minoans, especially their religion.
- The Mycenaeans built fortified settlements on hilltops, called citadels, with massive stone walls called "cyclopean walls" because the Greeks thought the giant Cyclops must have built them. Later, Greek city-states, like Thebes and Sparta, were built on these sites.

- The Mycenaeans' written language, Linear B, is the earliest form of written Greek, and their culture is considered the precursor to ancient Greek culture.
- The Phoenicians were a loose collection of city-states on the eastern Mediterranean who became master sea goers, established colonies as far away as north Africa, and dominated trade between other civilizations.
- The Phoenicians were famous for manufacturing ships, glass, and a very expensive purple dye called Tyrian purple.
- Alexander the Great eventually conquered the original city-states of Phoenicia. Still, their colony of Carthage would become the great Carthaginian Empire and battle Rome in the Punic Wars.

CHAPTER 7

The Greeks

Chances are, if you are reading this book, you live in a society dominated by Western civilization. **Western civilization**, sometimes called **Western culture**, refers to the values, politics, ethics, ideas, technology, social **norms**, and traditions of the Western world.

The Western world used to mean Europe—everything west of Asia and north of Africa. Then, gradually, explorers, settlers, and conquerors—prompted by their geography, religions, politics, and greed—expanded worldwide, taking their culture with them. Now, Western civilization refers to all of Europe, North and South America, Australia, and even Russia in Northern Asia—an enormous swath of the world. Now, while there may be a great many differences between the people in these places, there are also a tremendous number of similarities. And the staggering thing is that many, if not most, of these similarities have roots in the culture of ancient Greece.

The Greek word for their homeland was *Hellas*, so their culture is sometimes called **Hellenistic**. Technically, this refers to a period of Greek culture from 323 to about 30 BCE. Hints of Hellenistic culture, large and small, are found in our government, theater, writing, language, education, art, literature, science, math, architecture—we could go on, but you get the point.

What you are doing this very second is handed down to you from the Greeks. Remember, our friend Herodotus, the "father of history," was Greek. He was the first to record an accurate account of history (at least by his loose definition). By studying history, we are following in his tradition.

Whether you are reading this book for school or pleasure, we get the language to express that action from the Greeks as well. The word "school" comes to us (through Latin) from the Greek word *skholē*, which means—wait for it—"Leisure!" Surprised? Well, the Greeks thought of learning as a pleasurable and contemplative task, one for which you had to have *leisure* time to engage in thought, investigation, and discussion. So, over time, this word became associated with a place of learning. Even the words on this page are written in a script with roots in the Greek alphabet. These are just a couple of examples of how ancient Greek culture is tucked away inside almost every part of our own.

But why Greece? How did this ancient civilization, among all the others, manage to have such a significant and lasting impact on the world? There are many reasons for this, but here are the top two.

The Greeks spread their own culture through trade, conquest, and colonization. Alexander the Great alone was responsible for bringing the world the Hellenistic Period when Greece dominated Eastern Europe, Asia Minor, the Middle East, the Levant, *and* Northern Africa. As Greek culture took hold among other peoples, it was passed down within their civilizations.

Another reason Greek culture spread? Other nations loved it! Many cultures voluntarily adopted or copied certain aspects of Greek culture for various reasons. Some thought their art and architecture were beautiful; some thought their technology was advanced and improved; others thought their drama and literature were entertaining and refined. The Greeks made good things, and just about everyone wanted, secretly or openly, to be a little bit (or a lot) like them. Ancient Greeks were indeed the influencers of their day.

Perhaps no one was a bigger fan of the Greeks than the Romans. In the next chapter, we will examine the many things the Romans "borrowed" from the Greeks. So, with the spread of the Roman Republic and Empire, Greek culture spread even more throughout the geographic world and throughout the pages of history, down to us today.

The Rise of Greece

Just as we have with the other civilizations we've visited, let's familiarize ourselves with the where and when of ancient Greece.

Like so many other civilizations, geography drove Greece's rise to prominence. The sea gave them swift and easy routes to trade and expand. **Greece** juts out into the Mediterranean Sea on a peninsula. We have the **Adriatic** and the **Ionian Seas** to its west, which separate it from the Italian peninsula (ancient Rome). To the east, we have the Aegean Sea, which separates Greece from Türkiye (Turkey) today. In ancient times, that was Asia Minor or the Persian Empire. Here in the Aegean, we find an **archipelago**, or collection of small islands, called the **Cyclades**, and to the south, we have the island of Crete, the previous home of the Minoans. This area, around the Aegean, is where most of our exploration will take place, although Greece would also establish colonies as far away as modern-day Spain and India.

The Greek peninsula itself is divided into two main parts. The northern part was called **Macedonia** (or Macedon), and the southern part was called **Peloponnese**. Peloponnese is really a peninsula *on* a peninsula—connected to the mainland by an **isthmus**, or narrow strip of land, called the **Isthmus of Corinth**. Peloponnese is where our search for the ancient Greeks begins.

Before the Greeks were in Peloponnese, the Mycenaeans were there. We'll be exploring the Greek civilization beginning with the collapse of the Mycenaeans in about 1200 BCE, all the way through 31/30 BCE, when the Romans conquered the last Greek stronghold.

The Greeks were, of course, not an advanced civilization for this entire period. In fact, it was a long road from illiteracy and low technology to the height of their civilized accomplishments. Before we look at their time periods, let's take a closer look at the cultural legacy the Greeks left us in their wake.

Religion

The enormous volume of stories about Greek gods, goddesses, heroes, and monsters is what we call Greek mythology. It was their religion, and it served many functions for them.

It gave the different city-states a shared history and culture that bound them together despite their differences. It gave them explanations for the world around them and why things happened, like storms or seasons. It gave them a way of trying to control their lives by following rituals and making sacrifices to appease the gods. It also inspired them to achieve outstanding accomplishments with the idea that they, too, could earn immortality.

Greek mythology was created over time through oral tradition. It was a way for the Greeks to pass on stories of historical events like battles and other shared histories. There was a wide range of responses to the stories among the Greeks. Religiously observant Greeks may have mostly believed the legends. Others regarded them as mostly fiction. Some enjoyed them for entertainment purposes or for the sense of patriotism they inspired. But almost all Greeks, no matter how skeptical, were religious in some form.

The Greek Pantheon

If you lived in ancient Greece, there would be no aspect of your life that was not intertwined with religion. From entertainment to war to politics—religious ritual touched it all. There was a god or goddess for every occasion. This ensemble of a culture's religious figures is called a **pantheon**.

In addition to superpowers, Greeks gave their gods human characteristics, emotions, and even character flaws. Gods could be jealous, forgetful, vengeful, or careless. These human-like flaws must have made them seem very relatable to the Greeks. They were more powerful versions of people you knew or even of yourself.

The Greek pantheon consisted of twelve major gods and goddesses called **Olympians** because they were said to live on the sacred **Mount Olympus**.

The Olympians were:
- **Zeus**, father of the gods and controller of the weather;
- **Hera**, wife of Zeus and goddess of marriage and family;
- **Poseidon**, brother of Zeus and god of sea and storms;
- **Demeter**, sister of Zeus and goddess of agriculture;
- **Ares**, son of Zeus and Hera and god of war;
- **Athena**, daughter of Zeus and goddess of wisdom, war, and crafts;
- **Hephaestus**, son of Hera and god of fire;
- **Apollo**, son of Zeus and Leto and god of music and the bow;
- **Artemis**, twin sister of Apollo and goddess of hunting and nature;
- **Aphrodite**, the goddess of love and beauty, sometimes called the daughter of Zeus and Dione;
- **Hermes**, son of Zeus and Maia and god of many things, including trade, travel, thieves, domesticated animals, sleep, and more; and
- **Dionysos**, a popular favorite, the son of Zeus and Semele and god of wine, merry-making, and theater.

Greek Name (Roman Name)

Zeus (Jupiter)

Hera (Juno)

Poseidon (Neptune)

Demeter (Ceres)

Ares (Mars)

Athena (Minerva)

Hephaestus (Vulcan)   Apollo (Apollo)   Artemis (Diana)

Aphrodite (Venus)   Hermes (Mercury)   Dionysus/Bacchus (Bacchus)

It was a complicated family, to be sure. But these 12 were not the only cast of characters to keep track of by any means. There were many other gods and goddesses in this family tree besides those that resided on Mount Olympus. **Hades**, brother of Zeus and god of the underworld, is just one example. So is **Persephone**, Hades's wife, daughter of Demeter, and another goddess of agriculture. This is getting rather complicated, isn't it?

There were **heroes** too, like **Hercules**, who was half god, half human. The heroes helped the Greeks relate even more closely to the gods since they were half mortal like themselves. There were also the **Titans**, a whole other family of gods and goddesses who preceded the Olympians. Then, there were all of the **monsters**. These were not always scary, gross creatures as we think of monsters today. Instead, they were *any* mythological beast, like **Pegasus**, the winged horse, or the one-eyed **Cyclops** credited with building the enormous cyclopean walls.

The bottom line? There was much to keep track of between their religious figures and the endless stories about their antics and achievements.

Oracles

With all these gods and goddesses up there having all kinds of moods and controlling all manner of activities on earth, the Greeks wanted to know what they were thinking. So, it was common practice for people to consult an **oracle** to ask them for advice.

An oracle was a priestess who would consider your question, fall into a trance (sometimes caused by breathing natural gasses rising through a crack in the ground), and then let you know what the gods said about it. For example, if you wanted to know how the gods felt about you buying a piece of land, getting married, or starting a war—an oracle was the place to go.

The most famous oracle in the world was the **Oracle at Delphi** in the temple of Apollo. Anyone who had an important question and could make the trip, commoner or ruler, would consult her. Wealthy questioners would pay enormous prices to skip the line. This shows us how seriously the Greeks took their religion.

The Olympics

Today, we think of the **Olympic Games** as sports. When they originated in ancient Greece, they were just as much about religion. Every four years, from 776 BCE to 393 CE (That's over a millennium!), the Greek city-states gathered to hold athletic competitions in honor of Zeus. The location of the games was **Olympia**, named after Mount Olympus but actually in a very different spot on the Peloponnese. There was an enormous statue of Zeus and groves of olive trees on site. At the Games' closing, they sacrificed 100 oxen to the father of the gods. The Greeks highly valued physical fitness and competition, and the Olympic games connected these attributes to the gods and god-like characteristics. Showing off your strength, like Hercules, or your speed, like Hermes, was as close as you might get to being a "hero" on earth.

The Olympics began as a single event—a foot race called the *stadion*—which was held in an arena called the *stade* (note the connection to our modern word "stadium"). Over the years, additional events like chariot and horse racing, boxing and wrestling, javelin and discus throwing, and jumping were added. In time, games were held in a few other cities like Delphi, but the ones at Olympia were always the most important.

Javelin Throwers

The official prize for winners was a crown or wreath of olive branches, but, in reality, they received much more. City-states offered huge incentives for their young men to return victorious. Processions and banquets, free meals, invitations to join the elite social clubs, and sometimes even large sums of money.

The real prize, however, was fame and glory. To the Greeks, immortality was having your name sung in songs and told in stories—just like the gods and heroes—long after you were gone. The winner's name was listed in the official victor list; statues were carved of them; **odes** (poems) were written about them. So, again, we see a connection between sports and religion. Beating the best of the best at a footrace made you immortal. It makes you wonder if this connection between having your name remembered and everlasting life after death is one of the reasons why the Greeks achieved so much. Were they driven in science and other subjects, as well as sports, to see their names go down in history?

The Olympics was the most important cultural event in Greece. The calendar was even set by it. An **Olympiad** was the four year time period between the Games. Preparing for the Olympics was serious business. Athletes had trainers and needed to arrive at Olympia one month before the Games for training. When they got there, they had to declare that they had already been training for ten months. There were official judges and vendors to feed the mass of spectators who came to cheer their favorites. Speaking of spectators, it is estimated that over 45,000 people from far and wide traveled to watch the Olympics. This was possible for two reasons. First, the Olympics were in the summer, a slow time of year for agriculture, so that most people could spare the time. Secondly, a truce was declared, temporarily stopping all war between the city-states for a three-month period around the Games. It was illegal to carry a weapon in the territory around Olympia or disrupt the travel of any spectator or athlete in any part of Greece. The city-state of Sparta was banned from the 420 BCE Games for violating this truce.

One category of people, though, was always excluded from participating. Women could not compete in, or even watch, the Games. There have been some notable exceptions, however. One loophole allowed women to own the horses that competed in chariot races. Since the crown was awarded to the horse owner and not the chariot driver, women have technically won in this way—even though they didn't get to witness their victory. Eventually, games to honor Hera for female athletes were held at a different time of year.

Four of the seven Wonders of the World were in the Greek world—at least at the time they were built. So we know two things. First, the Greeks were masters at making impressively large and beautiful items. And secondly, they likely thought a lot of themselves. (The two most well-known "Wonders" lists were both written by Greeks.)

Statue of Zeus at Olympia

Nike

The statue of Zeus at Olympia was one of these Wonders. It was the actual must-see event for anyone attending the games.

This 4-story-tall Zeus, crafted from gold and ivory, was positioned in his temple so that he could "look" out and observe the ceremonies in his honor. Silver, glass, ebony, enamel, and jewels encrusted his robes and other details of the statue. Zeus was seated on his throne, and, in one hand, he held a **Nike**, the Greek's **personification** of Victory. Olympic-goers must have marveled at the god in whose honor the athletes competed!

Legacy

There is tremendous value in knowing a little bit about Greek mythology because of its sheer number of cultural references in our modern world. This is one of the best examples of how studying history can make you better informed about your own culture. Once you begin to look for these references, you will be astounded at how many you can find! Our planets and their moons bear the names of Greek gods or the Roman versions of them. So do many months of the year and days of the week. Atlas Van Lines; Nike shoes; Phoenix, Arizona; Trident gum—all throwbacks to Greek mythology.

And since we've mentioned the Romans, we should note that their religion and pantheon were borrowed heavily from the Greeks. Jupiter is their equivalent of Zeus. Venus is their Aphrodite. Mercury is their Hermes. So, if you look at all of the cultural references to Roman mythology and consider those originally came from Greece, the impact becomes even more impressive.

Philosophy

Have you ever heard anyone referred to as a "skeptic" (someone who has doubts or reservations about a topic)? Hint: we've seen the word "skeptical" in this chapter! What about "stoic" (enduring hardship without complaining)? Maybe you've heard someone label another person "cynical" (only concerned about themselves or distrustful of the motives of others). These are all words we get from Greek philosophy. They were actually the names different groups of philosophers gave themselves to describe how they looked at the world. But what are philosophers anyway?

Technically speaking, "**philosophy**" comes from the Greek words *philo*, meaning love, and *sophia*, meaning wisdom. So **philosophers** are literally "lovers of wisdom." Today, we tend to separate philosophy into its own branch of study; one concerned with brainy subjects, like ethics, reason, and logic, or metaphysical ones, like the origins of the universe or the true nature of reality. The same was true for ancient Greek philosophers; however, their philosophers might also study the natural world, astronomy, mathematics, physics, or any number of other subjects that we now consider separate domains.

Historians have noted that sometimes a civilization develops philosophy when there is a breakdown in religion, in other words, when someone questions the culture's religious explanations for things, like how the world came about, why natural disasters occur, why the sun rises every day in the east and sets in the west, and so on. This is precisely what happened in Greece. A fellow called **Thales** (about 585 BCE) is sometimes called the "First Philosopher" because, besides being an incredible astronomer and mathematician, he was the first to inquire into the origins of the universe. Thales did not accept the religious explanations that the gods created everything supernaturally. Instead, he used reason and an **empirical** approach based on observation to come to his conclusions—a true scientist! Thales decided that the origins of all things, or what he called the "First Cause," must have been water. As a side note, this is similar to the Mesopotamian and Egyptian creation stories. It is interesting to wonder if Thales studied or was influenced by these other civilizations.

Now, whether or not Thales was correct is really beside the point. He began a long tradition of thinking about things in a new way. Beginning with Thales, the Greeks became some of the first people to try to understand their world with logic, reason, and scientific inquiry. Not only that, aspects of their philosophies can be seen in many of the major world religions of today, including Christianity.

After Thales, it became increasingly popular in Greece to use one's *skholē*, or leisure time, to pursue knowledge or to thrash out answers to tough questions, like the origins of the universe. By the middle of the fifth century BCE, the Greeks had made an entire profession out of this. Early philosophers would travel from city to city and, for a fee, tutor the sons of private citizens and give lectures. These learned men were called **Sophists**.

They were also a bit like the world's first lawyers. Lawsuits were becoming frequent at the time, and Sophists provided the service of teaching people how to argue their cases in court effectively. They were so skilled in teaching the art of persuasion that it led to a reputation for being clever but fallacious (using faulty logic) to win an argument at any cost. Later, Greek philosophers would define themselves as "true" philosophers by distinguishing themselves from the shady Sophists.

Socrates

The Greeks admired beauty. You might even say they worshiped it. But one man from the city-state of **Athens** did not fit their mold of good looks. It was said that **Socrates** (470/469–399 BCE) had bulging eyes, a snub nose, and a pot belly. He wore dirty robes and always the same pair of sandals. In addition to his unkempt appearance, Socrates made a habit of hanging around Athens's *agora* (market) and tormenting the upper class with annoying questions. He would be called the "Father of Western Philosophy."

Socrates claimed to be ignorant or to know nothing. But, in fact, all of his questions were a clever plan. Socrates wanted people to question what they believed and *why* they believed it. He would start with a simple enough question, something like, "What is the noblest of arts?" And his subject (read "victim") would give an answer—perhaps, "Surely, it is sculpting," gesturing to a statue of a discus thrower nearby. Because Socrates tended to pick on the city's aristocrats, this man was probably used to thinking of himself as quite intelligent. He expected everyone within earshot to nod and whisper to one another about the wisdom of his response. But Socrates was just getting warmed up. "Why do you say that? Can you explain further?" Socrates's target might hesitate a moment and frown. Then, maybe, he would say something like, "Because the sculptor shows us the forms of the gods." He chuckled, thinking himself done with this fool, and started to walk on. "But don't the athletes train to perfect their bodies like the gods? Would not the living athlete be nobler than the maker of the marble statue then?" The man would halt mid-step, everyone's eyes on him, waiting to see how he would answer.

This way of going back and forth, each answer leading to more questions, came to be called the **Socratic Method**. Socrates's questions were designed to expose someone's hidden assumptions and biases and the weaknesses in their knowledge, reasoning, and logic. Socrates was trying to make people look within, question themselves, and bring to the surface all the hidden thoughts they took for granted. Socrates was famously quoted by his student, **Plato**, as saying, "an unexamined life is not worth living."

Socrates questioned people doggedly about any and every topic you can think of, from hot-button political issues to everyday affairs that didn't seem worth questioning. Not surprisingly, he made a few enemies doing this. But he also amassed a great many fans— the Twitter followers of his day. Many young, rich aristocrats had the time to spend in the *agora* and enjoyed hearing Socrates ruffle the feathers of the city elite. They became Socrates's students, and Plato would be the most famous among them.

Interestingly, Socrates never taught his students directly by instructing or lecturing them with facts. He always asked questions and prompted his students to reason their way to the result. He also never wrote anything down. Everything we know today about Socrates comes from the writings of his students, especially Plato. Today, the Socratic Method is used in universities, law and medical schools, and even in counseling and therapy.

But as well-known as his method has become, Socrates is just as famous for something else—his death. Eventually, the patience of Athens wore thin, and Socrates was charged with

impiety (lack of respect for the gods), introducing new gods, and "corrupting the youth." Instead of doing what was expected of him and giving an eloquent speech, declaring his innocence and begging for mercy, Socrates doubled-down. He told the court that he would never stop practicing his philosophy and, what's more, that he was doing Athens a favor. Like a fly on a sluggish horse, Socrates claimed, he kept the city aroused and alert, and maybe his "punishment" should be the free meals awarded to Olympic heroes. The audacity! Socrates was convicted and sentenced to die by drinking hemlock poison. Socrates accepted his fate, even though his friends offered to bribe the guards and let him escape. Instead, he chose to respect the laws of Athens, even if that meant facing death.

Plato

After the death of Socrates, several of his students immediately split off and formed different schools of philosophy based on his teachings. It's interesting to see how different these schools of thought are from one another, all based on the teachings of the same individual. The **Skeptics**, **Cynics**, and **Stoics** were all influenced by Socrates.

School of Athens

In a wooded garden close to his home, **Plato** (428/427–348/347 BCE) created his famous **Academy** of Athens. It was probably a *gymnasia*, where men would gather for intellectual discussion and physical exercise. Here, he taught his students and shared many of his writings, which would go down in history as some of the most important and influential writings of Western thought.

Most of Plato's writings are called **Dialogues**. These were conversations around a particular theme, and Plato usually put Socrates in the starring role. We can't be sure, however, whether or not these conversations were accurate recreations of Socrates's discussions and beliefs. Two of Plato's most famous *Dialogues* are *Republic*, his thoughts on the ideal society, and *Apology*, which some consider his masterpiece. In the *Apology*, we witness Plato's account of Socrates's courtroom speech in defense of himself.

While Socrates was trying to get people to see that whatever they claimed was "good" or "beautiful" or "true" was based on their own subjective opinion, Plato had a different idea. Plato was forever searching for the *Truth*, and he thought that it was out there if only we could access it. In his **Theory of Forms**, Plato suggests that there is a realm where the *true* version of everything exists. These perfected versions of earthly things are the Forms. What we observe in the world around us, he said, are merely reflections or shadows of this truth. In other words, we don't live in reality. If we see a horse, for example, and think it is beautiful, Plato says we are to realize that it is only an imperfect copy or reflection of the Form of a horse. This horse is only beautiful in as much as it relates to its *real* Form. He expressed this with a story called the **Allegory of the Cave** that still fascinates people today.

In the story, Plato compares us to people chained all our lives in a cave facing the wall. Behind us, there is a fire. Occasionally, people pass between us and the fire carrying different objects. These objects cast their shadows on the wall. We see the outlines of the people, food, animals, and plants they carry, but never the *real* objects. To us, this is our world, our reality. Then, one day, one of us escapes and gets out of the cave into the sunlight and sees the *actual* real world and all the things in it.

This person Plato likens to a philosopher (humble guy) who has grasped the true nature of Forms—the *real* reality—while the rest of us are still chained in the cave looking at shadows. When the philosopher returns to the cave and shares the shocking revelations of what *real* things are, the rest of us become angry, call him crazy, and resist his attempts to free us. We would rather continue to believe in our shadows. Insulting or not, the Allegory of the Cave makes for some very interesting discussions about perception, reality, and the difficulty of convincing other people to accept things they are not ready to accept.

The Romans destroyed Plato's original Academy in 86 BCE, but philosophers continued its tradition for nearly 1,000 years. Finally, in 529 CE, the Christian Roman **Emperor Justinian** ended it entirely by forbidding pagans from teaching publicly. Nevertheless, the Academy's impact endures in the writings of Plato, the philosophers it trained, and even in the use of the words "academy" and "academic" to describe education.

Aristotle

One of Plato's students at the Academy was **Aristotle** (384-322 BCE). Together, Socrates, Plato, and Aristotle form the triad of great Greek philosophers. Aristotle disagreed with Plato about his Theory of Forms, but this didn't seem to get in the way of his education. Aristotle came to be nicknamed "the man who knew everything" or simply "The Philosopher" or "The Master." He was so famous for his knowledge that he needed no other introduction.

Aristotle wrote on every topic, from agriculture to logic. He created the field of metaphysics and formed a standardized method for studying a subject, the precursor to today's scientific method. The classification system we use for naming organisms by genus and species (*Homo sapiens* or *Tyrannosaurus rex*) comes from him, too.

Aristotle's book, *Nicomachean Ethics*, written for his son Nichomachus, is required reading in Philosophy 101 classes today. It lays out his ideas about what it means to live a good life. Happiness was his highest ideal, but not how you might think. Happiness was not a momentary feeling to Aristotle. It was determined by the sum of how one lived their life. A life devoted to seeking virtue and being well-rounded might be considered a happy one. But just like the score of a football game can change until the last moment, with Aristotle, you could never be sure you'd lived a happy life until you'd gotten to the end of it.

It would be hard to pick which of Aristotle's contributions changed the world the most, but his most famous student would definitely make the list. Just as Socrates taught Plato and Plato taught Aristotle, Aristotle would become the private tutor of Alexander the Great. Aristotle was pro-war and considered non-Greeks barbarians and inferior to Greeks. It is believed that he encouraged Alexander in his military campaigns and thought conquest was an excellent opportunity for young Alex to live his best life in pursuit of that elusive happiness. Aristotle's influence can be seen in Alexander's habit of carrying books with him wherever he went, his skillful diplomatic wrangling, and his appreciation of art and culture. It is, perhaps, owing to Aristotle that Hellenistic culture spread throughout the world through the ambitions of his "greatest" student.

Incidentally, the ancient Greeks coined the phrase "barbarian." It was originally a derogatory term applied to all people who didn't speak Greek—Egyptians, Phoenicians, Persians, the whole non-Greek world. The word is an example of **onomatopoeia** (sounding like what it means). It is supposed to suggest how the unintelligible babble of these foreigners sounded to the Greeks—"bar, bar, bar." In other words, the Greeks were making fun of everyone else.

Science and Technology

The Greek philosophers didn't just sit around arguing about abstract concepts. They were practical people, too—true **"Renaissance men"** long before the Renaissance. Greek innovations in mathematics, engineering, physics, natural science, and more pushed human civilization forward by leaps and bounds.

Ancient Greek philosophers wrote about their discovery of fossils, developed early theories of gravity, and knew the earth was round. They built devices to raise and move water and made pulleys, cranes, and winches to lift marble blocks. In addition, they invented a portable sundial, a water-activated alarm clock, an odometer that measured distances over land, and a flamethrower!

There were far too many great Greek scientists and inventions to cover all of them in this book. But there are a few you should know about because they are referenced in Western society so frequently. So, let's look quickly at Archimedes, Pythagoras, and Euclid.

Archimedes

Here, ancient Greece gives us yet another "father." **Archimedes** (287-212 BCE) is considered the "father of mathematics." Born in the Greek colony of **Syracuse** on the island of **Sicily**, Archimedes' list of accomplishments is exhausting. He built a device that showed the current position of the planets. He invented the famous **Archimedes Screw**, a machine that pumped water out of the hulls of ships. Amazingly, it is still used today! And he frustrated the Romans for two long years, keeping them at bay with his war machines as they tried to capture the city of Syracuse.

Archimedean Screw

Much of what we know about Archimedes is **anecdotal**. He was famous in his own lifetime and often written about by contemporaries. Most of what we know combines his real achievements with stories that were probably embellished or quotes of questionable authenticity. True or not, they paint a picture of a fascinating man.

He was a master at the mechanics of leverage and is famously quoted as boasting, "Give me a place to stand, and I will move the Earth." He meant that he was confident that he could mathematically calculate not just the weight of the earth but the length of the lever needed to lift it.

We owe another famous quote to Archimedes—"*Eureka!*"—which means, "I have found it!"

In this story, the king of Syracuse, **Hiero**, had a problem. He had given a goldsmith some solid gold and commissioned a fine new crown for himself. When he received the finished crown, it weighed the same as the block of gold, but King Hiero was suspicious. Maybe the crown didn't seem quite the right size. Perhaps it wasn't the same rich yellow-golden color. Something about the crown made the king suspect that the goldsmith had mixed in some silver and kept the rest of the pure gold for himself. But how could he know for sure since the crown weighed exactly the same as the block of gold Hiero had given him? Well, King Hiero consulted with the smartest man in the city, Archimedes.

Certainly, Archimedes would have known the solution to the problem, but whether or not it came to him in the way the story tells is up for grabs. According to the legend, Archimedes pondered this problem as he prepared to take a bath. The bath was quite full, and as the mathematician lowered himself into the water, it spilled over onto the floor. *"Eureka!"* That was the answer! He was so excited that he rushed out into the street and off to tell Hiero without remembering to get dressed, shouting *"Eureka!"* all the way.

The solution? Fill a vessel with water to the very brim and lower the crown into it. Then, measure the water that spills over. Next, repeat the procedure with a block of pure gold that weighs the same as the crown. If the crown was pure gold too, the amount of spilled water would be the same. But if the goldsmith had substituted a lesser metal, the amount of spilled water would be more. This is because a larger amount of silver would be necessary to replace gold of the same weight. Unfortunately for the goldsmith, that was how the story went, and he was punished accordingly, thanks to Archimedes and his bath.

We'll never know whether this is all fact or just a legend about a brilliant man. But one part of the story rings true: Archimedes did seem somewhat absent-minded when he was trying to solve a problem. It is said that he would often forget to eat or bathe while engrossed in his work, and even his cause of death was related to total absorption in his work.

After two years of defeat at the hands of Archimedes's war machines, the Romans had finally captured Syracuse. Some time later, Archimedes was on the beach, fixated on drawing geometric shapes and calculations in the sand. A Roman soldier approached and commanded him to follow. Without paying the slightest bit of attention to who this person was or what they wanted, Archimedes simply replied, "Do not disturb my circles." The Roman soldier drew his sword and slew him on the spot for his **insolence**, which was more than likely just inattention. At least it can be said Archimedes died doing what he loved.

Pythagoras

Pythagoras (571- c. 497 BCE) was a philosopher and mathematician born on the Aegean island of **Samos**. He probably traveled to Egypt and Babylon in his younger days and influenced the likes of Plato and Aristotle. Herodotus references him but, for some reason, refuses to name him in his writings.

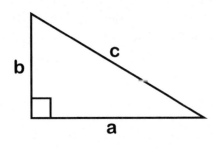

So why is Pythagoras relevant to us today? Well, he has left us his famous mathematical equation—the **Pythagorean Theorem**—which every elementary geometry student learns. With the simple and elegant $a^2+b^2=c^2$, Pythagoras explains the relationship of the sides of a right triangle to us.

$$a^2 + b^2 = c^2$$

Pythagorean Theorem

More practically, he tells us how far Suzie has traveled as the crow flies if she walks 4 miles east and then 7 miles north, a skill that will come in handy on standardized tests.

Euclid

The last great Greek mind we will peek into is **Euclid's**, a mathematician who lived around 300 BCE in **Alexandria, Egypt**, a Greek center of learning that rivaled Athens at the time.

While Euclid made many important mathematical discoveries in his own right, he is best known for his compilation of other people's findings. His book, *The Elements*, is the most widely used book on mathematics ever written and continues to be studied today. What made *The Elements* unique was its organized approach to teaching geometry from the basics, including definitions of terms. It was one of the earliest math textbooks.

Euclid took an approach to math that no one had ever taken before. He tried to figure out *why* certain mathematical ideas worked and if they applied in all circumstances. This made him a celebrity in Egypt with party tricks like calculating the heights of the pyramids.

These were just three of the many bright minds ancient Greece cultivated. Other civilizations admired and copied the Greeks for many reasons, but their advancements in technology and the sciences were absolutely near the top of the list. Is it any wonder they did, considering the gifts of knowledge the Greeks gave to the world?

Government and Society

The Greeks are fascinating because of the variety of their political systems. They shared a language, gods, and some customs. But, otherwise, each city-state, or **polis**, was independent and in charge of its own government and military. Only once, under Alexander the Great, was Greece united under the rule of a single Greek leader.

At one point, there were over 1,500 of these *poleis*, or city-states, in Greece. Each one consisted of a city or urban center, which might or might not be fortified. Common elements of a city were:
- An **acropolis**—a citadel or complex, usually for temples, built on a hill, usually the highest in the city. An example is the ruins of the **Parthenon** temple on the **Acropolis** in Athens. It is so famous that the proper noun "Acropolis" universally applies to this one.

Parthenon Temple

- An **agora**—originally an open-air place for people to gather and hear announcements. Later, it was the city marketplace. This was Socrates's favorite hang-out as he trolled unsuspecting Athenians with questions.
- A **gymnasium**—a building or outdoor area for men to partake in athletic exercise and training. We still use this word and its abbreviation "gym" today. Looking fit and being strong were very important to the Greeks. So, aristocratic men spent a lot of time at the gymnasium. Later, it would also be a place for teaching and philosophical discussion. It's where Plato set up his Academy.
- An **amphitheater**—an open-air venue with a central stage or performance area and tiered seating in a circular or half-circle shape. These were used for dramatic plays or for hearing court cases and political speeches. Theaters were an example of Greek excellence in science and technology. They could seat thousands of people and were perfectly designed for **acoustics**, allowing someone sitting in the very back row to clearly hear the person speaking—this in days *long* before microphones.

These trademark spaces defined the urban Greek city-state. Even their colonies far across the Mediterranean shared these features.

But a city-state was more than just the city. It also included the broad swath of agricultural land around the city. The Greek economy was based on agriculture, not trade, so land was massively important. Owning and controlling land was one way the elite families in a city-state could exert power over the poorer residents. This also gave the Greeks their reason to colonize. Unlike the Phoenicians, who set up colonies like stepping stones to enable trade by sea, the Greeks used colonies to alleviate overcrowding in city-states back home.

The Greek city-states show us at least four different types of government: **democracy**, rule by the people, **monarchy**, rule by a single ruler who inherits power, **tyranny**, rule by a single ruler who seizes power, and **oligarchy**, rule by a small, elite group. Of these, we will look most closely at democracy since the Greeks claim they invented that one and have handed it down to us. We will also compare and contrast two of the most famous and influential city-states, Athens and Sparta, which happen to be *extremely* different from one another.

Athens

Athens was (and still is) a coastal city. It takes its name from its patron goddess, **Athena**, goddess of wisdom and war, who gifted the olive tree to the city as a symbol of peace and plenty. Her temple is the world-famous Parthenon on the Acropolis.

Athens began as a small Mycenaean community. But it grew to become such a powerhouse that rival city-state, Sparta, felt compelled to go to war against it just to keep it in check. The **Peloponnesian Wars** (460–446 and 431–404 BCE) were essentially Athens and Sparta, with their respective allies, thrashing it out for control of the Peloponnese.

Athens was a fortified city surrounded by walls. It amassed a powerful navy, which it used to protect itself and other city-states around the Aegean from the ever-present threat of the **Persians**. In return, these city-states paid tribute to Athens, further increasing its power and influence nearly to the point of an empire. This alliance became known as the **Delian League** because they kept their treasury on the island of **Delos** in the **Cyclades**.

Despite its walls and navy, Athens was not known for its warfare. Instead, Athens's claim to fame was its culture. Their advancements in government, philosophy, drama, literature, art, mathematics, science, and more made Athens the seat of learning for the entire Western world in their day. Our companion, Herodotus, the "father of history," lived and worked there. So did Socrates, the "father of philosophy," and **Hippocrates**, the "father of medicine" (even though Imhotep of Egypt might also claim that title), just to name a few.

Their form of government, democracy, was probably the most original thing about Athenian culture. It was certainly one of their most important contributions to the world. But Athenian democracy was different from what we picture when we hear the word today.

The word democracy comes from the Greek *dēmos* or "people" and *kratos* or "rule"—literally "rule by the people." These "people," called the **Assembly**, would gather once a month, sometimes more, to debate and vote on matters that affected the *polis*—whether to go to war, how to organize food supplies, who should judge court cases, etcetera. The Assembly was not a representative form of government where people were elected to decide issues for us, like in the U.S. Congress. In Athens, *every* person voted on *every* issue—a system that would be impossible in today's modern, complex world. After discussion, they would vote by a simple show of hands. The majority won, even if nearly half of the people disagreed. But who were the "people"?

Well, it turns out that the word *dēmos* left out a lot of people. Not surprisingly, children couldn't vote. Slaves couldn't vote, and they made up a sizeable portion of the people. Athens was home to between 60,000 and 80,000 slaves at the height of its population, three or four for every Athenian household. Also, women couldn't vote. So, who could? Well, male citizens 18 years and older. These eligible voters represented about 10 to 20% of the population, and not even all of *them* could afford to take the day off work every time there was a vote. So, it is estimated that only about 3,000 people were actively involved in "rule by the people." But, in reality, the power was even more consolidated than that.

Of the 3,000 regular participants, about 100 of the top citizens—the richest, most popular, and best speakers—dominated the scene. This is where the sophists, with their tricky logic and flashy presentation, could shine. And if you were a good **orator** (public speaker), you could gain power and influence people by appealing to their emotions. It's where we get the word **demagogue**, *dēmos* (people), and *agōgos* (leading). Some philosophers, even at that time, saw the problem with this. Several wrote opinions critical of democracy, saying the people were too easily swayed by good speakers appealing to their emotions. Socrates, indeed, paid the ultimate price for crowds being swayed by impassioned speakers. This is a fundamental flaw of democracy that has persisted throughout history.

Sparta

Sparta Hoplite

Sparta, a land-locked city-state in the interior of the Peloponnese, had none of this "talking about our feelings" business. They were a culture centered around warfare. Their city was not walled, and that was on purpose. They thought that brave men made much better fortifications than hiding behind stones. They led their group of allied city-states called the **Peloponnesian League**, who paid tribute, not with money, but with soldiers under Sparta's command. Sparta's heavily armed Greek foot soldiers, **hoplites**, were the most feared in the realm.

Life in Sparta was extremely different from life in Athens. Until men were 30, they couldn't live with their families. Men lived separately in barracks, and everyone ate simple communal meals in mess halls. Today, the word "spartan" has come to mean simple and without luxury or comfort.

Young boys were raised by their fathers and, at age seven, went to live in the *agoge* or military training camp. It was a difficult life. Boys who exercised and trained for war were taught to read a little and were fed even less. Stealing food was encouraged, but you were never supposed to get caught! In this way, Spartans raised tough, ruthless, and crafty warriors. At age 20, the training got even more severe. Finally, at 30, you graduated as a full *hoplite* soldier and could participate in public meetings and live at home with your family.

Girls were raised by their mothers in a similar way. In Sparta, unlike Athens, women were equals. They could participate in all aspects of public life and often ran the household and the affairs of the city while the men were away at war. Girls were taught to read and sing, dance, and play instruments. But they were also expected to undergo the same physical fitness training as the boys. How else would they grow up to be mothers of strong sons?

One similarity Sparta had with Athens was a large slave population. Spartan slaves were called **helots**. Many of them were probably the native population that lived there before the Dorians, possibly Mycenaeans. *Helots* were the ones who cooked, cleaned, spun wool, and toiled in the fields. This left the Spartan men and women free to train, transact business, or go to war.

The Spartan government was quite different from the Athenian government, too. They had an oligarchy where two kings from different families would make military decisions and lead the army into war. Sparta had an Assembly to vote on matters as well, but they preferred to shout their votes rather than raise their hands. The Assembly's power seems to be more limited than the Assembly of Athens because they could not vote on any issue, just the ones that were put before them by the **Council of Elders**. This council was a group of 28 men over the age of 60 (plus the two kings, which made 30) that represented the different family groups in the city and served for life. The Council decided the voting issues for the Assembly.

To Spartans, being a great orator or seeking out the nature of reality was feckless business. They valued strength, discipline, and courage above all else. Greek philosopher **Plutarch** quotes Spartan mothers as telling their sons going off to war, "Come back with your shield or on it," meaning return victorious or die trying. It's easy to see from this sentiment why Spartans were the most fearsome force in Greece.

Art and Architecture

It's hard to walk around a modern city without seeing examples of Greek art and architecture. These might be the most observable contributions they have left for us. The Greeks mastered truly lifelike sculpture—the first **realists**. They created three **architectural orders** that dominated the building scene for hundreds of years and are still the go-to choice for classical construction. They didn't invent literature but evolved it into an entirely new form of artistic expression—the theater. Let's look at some of these a bit closer and learn how to recognize the fingerprints of the Greeks on our artistic world today.

Literature and Theater

Very early Greeks used Linear B to record their language. But about 800 BCE, they developed their own alphabet based on that of the Phoenicians and began writing down their oral traditions. We've seen the semi-historical mythological narrative before (*The Epic of Gilgamesh*). The Greeks did this as well but also added many new **genres** to the ancient library. Western philosophy, history, poetry, tragedy, and comedy were created or popularized through the writings of the ancient Greeks.

In the early days of Greek writing, the Archaic Period, myths and legends passed down from oral traditions were the most common literature. We've already been introduced to **Homer** (about 750 BCE) and his works, *The Iliad* and *The Odyssey*. These were so formative to the Greeks that Alexander the Great slept with a copy of *The Iliad* under his pillow.

A bit later in the Greek timeline, during the Classical Period, the tradition of reciting poetry developed into full-scale drama. Plays became a major form of both entertainment and education. Tragedies were the first type of play to develop, followed by comedies.

Some think that no one, except maybe Shakespeare, has mastered tragedy like the Greeks. These performances may have evolved from religious ceremonies since they

had mythological themes and often contained moral messages. One to as many as three male actors would don different costumes and masks to portray a variety of characters.

There could also be a chorus of as many as 15 men who would sing and dance but not speak. There also might be several non-speaking male performers. As you can see, theater performance was limited to men only. They were required to play the parts of women, too. It is debated whether women were allowed to be spectators or not.

Athens Theater Masks

After tragedies, the comedic genre came into form. These plays would make fun of well-known politicians and philosophers or use crude humor—not unlike the comedy of today. The surviving comedic plays offer great insight into the everyday workings of Greek life and the personalities and senses of humor of the average ancient Greek (man).

Plays were often performed along with religious festivals, especially for the god of wine and the theater, Dionysos. Competitions for writing the best plays became extremely popular. The prestige connected with winning was almost as sought after as Olympic glory.

One of these great Greek playwrights was **Euripides** (484-407 BCE). This Athenian began his career as an actor but, due to a weak voice, decided to focus on writing plays instead. His 90-some works were a bit different from those of his contemporaries. Some featured strong female leads or everyday people—not the usual aristocratic elite male star. He spiced up his stories with surprising plot twists, thought-provoking dilemmas, and intriguing immoral characters. His plays were extremely popular with the people, but, perhaps because they were so different, he didn't win very many competitions.

Histories were also a popular genre during the Classical Period and continued to be popular into the Hellenistic Period. **Herodotus** (484-425/413 BCE) appeared during this time, and **Plutarch** (45-50 CE-120-125 CE), who specialized in biographies, is the most famous historical author from this time. Much of what we know of the likes of Alexander the Great and Julius Caesar are from his writings.

Pottery

Pottery is one of the most useful and common artifacts for an archaeologist to learn about a society. It was available in ample supply, not valued by treasure hunters, and durable even when broken. Pottery styles also changed over time, making it possible to accurately date archeological findings based on pottery fragments. Greek pottery is no exception and displays this civilization's artistic and practical talents.

Amphorae for wine and olive oil were very common, as well as other jugs, pitchers, drinking cups, and plates. Most vessels for liquids feature vertical handles, a narrow neck, and some kind of foot or base. A three-handled **hydra** for water was another everyday piece. The Greeks crafted their vessels on potter's wheels, making each piece unique. The handprints of the makers are sometimes still visible on the insides of pieces.

Pottery, even for everyday use, was decorated. Looking at the decorative style is the easiest way to tell when the piece was made, although sometimes more than one style was popular at the same time. The earliest Greek pottery, Proto-geometric, was very similar to the Mycenaean geometric designs and was followed by full Geometric designs about 900 BCE. Then, in 700 BCE, plants, animals, and human figures began to make an appearance. They were painted in black on a light clay background, giving this style the name **Black Figure Pottery**. Next, in Athens around 530 BCE, potters began painting the backgrounds black and leaving the figures light, which allowed them to create more detailed pictures known as **Red Figure Pottery**. Popular motifs were, of course, mythological stories, gods and goddesses, athletes, and scenes from everyday life.

Greek Pottery Styles

Sculpture

If you look at the earliest Greek attempts at sculpting the human form, you might mistake them for Egyptian. They stand rigidly, face forward with little to no expression, arms sternly down at their sides, legs straight. But by the Classical Period, Greek sculptors had come into their own and created a unique style found nowhere else in the ancient world—one of stunning **realism**.

Bronze statue of horse and jockey

Greek statues were usually carved of marble or cast in bronze. Sadly, few bronze statues survive since the metal was valuable and could be melted down and made into other things. Most of the bronzes we have today are thanks to shipwrecks that kept them safe for 2,000 years under the sea. Broken marble is not terribly useful second-hand, so these are the statues we usually see in museums.

People were carved in action, usually poised as if they were just about to begin or finish a motion.

They were often life-sized, too, except for gods or goddesses, who were more commonly bigger than life. The attention paid to the tiny details of muscles and veins shows Greek artisans' great care and skill. They prided themselves in showing the idealized human form, particularly the male form, in all its glory. Here again, popular motifs were athletes and gods and goddesses. If the subject wore any, clothes were painstakingly rendered for a true-to-life effect. The fabric looks clingy and windblown as if it is still moving because the wearer has just draped it. Horses, an important animal in Greek mythology, were another popular subject.

Bronze of Poseidon or Zeus

Venus de Milo

Interestingly, the white marble figures in museums today are nothing like what the Greeks would have seen.

Most statues were painted in vivid colors. Hair and skin, expressive eyes, patterns on fabric—all these details came to life once the statues received their paint.

In addition to freestanding sculptures, Greek buildings, especially temples, were adorned with sculpted **reliefs** in a variety of places. **Friezes**, horizontal bands of sculpture, were used around the top of temples, above the columns, and just below the roof.

Block II from the West Frieze of the Parthenon

These long strips made terrific storytelling spaces. The **pediments** were another place begging to be filled with art. These triangular spaces on buildings, front and back, fill the gap in the A-frame roof.

Reconstruction of the Archaic Western Pediment of the Temple of Aphaia

Lastly, **metopes** were another place for sculptors to tuck in some impressive artistic messaging. Metopes are the blank spaces between the **triglyphs**—the three-sectioned vertical blocks that sometimes break up the frieze. Triglyphs represent the ends of the wooden beams that supported the roof, back when temples were made of wood.

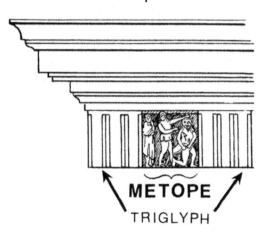

After the Greeks began constructing with marble, they kept the triglyphs for old-time's sake. The metopes, those spaces that alternated with the triglyphs, were the perfect place for vignette sculptures of different scenes, or they could work together, like pages in a book, to tell a tale.

One building that exhibited sculpture in all four places—freestanding, frieze, pediment, and metope—was the Parthenon in Athens. Both the amount and quality of sculpture on the Parthenon were unprecedented. In addition to Athena's massive gold and ivory statue, which took pride of place, there were 50 large figures in the pediments, 92 metopes, and 524 feet of frieze! Today, many of these priceless works of art can be seen in the British Museum.

This collection called the **Parthenon Marbles** or, more notoriously, the **Elgin Marbles** is the source of an interesting ethical debate. In the early 1800s, **Thomas Bruce**, the 7th Lord Elgin, was the British ambassador to the Ottoman Empire. He loved art and all things historical. So, while there, he "collected" many of these artifacts from the Parthenon and arranged for their shipment back to England. After being purchased by the Crown, they were displayed at the British Museum, where they remain today. Elgin has been widely criticized for vandalizing and stealing the artifacts, and the Greek government has frequently demanded them back. The British government argues that they preserved and protected them and are now the rightful possessors. If you had to judge, who would keep these priceless treasures? No matter whose side you take, the word "**elginism**" now means the taking of cultural treasures, usually from one country to a wealthier one.

Since we're talking about sculpture, this is a good time to look at another Wonder of the World from the Greek city-state of Rhodes. With its strategic island position, Rhodes was an essential trading port for the Greeks. Their patron god was Helios, the sun god, who rode his golden chariot across the sky each day. The city erected an enormous, or perhaps we should say *colossal*, bronze statue of Helios to guard their harbor and greet incoming ships. Its creation took 12 years, and it was finished in 280 BCE. This quickly became a tourist destination for ancients desiring to see the 100-foot tall "Colossus." But Helios didn't last long. An earthquake toppled him less than 60 years later. The fallen giant continued to attract sightseers, but, like so many other ancient bronzes, it was eventually carted away for scrap metal.

Architectural Orders

There are five **architectural orders**, or styles, of classic architecture. Three are Greek, and the other two are based on the Greek ones. If you ever visit Washington, DC, you should play "Name That Order." The city is full of examples, as are many state capitol buildings, city halls, and museums. But before we look at the three Greek orders, we should learn something about the vocabulary of architecture.

An order, or style, is determined by the type of **column** and **entablature** used.

A column is pretty straightforward—a tall vertical pillar supporting the roof. It might rest on a **base**, the lowest part of which is called the **plinth**. The long center piece is called the

shaft, which may or may not have grooves called **fluting**. At the top, there is a decorative piece called the **capital**.

The entablature is the portion of the building above the column and below the roof. It consists of three horizontal sections. The **architrave** sits directly on the capital of the column. It was originally a simple support beam, like the lintel of a door. Above that sits the **frieze**, which, as we have already seen, can be highly decorated. The top of the entablature that connects to the roof is called the **cornice**. It is a decorative molding that extends out from the building and serves the practical purpose of directing rainwater.

So there you have it—architecture 101! Different combinations of these elements give you the different Greek orders. Now that you're an expert, let's see what these orders are.

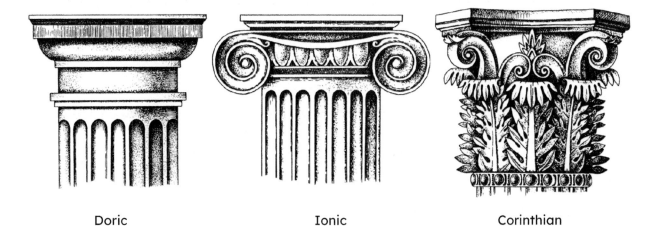

Doric   Ionic   Corinthian

Doric

The name "Doric" hails back to the Dorians, the low-technology tribes that settled in various locations, like Sparta, previously occupied by the Mycenaeans. So, the **Doric order** is, predictably, well, spartan. Squat fluted columns sit on no base and have a plain square capital. The frieze has the distinctive alternation of triglyphs and metopes, which may or may not be sculpted.

Ionic

The **Ionic order** comes from the Ionians, Greeks from Athens who colonized the northern coast of the Aegean Sea and developed their own art and architecture. This elegant style has taller, more slender columns than the Doric order. They also added a base. The most recognizable feature is the scrolled capital. The frieze is an unbroken band that typically contains a long sculptural element.

Corinthian

The city-state of **Corinth** claims the **Corinthian order**. What sets it apart from the Ionic order is the ornate capital, which sports a double row of leaves topped by four scrolls instead of two.

Temples were the best place to see these orders on display. Sometimes a temple was all one order, and sometimes it would be a combination of different ones. The Temple of Zeus at Olympia was Doric, and the Parthenon of Athena on the Acropolis at Athens was a mix of Doric and Ionic. The less famous but more prominent Athenian temple to Zeus—the **Olympieion**—is an example of the Corinthian order.

Another of the Greek Wonders is a stunning example of their architectural abilities. One of the things that made the Mausoleum at Halicarnassus unique among the other Greek Wonders of the World is that it was erected to honor a man, not a god. The city of Halicarnassus was an Ionian city-state (and the birthplace of Herodotus). However, by the 300s BCE, the city was under Persian control and ruled by Mausolus, its governor. When he died in 353/352 BCE, his wife, Artemisia, built a massive tomb for him in the Ionian order and filled it with sculptures.

Model of Mausoleum at Halicarnassus

Like the Colossus of Rhodes, this building would be destroyed by an earthquake. Some artifacts have been recovered, but its lasting legacy is the word **"mausoleum,"** meaning a large and impressive resting place for the departed.

Everyday Life

Although daily life would depend greatly on which city-state you called home, there were many similarities no matter where you lived in the Greek world.

Farmers in Greece grew different grains, olives, and grapes for wine. Since they lived close to the sea, fish were another common item on the menu. Greeks did not typically keep large herds of animals, but it was common for families to have just enough cattle, sheep, goats, pigs, or chickens for their own use. They usually made milk into cheese instead of drinking it. Ancient Greeks enjoyed a variety of fruits, vegetables, and nuts too. Pomegranates, apples, pears, onions, cucumbers, and almonds were common—a similar diet to other civilizations around the Mediterranean. One thing some ancient Greeks did *not* eat was beans. Greeks grew beans and often tilled them back into the soil for fertilizer, but it was not unheard of in their culture to believe that beans contained the souls of the dead and some people would avoid eating them!

Clothing was simple. Slaves might wear just a loincloth. The upper levels of society wore undergarments and a variety of simple tunics or robes that could be dressed up with belts, shaws, or jewelry. The most common everyday outfit was the **chiton**. There were Doric and Ionic styles of *chitons* just as there were columns. The garment was a cylinder of fabric you step into, fasten at the shoulder with a pin, and secure around the waist with a belt. In fact, all clothes—men's and women's—were mostly unsewn squares or rectangles of fabric that could be arranged, pinned, or draped in various ways to create different effects. This easy and elegant mode of dress was copied by many other civilizations around the ancient world, notably Rome, and has influenced dress styles to this day. Sandals were worn out and about, but people went barefoot at home. Athletes went barefoot as well. In fact, athletes often wore nothing at all as they felt they could perform better that way!

Free landowning men were the top tier of society. Some men might work in a trade, as a sailor, or in some other profession, but the landowners always controlled most of the wealth and power. They spent their day managing the work done on their estates by slaves, exercising at the *gymnasium*, and chatting with friends in the *agora*. And they might end their day at a *symposium*. These gatherings were a very important aspect of Greek culture. A *symposium* was like a dinner party hosted at the home of one group member. It was a men-only event. Women could be there only as entertainers—dancing, singing, and playing the lyre. Here, the men would recline on couches, eat, drink, and recite poetry or have political or philosophical discussions.

Women married at about thirteen or fourteen and spent most of their existence in the home, immersed in tasks like weaving and wool-work. They even had a women's-only section of the home, called the *gynaikon*. Respectable Greek women did not leave home without a male chaperone and did not have any interaction with men who were not family members. They *could* visit their friends in their homes, get water from the well, and attend certain religious festivals. They could *not* attend assemblies, vote, hold office, own property, make a will, choose their husband, or drink wine. Sparta was the exception to this, where women played a near equal part in society and enjoyed most of the same freedoms men did.

Despite the drastically different roles for men and women, boys and girls were treated a bit more alike. They were both educated in the basics of reading, writing, and arithmetic. After this, they moved on to literature, poetry, and music. Girls would receive more training in the arts like music and dancing. Young adult men would also study politics and rhetoric. By this age, girls were already married and at home. Athletics were essential to everyone's education—boys and girls alike.

Slaves, as we learned, made up a sizeable portion of the Greek population. From farming to shield making to statue carving—slaves made the wheels of the Greek life go 'round. These unfortunate laborers were acquired through war, kidnapping, or purchase, and Greeks, for the most part, felt this was just the way things worked. As we see from their superior attitude toward "barbarians," the Greeks thought *they* were the cultured and civilized portion of the human race and naturally fit to rule. However, it is believed that slaves were generally well-treated, often given skilled work, and could sometimes buy their freedom.

Grecian Time Periods

Greek civilization is usually organized into three major periods—the Archaic, Classical, and Hellenistic—spanning almost 800 years, plus about a 400-year "dark" period before that. Historically speaking, "dark" periods refer to times from which we lack written records. Our view of what happened during those times is "darkened." Some also associate dark periods with chaos, war, or backsliding in technology. While sometimes that is the case, it is not necessarily so.

The Greek Dark Ages — c. 1200/1100–800 BCE

Around 1200 BCE, we saw that the Mycenaeans on the Greek peninsula and Aegean islands were having some trouble. Whether it was from earthquakes, Sea People, or internal struggles, the Bronze Age Collapse was happening.

Around this time, tribes of people called the **Dorians** were moving down from the north into Peloponnese. At first, the Dorians were relatively low-technology people. Some historians say they were still in the hunting and herding stage when they moved in. But they did bring one significant advancement with them, iron weapons. The Greek Dark Ages are also referred to as the **Early Iron Age.**

The Dorians swept out any remaining Mycenaean strongholds and set up shop, sometimes on the same sites their predecessors had used like **Mycenae** and **Athens.** In some locations, the Dorians intermarried with the few native people who were left. In other places, such as **Sparta**, the Dorians created a militaristic power structure with strict divisions between themselves and the native populations. Here, the remnants of those native peoples became

serfs—non-free laborers, almost slaves, who worked in exchange for protection, food, and housing.

Around 1000 BCE, Greeks from Athens continued their migration into the Aegean islands and the western coast of what is now Türkiye (Turkey). They called this land **Ionia** and themselves **Ionians**. They were still Greek, but they would develop their own dialect, architectural style, and other cultural differences from the Dorians. (The most lasting example is seen in the Doric and Ionic columns.)

Linguistic and religious differences between the Dorians and the Ionians would sometimes lead to hostile divisions between the two groups. In some places, Dorians were prohibited from entering Ionian sanctuaries. This social fracture would set the stage for the upcoming wars between the city-states.

Speaking of war, do you remember the story of the **Trojan War** as told by Greek poet Homer in the *Iliad*? Well, different ancient Greek writers, including Herodotus, place the war between Greek city-states and the city of **Troy** sometime around the beginning of the Greek Dark Ages (roughly 1300—1100 BCE). Homer didn't write down this oral tradition until the beginning of the Archaic Period (about 800—700 BCE). We know this story is probably a mixture of myth and fact, but we can see from the timeline that the ancient Greeks were not even firmly established in the area when they say this war took place.

The Archaic Period — c. 800–480 BCE

Almost all of what we know of the Greek Archaic Period is about the city-state of Athens, and Athens, with its quick rise to democracy, was not exactly typical of the other Greek city-states. So what we say of this period is often true for Athens alone.

Everywhere you looked, this was a time of immense change for the Greeks in literature, politics, culture, art, architecture, foreign relations, and more. The Greek alphabet was invented during this time—a version of the Phoenician alphabet with the upgrade of vowels. This alphabet became the basis for many Western written languages, including ours. With this new tool came literature, poetry, and plays. Greeks began recording their oral traditions, and, sometime between 800 and 700 BCE, Homer gave us the *Iliad* and the *Odyssey*. They developed distinctive styles of pottery and sculpture, and the designs of temples were becoming more and more like the ones we recognize as Greek today. The Olympic Games began in 776 BCE, a major milestone in world history. And the Greeks began minting and using money for the first time.

A couple of key figures stood out from the rest in Athenian politics. **Draco** was an aristocrat of the 7th century BCE who was given the job of creating Athens' first set of written laws. The goal was to stop destructive feuds between families and to standardize punishments. Draco may have seen it as an opportunity to consolidate the power and land of the aristocrats. His laws were criticized for being unnecessarily harsh and favoring the wealthy. He demanded the death penalty for even minor offenses and was quoted as saying he considered these lesser crimes to deserve it, and he had no greater punishment for more important ones. This is where we get the term "draconian," meaning excessively harsh and severe.

Fortunately for the people of Athens, Draco's laws didn't last very long. **Solon** (640–560 BCE) came along. He was a trader, statesman, and poet. He is also called the "founding father" of Athens because, when he rose to power after proving himself in battle, he replaced Draco's laws and set the stage for democracy. Solon sympathized with the poor and debt-burdened population who worked the land owned by very few aristocrats. Along with canceling a lot of their debt, he made it illegal to sell yourself or a family member into slavery to pay a debt and freed the people who had. He also restructured the social classes into four groups based on how much agriculture they produced.

Depending on your class, you were assigned different civic duties and rights like serving on juries, holding political offices, or preparing business matters for the Assembly to discuss. The aristocratic elite, of course, didn't care for Solon very much because he leveled the playing field with the landowning middle class. Now, power was based on how much land you owned and what you produced, not just who your family was. So Solon did not create a democracy, but he planted the spirit of it in the people of Athens. In historical terms, changes came fast after that, and democracy was not far behind.

The population of Greece boomed in the Archaic Period. So did trade and colonization. This put the Greeks into more contact with the outside world, including civilizations like the Egyptians and the Phoenicians. But the neighbors that Greece had the most interaction with (and not in a good way) were the **Persians**.

The **Persian Wars**, sometimes called the **Greco-Persian Wars**, were a series of conflicts between the Greek city-states and their Persian invaders from the late Archaic Period through the Early Classical Period.

Across the Aegean Sea in Asia Minor, **Cyrus II**, also known as **Cyrus the Great** of Persia, began the **Achaemenid Empire** in 559 BCE. And, as we know, you can't have an empire unless you have other nations to rule. So, he also began expanding his kingdom, **subjugating** the Greek colonies on the eastern coast of the Aegean. Sparta made some diplomatic protests. But, overall, Greece did nothing about this.

After Cyrus, a man named **Darius I** took the throne. He was the son of a mere provincial governor. But with a bit of crafty plotting and some murdering, Darius seized power and picked up expanding the empire where Cyrus left off. His borders crept ever closer to the Peloponnese, swallowing Ionia, Macedonia, and many of the Cyclades. Then, he set his sights on Athens, but this was as far as the mainland city-states were willing to let Darius go. He had to be stopped. Finally, something Athens and Sparta could agree on! They promised each other that they would be allies against Persia.

In 490 BCE, Darius launched a full-scale invasion of the Peloponnese and landed his ships at the plains of **Marathon,** where he was met by the much smaller Athenian army in what is known as The **Battle of Marathon**. This battle has gone down in history for a couple of reasons.

First, the steadfast Athenians defeated the Persians against overwhelming odds. They were outnumbered by about 8 to 1. The Persian soldiers, exhausted from their voyage and not troubled by the tiny Athenian army, made camp and relaxed. The Athenians, sensing that this was their moment to strike, didn't wait for reinforcements, attacked, and emerged the victors.

The second reason we remember the battle is because it is the legendary origin of our marathon footraces. The story goes that the fastest Athenian messenger carried news of the Persian invasion to Sparta, asking for reinforcements. This runner supposedly traveled the 140 or so miles in only two days! *After* the Athenian victory, a second runner made the 26.2-mile trip from Marathon to Athens to inform them that the Persian fleet had fled and might be on its way there. According to legend, upon delivering his message to the Athenians, the poor messenger collapsed and died. Today, we hold marathon races that are 26.2 miles long in honor of this feat.

The Athenians may have found glory on the plains of Marathon, but the Greco-Persian Wars had only just begun. Only ten years later, in 480 BCE, Darius' son, **Xerxes I**, was back for more. And if you thought the odds were bad for the Greeks at Marathon, wait until you hear about **Thermopylae.**

The **Battle of Thermopylae** is such a real-life action-adventure tale that it has inspired many fictionalized accounts, including comic books and a movie. Of course, many artistic licenses are taken with these, so they should not be relied on as history *per se*. But they do make fantastic inspiration for historical studies!

Xerxes spent four years amassing an enormous army and then had to march them around the Aegean Sea, so Greece knew they were coming. Nevertheless, the Greeks were not as well prepared as they might have been. After quite a bit of talking and deal-making among the city-states, about 6,500 soldiers were sent to try to hold off the entire Persian army at a small mountain pass called Thermopylae. Among these, the only professional fighting force was 300 troops from Sparta led by one of their kings, **Leonidas**. That's it. Three hundred trained soldiers (plus some others) against some 80,000 Persians.

The reasons why the Greek response was so small are many and debated. It's possible that some city-states were unwilling to send many troops so far north. Also, the invasion coincided with a religious festival when fighting was prohibited. At any rate, this tiny contingent was supposed to hold the Persians at Thermopylae, a narrow mountain pass, until a proper army could be mustered.

When Xerxes arrived at Thermopylae, he set up camp, expecting the Greeks to run in fear. When they didn't, he sent an emissary to ask them to lay down their arms, saying there would be no bloodshed if they did. Leonidas's famous reply was simply, "Come and get them," and the battle was on.

For three days, amazingly, the Greeks, led by Leonidas and his 300 Spartan **hoplites**, held the pass. Unfortunately, though, a saboteur was working behind the scenes. A local shepherd, hoping to be rewarded by Xerxes, informed the Persian army of a hidden mountain path used to herd sheep that would allow them to encircle the Greeks and attack from all sides at once. This, of course, the Persians promptly did. All remaining Greeks, King Leonidas included, fell in battle. As a result, the Spartans did not have the victory at Thermopylae that the Athenians did at Marathon.

The Persian army continued forward and destroyed Athens in 480 BCE. But finally, Persia was defeated on Greek soil in 479 BCE once and for all. The combined Greek armies forced the Persians to withdraw. And in 478 BCE, Athens and other city-states around the Aegean formed the **Delian League** intending to defend one another from any further Persian encroachment. The Greek Classical Period was ushered in.

Also during the Archaic Period, sometime around the 6th century BCE, the Temple of Artemis, goddess of hunting and childbirth, was constructed (for the first time) at Ephesus in Ionia. It quickly made the list among the world's Seven Wonders. The temple was twice the size of any others like it and sported 127 beautifully carved columns. The temple was destroyed and rebuilt twice before finally meeting its end at the hands of a Christian mob in 401 CE. But its most infamous destruction was when it was intentionally burned—much to the horror of the Ephesians—in the 4th century BCE by a fellow named Herostratus. He allegedly confessed to doing it just for fame. The judges sentenced him to death and ordered that his name never be uttered. Yet, ironically, history has remembered him anyway. Another interesting fact—the fire happened on the same night that Alexander the Great was born, a coincidence some would consider an omen of his destined conquering of the area.

The Classical Period — c. 480–323 BCE

Classical Greece is Greece in its **Golden Age**. In this period, the Greeks gave us philosophy, democracy, lifelike sculpture, dramatic plays, and more. It was also a time of conflict. It began toward the end of the Greco-Persian Wars, lasted throughout the **Peloponnesian Wars** when the city-states fought each other, and ended with the death of Alexander the Great.

The destruction of Athens was the defining event that marked the beginning of the Classical Period. This catastrophe was an opportunity for one man named **Pericles** (495–429 BCE), to step forward and shine. Pericles was the Athenian son of a war hero from the Persian Wars. He established himself early by contributing to the arts and making several deft political moves. In 443 BCE, he was elected to the powerful position of Athenian general, a title he would hold nearly the rest of his life. He would later be called the "first citizen" of Athens.

Athens was the head of the **Delian League**, the alliance with Ionian city-states around the Aegean Sea against the Persians. The deal was that each city-state had to either contribute soldiers or pay a tax to Athens, who would, in turn, protect them from future Persian hostilities. Most city-states preferred to pay the tax. Even though Persia wasn't attacking, Athens was raking in the money. Their city had been pretty much reduced to rubble, but it was quickly growing quite rich.

Pericles felt it was only right to use the money from the Delian League to rebuild Athens. The other member city-states objected. That money was for their defense! But Pericles reasoned that the money was to ensure the other city-states were safe from the Persians, and the Persians weren't attacking. Therefore, Athens was doing its job and could spend that money how it saw fit. Hmmm.

Bust of Pericles

In 460 BCE, a massive restoration and improvement of the *agora* began. From 447 to 432 BCE, the magnificent Parthenon on the Acropolis was constructed and dedicated to the goddess Athena. Other temples were built as well. And Pericles didn't just build buildings; he also built Athenian society and culture. He encouraged and funded playwrights, sculptors, philosophers, inventors, and more. Athens became *the* city to come to for inspiration and free reign to create. He was a big believer in democracy and allowed more Athenian citizens to participate by paying them for civic duties like serving on juries. Thanks to Delian money and Pericles's leadership, Athens reached its **zenith**.

But another city-state was looking at the Golden Age of Athens with suspicious eyes. Sparta, who led their alliance of city-states, the **Peloponnesian League**, started to feel that Athens was becoming a little too much like an empire. The large navy and extra fortifications that Athens was constructing were particularly disturbing.

In 460 BCE, right about the time Pericles was rebuilding the agora, the **First Peloponnesian War** (460-446 BCE) broke out. Even though the argument was really between Athens and Sparta, Athens and Corinth (Sparta's ally who also had a navy) did most of the fighting. Pericles, ever the hero, led the Athenians in several battles, but neither side could gain a real advantage. Eventually, an uneasy truce was called, and the **Thirty Years' Peace** followed in 446 BCE. Truthfully, though, skirmishes continued to erupt, and this period was never actually peaceful.

In 431 BCE, an all-out war between Sparta and Athens broke out again, more intense this time. It was the **Second Peloponnesian War** (431–404 BCE). Sparta would emerge the victor, but Pericles would not live to see that defeat. This is because, in 430 BCE, another, more terrifying enemy than even the Spartan *hoplites* was sweeping north from Africa toward Athens—the plague.

Experts are still not sure exactly which disease or combination of diseases arrived in Athens in 430 BCE despite a detailed description of symptoms by the historian **Thucydides** who survived it. We do know that over a three-year period, it killed approximately a third of the population of Athens—about 100,000 people—Pericles included. Sparta even delayed an invasion just to avoid the plague.

Devastated by illness and without their longtime leader, Athens would continue to muster a response to Sparta for several long years. The Second Peloponnesian War raged all over Greece. At last, Sparta emerged victorious. Athens was forced to humble itself with embarrassing concessions, like rebuilding a fleet of no more than 12 ships. But Sparta wouldn't celebrate long. The victory had exhausted and depleted the entire peninsula. All of this infighting would leave the door open for some neighbors from the north, the **Macedonians**, to waltz right in.

Macedon was a Greek kingdom north of the Peloponnese. Macedonians were probably the first to refer to themselves as *Hellas*, eventually giving us the term "Hellenistic" to refer to all things Greek. The rest of the Greek city-states thought Macedon's monarchy was unsophisticated and behind the times. So they didn't take them very seriously. The only important thing about Macedon, they thought, was that it was a great place to get timber for ships. Then, in 359 BCE, **King Philip II** took the throne, and he would be taken seriously.

Philip reorganized, re-outfitted, and retrained an expanded Macedonian army. He also remade his capital, **Pella**, and invited philosophers and artists to fill his city with culture. One special invitee was Aristotle, who Philip selected to personally tutor his son, the young **Alexander**.

Between 357 and 338 BCE, Philip slowly conquered the rest of Greece. After he and 18-year-old Alexander defeated Athens and Thebes in 338 BCE, he started planning his invasion of Persia. Before he could act on this plan, however, he was assassinated in 336 BCE. Philip left the throne of this burgeoning empire in the hands of well-trained and well-educated Alexander, already on his way to being Great.

Alexander's greatness seemed destined to be. Historians tell us a brilliant star gleamed over Macedon when Alexander was born. Then, there was that whole burning of the Temple of Artemis that night, too. Alexander loved these "signs and wonders" and his family tree that claimed ancestry from his favorite heroes, Hercules and Achilles. Alexander believed he was a demigod, frequently referring to Zeus-Ammon as his true father. This belief filled him with confidence and drove his every action.

Alexander's youth leaves us with several anecdotal stories that seem to foretell his meteoric rise to power. It is said that, by age seven, he was boldly interviewing visiting officials about the strengths and weaknesses of Persia.

One of the most famous stories about young Alexander takes place when he was about 11 or 12. A visitor presented a fine horse for sale to his father, King Philip. The horse was incredible: black, fierce, larger than any horse from Macedon, and also three times the usual price. The problem was that the horse was unmanageable. The handlers could not control it, and, as it bucked and reared, Philip ordered the horse to be taken away. Let us imagine, with help from Plutarch the historian, the exchange that happened next.

> Alexander, who had been keenly watching, stepped forward. "What a shame to lose such an excellent horse because no one has the boldness to manage it."
>
> Philip laughed. "Do you insult your elders by thinking you can do better than they do?"
>
> Alexander looked from the horse to his father and back again. "If I cannot tame him, I will pay for him."
>
> The crowd, which had gathered around, laughed. They could not wait to see this! Philip shook his head but gestured toward the horse, knowing his son was determined to try.
>
> As Alexander approached the horse, pawing the ground and pulling at its reins, he smiled. He has noticed something no one else has—the horse is afraid of its shadow. Slowly, Alexander took the reins and turned the horse toward the sun, so its shadow was behind it. Then, with his characteristic self-assurance, Alexander mounted the horse and rode it as the stunned crowd watched.
>
> According to Plutarch, as Alexander dismounted, Philip said, "O my son look thee out a kingdom equal to and worthy of thyself, for Macedonia is too little for thee."

Alexander named his horse **Bucephalus**, perhaps the most famous horse in history. The keen observation and problem-solving skills he used that day would help him conquer most of the known world.

Alexander the Great earned his title by being great at both diplomacy and military tactics. He expanded his empire from the Greek city-states through Asia Minor, down the Levant, into Egypt, and then turned back toward Mesopotamia. His final empire extended far beyond Babylon to present-day India.

Alexander and Bucephalus

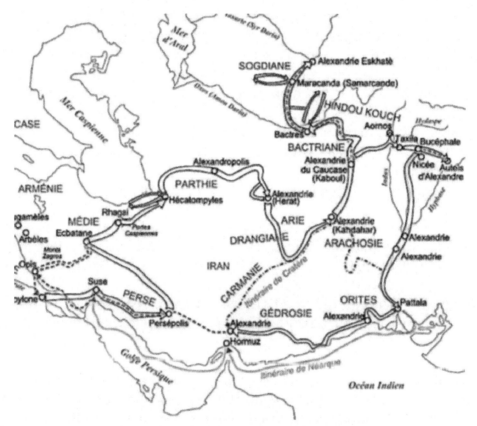

Map of Alexander the Great's Conquests

We have already looked at examples of his cunning war strategies and shrewd diplomacy in Tyre, Egypt, and Babylon. We could, once again, easily fill the rest of this book with his military exploits. So many volumes have already been written about them.

Instead, we'll spend our remaining time with Alexander by noting his lasting legacies. In addition to founding several cities, he named or renamed many of them after himself (and one—Bucephala—after his horse). His most famous namesake city, Alexandria, Egypt, would become the new Athens as a center of learning and culture.

And that was Alexander's real impact—culture. His empire, even after it was fractured, spread the Greek language and culture across the world. Those are the cultural ripples we see all around us today.

Alexander died of a sudden and unknown illness in 323 BCE as he planned to conquer Arabia. Unfortunately, he had never named an heir, so his empire was ultimately divided among his four generals. The most famous of these, **Ptolemy**, would take Egypt and begin the dynasty of Greek pharaohs. But, since we've already met them, we will stick with Greece's story and see what happens to the people around the Aegean Sea in the Hellenistic Period.

The Hellenistic Period — c. 323–31/30 BCE

The Hellenistic Period was still a time of expansion, learning, and innovation, even if it looked slightly different from the Classical Period. Let's look at a few of the main differences between these eras.

Politically, the city-state was no longer the main form of government. Instead, kingdoms formed where power was more centralized. Four of Alexander's generals had split his empire after his death. One was quickly overtaken by another, leaving three empires—the Ptolemies in Egypt, the Seleucids in Persia, and the Greek homeland, Macedonia. Although these states were separate entities, they were united in their Greekness.

In these empires, an everyday, or **colloquial**, form of Greek called *koine* was spoken by just about everyone. This made travel and trade throughout the entire Mediterranean region quite easy. Greek colonies popped up everywhere. (Overpopulation was still a problem back home.) Kings liked to display the wealth and exotic luxuries from all this trade, and they financed grand palaces, zoos, and libraries, including the famous **Library at Alexandria**. Great works of literature were collected from all over and copied into Greek.

Art was different, too. Greek realism became even more real. Sculptures started showing people who actually looked like real people, wrinkles and all, instead of just gods and heroes in idealized forms.

Athens was no longer the magnet for academics and philosophers. Weakened by years of war, it was now a shadow of its former self. Democracy was gone, and Athens suffered the insult of Macedonian soldiers stationed at its port.

Greek Realism

That didn't mean that the academics and philosophers weren't around! On the contrary, Alexandria was the new epicenter of learning, and brilliant minds flocked there to work and discuss together. It was the age of Archimedes and Euclid. Followers of Socrates developed Stoicism, and those of Plato developed Skepticism. Greek poetry reached its height in this period as well.

During the Hellenistic Period, something else was happening outside the Greek world—something that would become very important to history. A new power was rising. Rome had started as a simple city-state, but it had grown and quickly encroached on Greek colonies on the southern tip of Italy and the island of Sicily. We saw this in the story of Archimedes and the Roman conquest of Syracuse that spelled his demise in 212 BCE. Rome was also involved in the Punic Wars with the Phoenician-colony-turned- empire of Carthage between 264 and 146 BCE. When Rome emerged victorious, it cemented them as the new masters of the Mediterranean.

Different parts of the Greek world responded differently to the growing Roman Republic. Athens was desperate to overthrow Macedonian rule. They, along with several other city-states, gladly accepted Rome's help in the **First** (214-205 BCE) and **Second** (200-197 BCE) **Macedonian Wars** against **Philip V** of Macedon, essentially inviting in the Romans. Athens regained their independence for a while. Rome, with tongue in cheek, celebrated the "free Greeks" while establishing a foothold on the peninsula, which they were not about to let go.

Rome annexed the Greek peninsula in 146 BCE. In the 80s BCE, Athens made another stand for freedom, this time against Rome, by allying themselves with **King Mithridates VI** of **Pontus**. This was a mistake. In 86 BCE, the Roman general **Sulla** laid siege to Athens and eventually sacked it with enormous loss of life and destruction of buildings.

The story of Roman expansion throughout the Greek world genuinely belongs in the story of Rome. So, let us finish by saying that scholars usually end the Hellenistic Period in 31 or 30 BCE when Rome finally took over the last remnants of Alexander's empire. This happened at the Battle of Actium when Roman leader **Octavian** (soon to be **Emperor Augustus**) defeated **Cleopatra**, the Ptolemaic queen of Egypt.

Decline and Fall

As you see, the decline of ancient Greece is a complicated thing. It probably began with the death of Alexander the Great. Yet, there is also an argument that, with the spread of the Greek language and Hellenistic culture, it was still rising at that time, too! After Alexander's empire splintered, Greece's decline became the story of three or four kingdoms' separate declines.

Hundreds of years of war had taken their toll on the Greek homeland on the Peloponnese. It's interesting to wonder how history may have been different if the city-states had indeed come together and avoided fighting one another. Even still, Rome seemed like an unstoppable force. Likely, they would have overtaken Greece eventually anyway.

Did Greece ever actually fall, though? As we look around us today, ghosts of the ancient Greeks whisper to us from every corner. Ironically, there was no bigger fan of Greek culture than the Romans. They incorporated their art, architecture, and their gods into their own. In our final chapter—The Romans—we will see how they did this *and* put their own stamp on Western civilization.

Historical Highlights

Here we go! What do you think should make the list of the most important things to know about the ancient Greeks? Here are our picks:

- The ancient Greeks were a collection of independent city-states that often fought each other on the Mediterranean peninsula called the Peloponnese, as well as the Cyclades and other areas around the Aegean Sea.
- The Greek pantheon consisted of twelve major gods and goddesses called Olympians because they lived on Mount Olympus. The head of this family of deities was Zeus, the god of weather. Greek mythology contains many other characters besides the Olympians, including demigods, heroes, monsters, and other mythological creatures.
- The ancient Olympic Games, held every four years at Olympia, were a religious festival honoring Zeus. His statue was one of the Wonders of the Ancient World. Athletes competed for fame and glory. The Greeks even called timeout on their wars to hold the Games.
- The Greeks laid the groundwork for Western philosophy and scientific thought. Socrates, Plato, and Aristotle made up the triad of Greek philosophers, while men like Archimedes, Euclid, and Pythagoras excelled in science, technology, mathematics, and astronomy.
- The two most famous city-states were militaristic Sparta and culture-loving Athens. They sometimes joined forces, for example to defeat Persia, but more frequently

fought one another. Athens is considered the birthplace of democracy, albeit in quite a different form than we think of today.

- The Greek alphabet has become the basis for many Western written languages, including our own. Our spoken language includes many Greek words, too!
- Greek art, literature, and architecture influenced styles around the world to the present day. They invented dramatic and comedic theater, perfected realistic sculpture, and created three orders of classical architecture: Doric, Ionic, and Corinthian.
- Homer's epic poems about the semi-legendary Trojan War, the *Iliad* and the *Odyssey*, became fundamental to the Greek's self-identity, how they viewed their history and their heroes. Alexander the Great would sleep with a copy of the *Iliad* under his pillow.
- The Greek city-states fought the invading Persians for many years in the Greco-Persian Wars. Sometimes they were successful, like in the Battle of Marathon, and sometimes they lost, like in the Battle of Thermopylae. Eventually, Persia was ousted, and Athens formed the Delian League to protect against future invasion.
- Taxes from member states of the Delian League made Athens rich! They used the money to rebuild their city, including building grand temples like the Parthenon on the Acropolis, all under the management of their leader-general, Pericles.
- Sparta grew suspicious of Athens' new wealth and power. This eventually led to the Peloponnesian Wars between the two rival city-states and their allies.
- King Philip of Macedon took advantage of the fact that the other Greek city-states were weakened by years of war. He took over the entire Greek peninsula. His son, Alexander the Great, would continue his campaign, conquering all the way to Egypt in the south and India in the east.
- After Alexander's death, Hellenistic culture and the Greek language continued to spread around the known world. Greek colonies were everywhere, like Alexandria in Egypt and Syracuse in Sicily.
- Rome eventually conquered the Greek world, although they assimilated much of Greece's culture and religion into their own.

CHAPTER 8

The Romans

We have arrived at our final destination for this book—ancient Rome! Let's look around.

Like Greece, Rome sits on a peninsula—the boot-shaped one—that juts out from the northern Mediterranean coast. Today, we call this "boot" **Italy**. The ancient Romans referred to it by the same name, only Latinized, **Italia**. To the east, or along the "back" of the boot, we have the **Adriatic Sea**. Under the sole of the boot, we have the **Ionian Sea**, which separates ancient Rome from Greece. Along the west side, or front of the boot, we have the **Tyrrhenian Sea**. All of these smaller seas are just different sections of the Mediterranean. There are three large islands around Italia, too—**Sicilia** (modern-day Sicily), which gives the impression Italia is kicking it like a football, **Sardinia**, and **Corsica**.

The geography of **Rome** is central to its long history. The city lies about 15 miles inland from the Tyrrhenian Sea on the **Tiber River**, about mid-way up the front, or west coast, of the boot. The city of Rome was built on seven hills that sit on the east side of the river. Each hill was given a name in ancient times, which it still holds today: **Palatine Hill**, **Capitoline Hill**, **Aventine Hill**, **Caelian Hill**, **Esquiline Hill**, **Quirinal Hill**, and **Viminal Hill**. We'll visit some of these hills on our journey in this chapter.

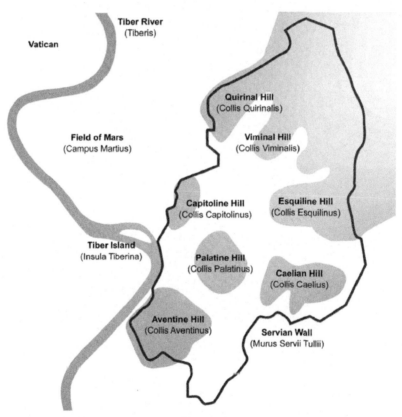

Seven Hills of Rome

The story of the Romans begins in the 700s BCE on these hills in a marshy swamp. By 117 CE, however, the Roman Empire stretched from modern-day England to Iraq. They were one of the most successful imperial powers in history, leaving their mark across Europe, Asia, and Africa.

Their mark was lasting, too. The government of the United States of America is based on some aspects of the Roman Republic. Today, over 900 million people worldwide speak a "Romance" language. These aren't lovey-dovey ways of communicating. They are languages, like Spanish, French, and Italian, derived from "Roman" Latin. English is not one, although it has *many* Latin words. Rome is even responsible for the rise of a major world religion—Christianity.

The Rise of Rome

Befitting its future status as a legendary empire, Rome begins with a legendary founding:

Once upon a time, there was a city called Alba Longa ruled by good King Numitor, who had a son, Aegestus, and a daughter, Rhea. Not long after Numitor took the throne, his jealous brother, Amulius, conspired to overthrow him. Amulius wanted to ensure that Numitor had no heir who might avenge him and claim the throne for themself. So, he had Aegestus killed and sent Rhea to be a priestess of the Roman goddess Vesta. Rhea was not supposed to marry or have children during her service there. However, the Roman god of war, Mars, had other plans.

Mars and Rhea would have twin sons, **Romulus** and **Remus**. Rhea tried to hide the boys from her uncle, Amulius, but he found out and ordered them to be drowned in the Tiber River. They were placed in a trough and left, but fate intervened (similar to Sargon of Akkad's story). Instead of sinking, the trough floated downriver and came to rest under a fig tree. Here, a mother wolf and a woodpecker, animals sacred to Mars, would feed and care for the boys. Then a shepherd, Faustulus, found and raised them (a gardener raised Sargon).

Romulus and Remus

Once adults, the brothers returned to Alba Longa and liberated the people from the evil King Amulius, returning their grandfather, Numitor, to his rightful place on the throne. But their most remarkable work was yet to come!

Romulus and Remus wanted more than just to be princes of Alba Longa until their grandfather died. So, they decided to found their own city at the location where the wolf had rescued them along the Tiber (the seven hills). But they could not agree on which hill to build the city on or who would be the king. So, they each staked claim to their hill of choice and waited for a sign from the gods.

As the legend goes, Remus saw six vultures flying overhead and took this as the sign that *he* was the chosen king. But, next, Romulus saw 12 vultures and claimed *he* was the gods' favored one. Soon, the brothers were arguing about who saw the better sign—seeing vultures first or seeing more of them. Finally, Romulus decided to go ahead with his building project on what would be named Palatine Hill.

Sometime later, Remus and his buddies went to look at how Romulus's city was coming along. There was already a wall going up. Remus decided to poke some fun at his brother by jumping over his wall, but the joke didn't go over as planned. Romulus became enraged and slew his brother, establishing himself as the sole ruler of his new city that would take his name—Rome.

Romans date this legendary founding to the year 753 BCE. There are several noteworthy parts of this story. Because Romulus's father was a god, Romulus was technically a demi-god, a point that Roman leaders who claimed a relationship with him did not want people to forget. And it wasn't just any god. Rome was founded by a son of Mars, the god of war. This, along with Romulus's short temper, gave Rome a legacy of violent domination right from the start. The story also introduces us to some of the finer points of Roman culture, like looking for signs from the gods by observing birds.

The reality was that Rome grew slowly from a group of farmers and traders called the **Latins**. Controlling the Tiber River at this strategic location near the sea allowed these early Romans to control trade in the entire area. Early Romans had a lot of interaction with people to the north called the **Etruscans**. Eventually, Rome would assimilate the Etruscan people and culture into their own as they began their spread throughout the peninsula of Italia.

Religion

Early Romans were polytheists, worshiping a variety of gods and spirits. They also integrated many foreign gods into their pantheon, especially those of the Greeks. The Romans were usually tolerant of the religions and gods of the people they conquered unless those religions presented a political problem. They liked to equate foreign gods with their own. For example, they saw Mars, their god of war, as the same as Ares, the Greek god of war. This practice helped assimilate other cultures into the Roman Empire. Gradually, however, Rome gave up its paganism for monotheism. The Roman Empire shifted from persecuting Christianity to tolerating it to adopting it as the official state religion.

The Roman Pantheon

You will no doubt recognize some familiar names among the Roman pantheon! Of course, we have already met **Mars**, the god of war, but there are other gods and goddesses you will know, too.

As we've learned, ancient civilizations studied the night sky. The Babylonians looked at a vast bright object and called it Marduk, after their chief god. They tracked its position to determine what the god's plans were. The Greeks looked at the same night sky and tried to discern the mysteries of the universe. They called that same bright object after their chief god Zeus. The Romans were no different. They named this object Jupiter, the name we use today.

In all, six of the eight planets in our solar system are named after Roman gods. Only Uranus and Earth are not. **Jupiter** was the Roman's supreme god, one they adopted from the Etruscans. He was the god of thunder, storms, and weather, so it makes sense that the Romans associated Jupiter with Zeus. Jupiter's son, Mercury, was the god of commerce and associated with Hermes. **Venus**, the goddess of love, was the equivalent of the beautiful Aphrodite. **Saturn** was the god of agriculture—the Greek Cronos. **Neptune** was Poseidon, the god of the sea.

Of course, we can see many more planets and celestial objects with modern technology than ancient people could. But we have continued the tradition of naming many of them after Roman gods or demigods. Dwarf planets **Pluto** and **Ceres** are the Roman god of the underworld (Greek Hades) and goddess of corn and the harvest (Greek Demeter), respectively. Even the moons of Mars, **Phobos** and **Deimos**, take their names from the sons of the war god they orbit. Their names, fittingly, mean "fear" and "dread" respectively.

Many other Roman gods did not get planets named after them. For example, **Juno** is Jupiter's wife, associated with Hera, and **Minerva** is his daughter, the equivalent of Athena. **Bacchus** was Dionysus, the famous god of wine.

Capitoline Triad of Juno, Jupiter, and Minerva

The fact that many ancient civilizations had gods or goddesses for the same things was a powerful tool for the Romans. Instead of asserting that their goddess of love, Venus, was better than the Greek goddess of love, Aphrodite, the Romans found common ground. If a Roman was visiting (or conquering) a Greek city-state, they might observe, "Oh, you worship the goddess of love just as we do. We call her by a different name, but no matter. I will pop into your temple and make a sacrifice to her here in your city." A great way to win friends and influence people in the ancient world.

Roles and Rituals

In addition to worshiping gods and spirits, **ancestor worship** was an enormous part of Roman religious life. They believed that the souls of dead family members could have power over events in one's life and that these spirits would return and assist those who honored them. Wealthy Romans would display images of departed loved ones prominently in their homes. These were either carved busts or wax **death masks**. A death mask was made while the person was still alive. A plaster cast of their face was prepared, and then melted bee's wax was poured into the cast to recreate their exact likeness. At their funeral, an actor would wear the mask to represent them in the funeral procession and may even speak as the departed. Then, the mask would be displayed and honored in the entry of the family's home next to a label listing the person's greatest titles.

Ancestor worship was closely linked to another aspect of Roman religion, the worship of the emperor. When **Julius Caesar** died in 44 BCE, he was declared "divine." His successor **Augustus**, the first official emperor of Rome, was also revered after he died. This began the **Imperial Cult**, a tradition of granting god status to popular emperors upon death. However, not every emperor received this honor. Some arrogant emperors, like **Nero**, who we will hear more about later, even considered themselves gods while still living! A handful of particularly unpopular rulers (also Nero) were skipped over in the deification tradition.

To the Romans, it did not matter so much whether you expressed strong feelings of personal belief and devotion to the gods. What mattered is what you did and how you did it. Sacrifice, prayer, and other rituals were the key to gaining the gods' favor, and these needed to be carefully observed. In respecting the gods of the nations they conquered, the Romans also expected their gods to be respected. This was one reason the monotheistic Jews and Christians were persecuted under early Roman rule. They refused to do what other conquered peoples did and pay tribute to the Roman pantheon.

There was no priest class in Rome. Instead, various priestly jobs were considered public offices to which one could be elected. The most important were the *pontifices*, who made religious laws and judged spiritual matters. Eventually, the emperor would hold the title of *pontifex maximus* or chief priest. Some lesser priests made sacrifices or performed other religious rituals. These included fun jobs like "reading" animal entrails or birdwatching, both popular methods for determining the future.

One religious role unique to the Romans was the **Vestal Virgins**, who served **Vesta**, the goddess of home and hearth. She is closely associated with the Egyptian goddess Bastet. Vestal Virgins had the critical job of keeping the sacred fire burning in Vesta's temple. Some think they were also the keepers of divine secrets known only to them. Girls could be chosen for this job as young as six and began their 30-year career no later than ten. During this time, they were forbidden to marry under penalty of death. Even after they served their 30 years, few of them did marry as this was considered bad luck.

Regarding divining the future, the Greeks had their oracles, but the Romans had sacred chickens. Birdwatching was serious business for the Romans. They kept an entire flock of chickens, and priests to handle them, to read fortunes.

In Chapter 6, we learned that the Romans fought Carthage, the great naval power, to control the Mediterranean in the Punic Wars. During the first of these wars, Roman Commander Publius Claudius Pulcher took some sacred chickens along on the voyage. As he was preparing to attack, one of the priests informed him that the holy chickens were refusing to eat—a bad omen. (Maybe they were seasick?) A prudent Roman commander would have rethought his battle plan. But headstrong Publius Claudius was not to be put off by some sullen chickens. He declared, "If they will not eat, let them drink!" So, he had them thrown overboard. Disaster ensued. Of his 123 ships, Publius Claudius lost all but 30, including his own. He was fined and accused of treason upon his return to Rome. Perhaps, he should have respected the sacred chickens.

From Paganism to Christianity

Judaism and its offshoot, Christianity, were entirely at odds with the Roman religious tradition. These religions were devoted to a single god, and followers refused to recognize any other, particularly deified dead emperors. This worried, angered, and offended the Romans. They unfairly blamed all sorts of calamities on Jews and Christians for refusing to sacrifice to their gods.

Suspicion led to harsh treatment, which led to downright persecution. Under the rule of Emperor **Diocletian** (r. 284-305 CE), Christians endured eight years of systematic destruction, later called the **Great Persecution**. Like most persecutions in history, it started slowly and then escalated. First, anyone working for the government or military who would not sacrifice to Roman gods was forced to resign. Next, Christian texts and churches were burned. Finally, Christians themselves were killed for their beliefs. Fortunately, this ended in 305 CE when Diocletian gave up his throne due to a severe illness. Then, in 312 CE, the future of Christianity took a drastic turn for the better.

In 312 CE, Emperor **Constantine I** (later **Constantine the Great**) was preparing to face down an enemy at the **Battle of Milvian Bridge**. According to later writings, Constantine saw a cross of light in the sky and, that night, in a dream, was told that he would conquer under that sign, the symbol of Christianity. The next day, he had all the Roman banners replaced with ones bearing the cross and marched his troops to a resounding victory. In 313 CE, Constantine issued the **Edict of Milan**, legalizing Christianity throughout the empire. He rebuilt churches destroyed by Diocletian, invited church leaders to the **Council of Nicaea** to settle internal disputes, and was baptized as a Christian on his deathbed.

In 380 CE, Emperor **Theodosius I** made Catholic Christianity the Roman Empire's official religion and closed pagan temples. Today, the faith is claimed by 2.8 billion worshipers worldwide! Constantine's actions set Christianity on a course to become a leading world religion.

Class Structure

Before we look at the Roman government, it's important to understand the Roman class structure.

The most important social unit was the family, and the most important part of the family was the father. The father was the head of his household in all respects, and his word was final on all things. He had complete authority over raising the children, which continued for as long as he lived—even after his children had grown up and had families of their own! Women were, for most of Roman history, second-class citizens. This is true in a literal sense. Unlike in Greece, women *were,* at one point, considered citizens, but they had no rights or actual power.

Being a Roman citizen conferred several benefits, not the least of which was the right to vote (unless you were female). Speaking of citizens, being able to call yourself a citizen of Rome was a valued status. Initially, citizens were males, age 15 and older, who descended from one of the three original tribes of Latins. As Rome expanded its borders, so did this definition. However, one thing remained the same. Every citizen was required to register every five years and declare their family size and possessions. That way, Rome could count and rank (and tax) each person in each family according to the strict social hierarchy they adored. This accounting was called a *census*—today's forbearer of our 10-year census.

Beyond male or female, citizen or non-citizen, there was another important class distinction: *patrician* or *plebeian.*

Patrician comes from the Latin word *patres,* meaning "fathers." Initially, these were the land-owning nobles who were advisors to the early kings of Rome. They evolved into the Roman aristocracy or upper class. One had to be born a *patrician,* and this privileged birth came with a hereditary right to govern. If a father was the head of a family, then *patricians* were the heads of society.

Plebeians or *plebs* were commoners, basically everyone who was not a *patrician.* This did not mean, however, that *plebeians* were poor, though sometimes they were. They might be merchants, tradesmen, or property owners. Some became very wealthy, and it was even possible to find successful *plebeians* who were more affluent than their *patrician* neighbors. But, in the days when kings ruled Rome and the early years of the Roman Republic, *plebeians* did not have any power to speak of.

This dividing line in society was strictly enforced until the **Conflict of Orders**, which began about 500 BCE. This conflict was a power struggle between the two classes that lasted over 200 years. It started when the *patricians* wanted to go to war against a neighboring tribe and the *plebeians*, who made up the majority of the fighting force, refused to go until they were given an equal say in the government.

Reforms came about slowly, but they came. By the end of the Conflict of Orders, *plebeians* had achieved equality—they could be elected to the highest positions of power. Plebeians were eventually allowed to marry patricians, allowing one's family to climb the social ladder.

However, another group of people in Roman society was not fortunate enough to achieve equality—the enslaved. As in Greece, it was possible to be a skilled slave, working as a craftsman or tutor. As a slave, you would likely be digging in a mine or toiling to build a road. Household slaves were used to performing any or all of the work that family members did not want to do themselves. They were considered the property of their owners, who could punish or even kill them at will. There was hope, though. Roman slaves could earn and buy their freedom. Once free, they could become citizens, and their children could even hold public office.

Once, the Romans considered passing a law requiring slaves to wear uniforms. That way, they could quickly identify them as slaves. Interestingly, they decided not to do this because they realized that the slaves could *also* identify other slaves and see *how many* there were. The Romans were afraid the slaves would organize and revolt.

Rome's Most Famous Slave

Slave revolts were a constant worry for the Romans. This fear was made worse thanks to a man named **Spartacus**. Most of the time, revolts were isolated, and slaves were quickly brought to order. Still, Spartacus led such a large and threatening revolt that Rome assigned two of its top generals to put the **insurrection** down.

Spartacus was a soldier from an area near Macedonia called Thrace. He was intelligent and strong. So, when the Roman army enslaved him, he was sent to train as a **gladiator**. Gladiators were subjected to harsh treatment to prepare them for fighting in the arena, and, understandably, Spartacus wanted out. This life was a horrible existence.

The plan was, at first, not to revolt but to escape. Spartacus formed an escape plan that included about 200 men. Of course, with so many people involved, someone told the authorities. Once their plan was discovered, Spartacus knew they would have to fight for their freedom or be executed. Armed with kitchen knives and spits (the long metal poles used to rotate meat over a fire), Spartacus and 78 others fought their way out. After capturing some real weapons and fleeing to the countryside, Spartacus was elected the group's leader. Surprisingly, many others joined him—farmers, shepherds, and other slaves came from all around. Soon, Spartacus commanded a rag-tag army of 70,000!

For over two years, 73–71 BCE, Spartacus and his army tore around the Italian countryside, pursued by the Roman armies. The Roman generals underestimated Spartacus's skill as a military commander. They grew increasingly frustrated and alarmed as Spartacus and his band of slaves racked up victory after victory against the professional Roman soldiers. In a display of power and irony, Spartacus held his own gladiatorial games to amuse his troops with captured Roman soldiers. He was, indeed, a real threat to the city of Rome itself. Spartacus, however, did not want to invade Rome. Instead, he desired to cross the Alps and return to his homeland in Thrace. Many in his army, however, wanted to continue to pillage Italy.

Eventually, Spartacus's fortune ran out. After evading or defeating Roman armies repeatedly, he was killed in battle. History has remembered this soldier from Thrace as a champion for freedom and a symbol of defiance against enslavement. Rome would not soon forget this lesson. They took steps to prevent another rebellion, including lowering their dependence on slave labor.

Spectacles

While the Greeks had their Olympic Games, the Romans had their **spectacles**, and I'm not talking about reading glasses. These were action-packed shows like chariot races, mock battles, and fights. Gladiators might fight one another to the death or fight wild animals, from ostriches to lions. These were also events to execute prisoners or **martyr** Christians. Notice the link between "spectacle" and "spectacular," meaning dramatic and eye-catching—the more lavish and bloody the spectacle, the better.

Romans, men and women, *patricians* and *plebeians* alike, loved the spectacles, and the Roman rulers knew it. They built massive venues to host them and sponsored shows that sometimes lasted for days. The emperor of Rome might hold spectacles to celebrate a birthday, a battle victory, or a visiting dignitary from a foreign land. But spectacles were also held all over the Roman empire and often just for entertainment. They kept the people happy and the emperor popular!

Spectacles were usually held in one of two venues: amphitheaters or **circuses**. Fortunately, these are some of the best surviving architectural examples from ancient Rome.

The **Colosseum** in Rome was the largest amphitheater. It was, in fact, two amphitheaters put together to form an oval—the Romans' preferred arrangement. It is four stories tall and, in its day, seated 50,000 people.

Section and Elevation of the Colosseum in Rome

A visit to the Colosseum would have been truly spectacular! Underground, a series of hallways, holding cells, and trap doors, allowed the performers and wild animals to move around and appear in the arena at just the right time and place. Emperors even flooded the Colosseum and staged mock sea battles with real boats and a manmade island where sailors would jump out and fight one another hand-to-hand. Emperor **Commodus** himself performed in the arena hundreds of times.

Rome's **Circus Maximus** is an example of the other style of venue. Notice, again, the similarity of *circus* to the word "circuit," meaning a closed loop or ring. Circuses were long, narrow ovals, usually used for chariot racing. But fights and other types of shows could be held there, too.

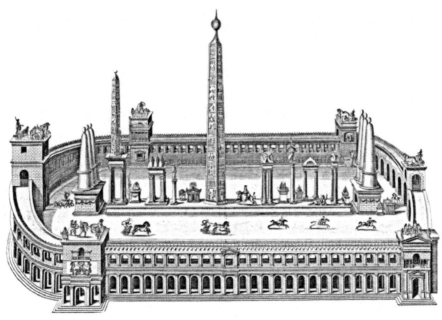

Circus Maximus

Gladiators like Spartacus played a starring role in these spectacles. They held an interesting place in Roman society as well—they could simultaneously be superstars and members of society's rock-bottom class.

Gladiators were housed and trained in special gladiator schools, which were more like prisons. Despite the poor living conditions, though, they did receive the best medical care available at the time. After all, they were an investment, and everyone wanted them to perform well.

Gladiators were named for the **gladius** or short sword they often used. Most were slaves, war prisoners, or criminals condemned to death. Rarely, women were gladiators who chose the profession to gain financial independence or fame.

Samnite, Thracia, Myrmillo, and Retiarius

There were about two dozen types of gladiators, recognized by their armor and weapons. The four most popular types were the **Samnite, Thracia, Myrmillo,** and **Retiarius**. A *Samnite* had a sword or lance, a large shield, an armored right arm and left leg. He was often paired against a *Thracia* with a curved blade and a small shield. These pairings were designed to pit a heavily-armed but slow gladiator against a lesser-armed but quicker one. The *Myrmillo* and *Retiarius* was another frequent matchup. The *Myrmillo,* also called the Fishman, had heavy armor and a fish on his helmet. His combatant, the *Retiarius*, wore only a shoulder pad and would try to catch his "fish" with a weighted net and stab him with his trident.

If a gladiator won his fight, he might receive a silver dish heaped with prize money. A long, successful career might mean a gladiator could buy his freedom. If a fighter knew he was coming out on the losing end, he could drop his sword and ask his opponent for mercy. If the emperor were in attendance, he would decide the loser's fate. The crowd would weigh in with their opinion. Then, the emperor would deliver his verdict with a thumbs-up (he lived to fight another day) or a thumbs-down (he was put to death).

Today, we might wonder why Romans wanted to watch such violent entertainment, but life in Rome was hard, and suffering and death were just an accepted part of it. Spectacles were a rare opportunity for someone to escape from the troubles of their own everyday life. They could sit in a beautiful venue, look at the architecture around them, cheer for the reenactments of Rome's battlefield victories, and feel proud that they lived in the greatest empire the world had ever known.

Around 100 CE, after the Roman Republic gave way to the Roman Empire, one writer, **Juvenal**, observed that the people no longer seemed to care about their rights or their government. The people, he wrote, care only about two things, "bread and circuses." This referred to the food distributed to the public by the state and the state-funded spectacles. Today, "bread and circuses" refers to anything used to keep a crowd happy or distract them from more important matters.

Government

The United States owes the structure of its government, a constitutional republic, and many of our beliefs about how it should operate to ancient Rome. The Greeks gave us democracy, but the Romans took that idea and formed it into representative government. Representative government, however, didn't come about all at once. As we've already seen, Rome began under the rule of kings. Now, let's look at how time took Rome from a kingdom to a republic to an empire.

The Kingdom of Rome

Rome did not have a hereditary kingship, at least in the beginning. Rather, the people elected kings, who, once elected, had absolute power. Unfortunately, we don't have a lot of written records from Rome's kingdom days, but later writings reflect that Rome had seven kings beginning with Romulus.

By the time the seventh king rolled around, the Romans had seen the dangers of being ruled by the whims of a single individual, and they wanted no more of it (not unlike the United States did centuries later). The last king, **Tarquin**, was overthrown in 509 BCE, and a new system of government was established, which the Romans called *res publica,* being governed as a republic.

The Roman Republic

Three significant changes occurred in the Roman government under the Republic. First, the Roman Senate went from having a minor advisory role to being Rome's primary governing body. Second, a complex hierarchy of positions, called **magistrates**, was created to act as the executive branch instead of a king. And third, the *plebeians* rose up and demanded their own representation in the government.

The Senate

Romulus created the **Roman Senate**, a group of 100 men who advised the king and carried out his orders. After the kingship was done away with, the Senate was kept around to advise the *consuls*—the top role in the magistrate pyramid.

Senators were exclusively patricians, at least in the beginning. Their number fluctuated and grew to as many as 900 senators during the time of **Julius Caesar**. Most of the time, there were around 300. They served for life and were afforded special privileges like the right to wear robes of Tyrian purple.

During the kingdom years, the Senate did not have much power. But as its influence over the role of **consul** grew, so did its power. This was the most powerful branch of government during the years of the Republic, and it had final say over money in the treasury.

Magistrates

The highest magistrate role one could hold (during non-emergency times) was that of *consul*. This was, essentially, the replacement role for the king. Every year, two *consuls* were elected who served together, balancing one another's power. One month, one *consul* had a higher rank. The following month that superior position switched to the other *consul*, and back and forth the power would go.

Consuls had great civil and military authority, but two things limited their actual power. First, they only served for a year. Second, the Senate still advised the *consuls* just as they had the king. Because Rome had a tradition of electing *consuls* to the Senate when their term was over, the *consuls* rarely disregarded the Senate's advice. This was their future job.

There were other lesser magistrate roles as well. If you study Roman history further, you will run across many of these titles, like *praetor*, *quaestor*, and *aedile*. These roles assisted the *consuls* with duties like managing finances, constructing temples, or even planning entertainment like spectacles.

If you were a young *patrician* man with aspirations to be a *consul* or senator, you needed to follow the *cursus honorum* or "course of honors." This was a sequence of military and government roles you were supposed to hold to climb the political ladder. There were minimum ages for each job. For example, during the Republic, you had to be at least 43 to be *consul*. By the time you reached that position, you would have a wide range of experience. We have similar requirements in the United States—25 to be a Representative, 30 to be a Senator, and 35 to be President.

Assemblies

How were magistrates chosen? Well, jobs like electing magistrates, deciding when to go to war, and making laws were vested in the hands of the people, more or less, through **Assemblies**. These **legislative** bodies were not **democratic** in the strictest sense, meaning each person did not vote individually on each issue. Instead, they were divided into blocs of men that voted as a unit.

First, there was the aristocratic *Comitia Centuriata*, or **Assembly of Centuries** (so called because it was divided into blocs of 100 men). This assembly was heavily weighted in favor of the wealthy and was a military group—soldiers only. They decided on crucial matters like when to go to war and who would be *consul.*

One interesting fact about Rome is that the city itself was considered consecrated ground. Within this sacred boundary, called the *pomerium*, weapons were prohibited. Generals were forced to resign from their armies before entering, and even soldiers lost their status and were considered civilians while inside. Due to this, the aggressive Assembly of Centuries met outside the city at an exercise area called the **Field of Mars** rather than in the Roman Forum as other Assemblies did.

The **Roman Forum** was a rectangular space of land between the Palatine and Capitoline Hills. It started as a marketplace, similar to the Greek *agora.* Public events began to be held here in about 500 BCE when the Republic began. Soon, it became the city's central meeting place and the site of important religious, political, and social gatherings. Most important temples and landmarks were built around the Forum, like the Temple of Saturn, the Temple of Vesta, the House of the Vestal Virgins, and the **Senate House**—called the *Curia.* Many of Rome's triumphal arches, monuments, and statues were placed here. One of Rome's most important roads, the Sacred Street or ***Via Sacra***, led from Capitoline Hill through the Forum and to the Colosseum.

Next in importance, the *Comitia Tributa*, or **Tribal Assembly**, was comprised of civilians and organized according to the various ancestral tribes that citizens belonged to. This group voted on laws, elected minor magistrate positions, acted as a court of appeals for petty crimes, and handled other small business matters.

Plebeian Representation

So, all of this was well and good for the *patricians*, but what about the *plebeians*? Right about the same time the Romans kicked out their king and set up the Republic, the Conflict of Orders erupted. The *plebeians* were tired of the *patricians* deciding everything. After all, they made up most of the army and did most of the actual work there!

Gradually, the *plebeians* won equality. In 451 BCE, Roman laws were first written down on bronze tablets called the **Twelve Tables**. These tablets laid out the rights and responsibilities of *patricians* and *plebeians*, and they were put on public display for everyone to read in the Forum. No longer could *patricians* rule over *plebeians* with vague and changing verbal "laws."

Plebeians also received their own Assembly, the *Concilium Plebis* or **Council of the Plebs**. At first, they could make laws pertaining only to *plebeians*. But by 287 BCE, their laws carried the same weight as those of the other assemblies and applied to everyone. They could hold their own trials for minor crimes, and, most importantly, they could elect tribunes.

A **tribune** was essentially a *consul* for the *plebians*. They served for one year, and their job was to protect *plebeian* interests. Their main power was the ability to veto laws created by magistrates that unfairly affected *plebeians*.

By 367 BCE, a law was passed that said one of the two *consuls* must be *plebeian*. Because, by then, *consuls* automatically became senators when their term was up, this meant *plebeians* could also serve on the Senate. Of course, *patricians* would always be the aristocrats of ancient Rome, but the *plebeians* finally achieved equality under the law.

The Roman Empire

Unfortunately, the groundbreaking system of representative government realized by the Roman Republic was not to last. You see, there was a built-in loophole to the balance of power in Rome, a backdoor to the throne if you will. Romans realized that their bureaucracy was complicated. There were lots of different people in different roles all having to get permission to do things from other groups of people. This would not work very well in a crisis. So in times of emergency, the Senate could appoint a **dictator** who had absolute authority to manage things for only six months. Some people held this office honorably, and some people exploited it. Julius Caesar, the last person to hold the title, convinced the Senate to name him dictator for life in 44 BCE. He was emperor in all but name.

This turned out to be a step Rome could not turn back from. As we will see a bit later, Caesar's successor, **Octavian** (**Augustus**), would take things a step further and was *actually* declared emperor in 27 BCE. The rest of Rome's history is its imperial history.

During the Roman Empire, the Assemblies lost their power and practically disappeared. The Senate remained, but mostly in a ceremonial role. Its presence gave the appearance that some balance of power still existed. Senators did still vote on laws put forward by the emperor, but few would openly oppose him. The Senate also, technically, elected new emperors and was, therefore, the source of their power. In reality, once elected, the emperor had supreme authority.

The Roman Justice System

Initially, Rome did not have dedicated courts for trying criminal and civil offenses. Instead, the different Assemblies handled these matters. By the late Republic, standing courts existed in Rome and its outlying territories to handle legal cases.

Although our laws, remedies, and court systems look very different from ancient Rome's, we do get much of our legal science and terminology from them. Things like:
- precisely worded laws and documents to avoid misunderstanding,
- a system to appeal a verdict or decision,

- legal experts who people could consult for advice,
- preliminary hearings, and
- presenting evidence and witnesses

are all ideas we take from the Romans.

Perhaps their greatest gift to the modern world is the idea that every citizen should know their rights and that the government should have systems in place to uphold those rights.

If you study Rome's history long enough, you will undoubtedly run across the letters SPQR. These four letters were chiseled into buildings and emblazoned across the battle standards of Roman soldiers. They stood for what Rome saw as its best and most authentic self— the equivalent of our own "We the People . . ." Until the emperors consolidated power in their own two hands, these letters stood for who really mattered—*Senatus Populusque Romanus*—the Senate and the People of Rome.

Infrastructure and Technology

Rome was known for taking the technology and culture of other civilizations and adapting or improving it for their own uses. They did this, in particular, with innovations from the Greeks and Egyptians.

As Rome conquered the world, it also put its technology to good use. Many small rural cities were transformed by the upgrades in infrastructure that the Roman army brought with them.

Cement and Concrete

The Romans did not invent cement and concrete, but they did make much better versions of them. Their new recipes created bricks that were lightweight, durable, and, most importantly, waterproof. This allowed them to tackle building projects that were simply not possible before, which, in turn, revolutionized Roman life.

Aqueducts

Waterproof building materials could be used for piers and harbors, fountains, public bathhouses, *and* **aqueducts** that brought fresh water from mountaintops to Roman cities. An ample, reliable fresh water supply meant Roman cities could sustain more people— making them even more urbanized.

Aqueduct

Aqueducts, manmade channels for transporting water, were not a Roman invention either. But the Romans harnessed their power in ways never before seen. Some Roman aqueducts were over 60 miles long. They tunneled through mountains and crossed deep valleys.

This was also an impressive display of Roman math and engineering skills. Aqueducts worked using gravity. So Romans needed to precisely calculate a gentle slope for the water to roll down, from the mountain springs to the city fountains, then accurately build according to those calculations.

Arches and Domes

Another innovation needed to make aqueducts—**arches**—was made possible by Roman concrete, too. Once again, Romans were not the first to use arches, but their strong and lightweight concrete meant they could create larger ones that spanned longer distances. They used arches in their aqueducts and bridges that crossed broad, deep valleys.

They also used a variation of the arch—the **dome**—to build magnificent buildings.

Arched Bridge

Interior View of the Pantheon Dome

Arches and domed ceilings became the trademarks of Roman architecture. The winning combination of light concrete and strong arches allowed them to build enormous structures, like the Colosseum, that were previously unimaginable.

At first glance, it can be difficult to tell the difference between ancient Greek and Roman architecture. The use of arches and domes is the biggest clue that you're looking at a Roman building. The Romans continued to use the Doric, Ionic, and Corinthian orders with a couple of variations. They created a **Tuscan order**, which looks much like a Doric column but is more slender without fluting on the shaft. They also made a **Composite order** that combines the Corinthian capital with the Ionic for a more ornate look. One final clue, the Romans liked to use marble in a big way. The Temple of Jupiter Stator in Rome was the first to be made entirely of this beautiful stone.

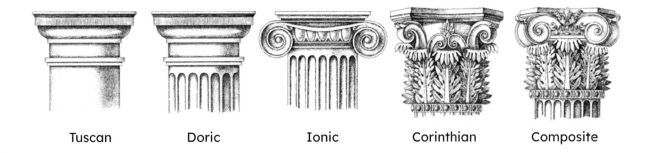

| Tuscan | Doric | Ionic | Corinthian | Composite |

Roads

One bit of Roman technology and infrastructure that stands out from all the rest is their roads. There is a reason we have a saying, "all roads lead to Rome," meaning all paths eventually arrive at a common destination. The Roman road network, much of which can still be seen today, transformed life for everyone across the empire and enabled Rome to conquer and hold its vast territories.

There were, of course, roads before the Romans came around. Before Rome, roads were little more than dirt paths. They were not very good and were way longer than they should have been because they had to wind around mountains, swamps, valleys, and rivers. The Romans fixed all of that. With their math skills, Romans calculated the shortest, straightest route between two destinations. Then, with their workforce and engineering skills, they built flat, straight roads between them. They cut through mountains and crossed gorges with their arched bridges and tunnels. They drained swamps and sliced through forests.

The roads themselves were different than anything seen before, too. They were built for a purpose. Like today's roads, there were wide highways, city streets with sidewalks, and simple country roads. First, the land was cleared and leveled. Then, curb stones were laid to mark the edges of the road. Next, the area between the curbs was filled with layers of gravel that were compacted to create a stable base. Finer gravel and sand were added, and, finally, paving stones were laid on top. Over time ruts formed in the roads from the wheels of carts and chariots. Later travelers would ride in the ruts to keep their wheels in a straight line. This also helped them to keep from tipping over. Mountain roads were grooved for better traction. All streets were sloped toward the sides, so water ran off and didn't puddle in the middle.

Roman roads were built by a combination of people. Soldiers constructed many of them as they expanded the empire, linking Rome with its newest acquisitions. Slaves also built and maintained roads and other infrastructures like bridges and aqueducts; sometimes, the government would contract with private companies for the job.

Appian Way with Wheel Ruts

The first and most important Roman Road was named the *Via Appia*, or **Appian Way**. It ran hundreds of miles along the length of the Italian boot, connecting Rome to the "heel" of Italy at the Adriatic Sea. You can still stroll along portions of this ancient highway outside of Rome today.

During the height of its empire, the Roman road network stretched for over 75,000 miles! The roads themselves are remarkable enough, but their effect on civilization was equally impressive. Rome built its roads mainly to enable its army to move efficiently from place to place. Military units could travel up to 20 miles a day on these roads. Rome quickly dispatched troops to quell uprisings and maintain its grip on the empire. The streets kept the army supplied as well. Wheeled vehicles could quickly transport the food, weapons, and other essential items that the soldiers needed. Communication was sped up as well. Posthouses at regular intervals allowed government officials to switch their tired horses for fresh ones. This meant messages could be passed along at great speed.

This speed and ease of movement benefited more than just the Roman army. Anyone living near a Roman road was affected—and that was just about everybody. Mile markers along the way showed the distance to the next town and gave travelers other important information, like the best places to stop. The roads were patrolled, so people no longer had to fear being robbed anytime they went somewhere. Moving goods and people from place to place suddenly became easier, safer, and faster, so travel and commerce increased. The Roman economy flourished in large part because of the Roman roads.

Other Roman Innovations

The Romans weren't just all about building things. They applied their technological and scientific skills in other areas as well.

They pioneered advances in farming and animal husbandry. They knew how to rotate crops, fertilize with manure, prune and graft trees, and even genetically modify plants and animals by crossing different varieties and selective breeding.

Healthcare was another area where the Romans went where no one had gone before. They created field hospitals for their army and successfully treated battlefield injuries, at least compared to any previous army. They undertook complicated surgeries, like cataract surgeries and cesarean sections. And they understood the importance of sanitation and disinfecting instruments—a concept not fully embraced by the medical profession until the 1800s.

Although the Romans brought war and conquest, it wasn't all bad news. The technology they brought raised the standard of living for millions of people within their borders. And the infrastructure they built allowed civilization to take the next step forward.

Writing

Like so many other things borrowed from the Greeks, the Romans adopted the Greek alphabet and used it for Latin. This was the infancy of our modern Western alphabet, although the Romans had only 23 letters to our 26. Then, they used their 23 letters to contribute all kinds of writings to the library of civilization—poetry, histories, dramas, comedies, philosophy, and more.

Rome also gave us brand new formats for writing. Until this point, writing was done on bulky clay tablets or awkward papyrus scrolls. Then, the Romans invented the codex—a stack of pages bound together—which became the forerunner of our modern books. The first codices were wax tablets that someone could wipe smooth and reuse. Next, the wax was replaced by bound pages of animal parchment, then, finally, by paper.

They also gave us newspapers. The *Acta Diurna,* or **Daily Acts**, were inscribed into tablets and set up in busy public places. One might stop by the Forum to read about Rome's latest military victory, who won the gladiatorial event last week, or which important person just died.

Art

As we look at Rome's cultural contributions to the world, it is an excellent time to talk about Roman art. The Romans highly admired Greek art. They collected it in droves, and, when they couldn't collect it, they copied it. Many Roman families displayed miniature copies of Greek statues. In the 1600s, art critics realized that the Roman pieces they had long admired were copies of Greek art or, at least, inspired by it. This led to a diminished reputation of Roman art. However, there is much to admire about it in its own right.

In addition to highly realistic statuary,

Bust of Marcus Aurelius

they decorated the inside of their homes and other buildings with stunning wall paintings. Bold colors, authentic details, and intricate designs might cover every inch of wall space. They also mastered mosaic art. Floors, vaulted ceilings, and even columns were decorated in tiny pieces of glass and stone arranged into pictures. Small details were painstakingly rendered with pieces as small as 1 millimeter—making the finished piece look almost like a painting.

Roman Mosaic

The Military

We've already talked a lot about how the Romans conquered vast swaths of the ancient world and expanded their empire from Britain to the Middle East. Now, it's time we look at how they accomplished this—their military.

During the early days of Rome, soldiers were recruited from the land-owning class and served only for the duration of a war. By the mid-Republic years, this strategy was no longer working. So, Rome formed a professional army of paid soldiers enlisted from all classes, giving them a younger and larger pool of people to recruit from.

The average soldier was called a **legionnaire**. He was a citizen, typically recruited around age 18 to 20. A *legionnaire* signed up to serve for 25 years. During that time, he was paid, according to some records, the equivalent of roughly $4.50 to $8.50 a day. This may seem like a small amount of money to risk your life for, but the job offered stability, guaranteed food, medical care, and a chance to travel the world. If you made it all 25 years, you also received a bonus and a piece of land on which to retire. There was even the possibility of receiving a share in the spoils of war if your unit was successful and your commander was generous.

Auxiliaries were non-citizen soldiers. They were paid less than *legionnaires* and placed on the frontlines of battle because they were considered less valuable. However, if you survived your 25 years as an *auxiliary*, you were rewarded with a certificate granting you *and* your children Roman citizenship—a prize many thought worth the risk.

Legionnaires were organized into **legions**, groups of between 4,000 to 6,000 men. Each *legion* contained different fighting forces, from artillery to infantry, to archery, to cavalry units.

Every *legion* also had its own **standard**. This was the *legion's* flag or banner. It was used as a rallying point for troops and also for communication.

Roman Legion Standard

Far-flung soldiers in battle could be commanded by raising, lowering, or waving the standard. Standards of the Republic carried the "Senate and People of Rome" acronym, SPQR. They also had a bronze or silver totem animal on top of the standard pole. The most well-known totem is an eagle with outstretched wings, a symbol we also use in the United States. Standards were a point of pride for the Roman army, and it was a disgrace if your standard was captured. Battles were fought just for their return.

Centurion

Legions were further divided into centuries, groups of around (but not always precisely) 100 men. Centuries were led by officers called **centurions**.

A *centurion* had a tremendous amount of responsibility. They trained the soldiers, assigned them their duties, maintained discipline, and doled out punishments. They also handled administrative jobs like procuring provisions, camp organization, distributing camp passwords, or escorting prisoners. A *centurion* won his soldier's loyalty and respect by leading by example. They were expected to show bravery under the direst of circumstances.

Centurions were compensated for their risky and stressful job. They were paid anywhere from five to eight times what a *legionnaire* was paid and typically received a portion of war booty. After retirement, a *centurion* might also have the option of moving on to a much more illustrious career. Some were named provincial governors. Some joined the **Praetorian Guard**. This elite fighting force protected generals during the Republic years, but they are better known as the emperor's personal bodyguards. They were the only military members allowed to serve and carry weapons within the sacred *pomerium* of Rome.

Legionnaires and *centurions* wore helmets with the iconic red plumed crests made of dyed feathers or horse hair. One ancient historian commented on this psychology, saying that the crests made the soldiers look much taller and fiercer than they actually were. In addition to a helmet, most Roman soldiers wore body armor to protect themselves. Although different fighting units had other weapons, a *pilum* or heavy spear was the most common equipment. These were thrown at the enemy first. Next, the soldier went to their *gladius*, or short iron sword, for close hand-to-hand combat. Some soldiers had large rectangular shields, while others had smaller round ones called a *scutum*. These were inscribed with each soldier's name and military unit—the ancient equivalent of today's dog tags.

The Roman army was one of the most effective and feared fighting forces the world had ever seen. They employed battlefield entrenchments, fortifications, catapults, and other siege weapons with alarming ferocity. *Legionnaires* fought in formations and used various well-rehearsed strategies depending on the situation. For example, if surrounded, they would form a hollow square with each man facing out. Roman commanders generally preferred the full-frontal attack after a proper reconnaissance of the enemy. And they often tempered this shock-and-awe approach with tempting offers of mercy upon peaceful surrender.

Much of the army's success is owed to their organization in preparation and training. They were organized while on the road as well. Camps were fortified and had their own hospitals, doctors, storage buildings, and food supplies. One benefit of building roads wherever they went was that the army didn't have to depend on local resources to feed and supply themselves. They set up supply chains that kept the army provisioned anytime, anywhere, for however long it took to get the job done.

A *very* successful Roman military commander might be awarded the honor of a lifetime—a triumph. (Eventually, this honor was reserved for the emperor alone.) A triumph was the spectacle of all spectacles—a parade through the streets of Rome, in which a returning war hero was celebrated *almost* as a god. In addition to all the dignitaries of Rome, the parade would include the commander's spoils of war. Everything certain to wow the crowd was included: wild animals, captured slaves, high-ranking enemy army or royal family members, and, of course, all the gold, silver, art, and other valuables that could be wrangled home. The highlight of the triumph was the victorious general, decked in purple robes and riding in a chariot. A slave would stand behind him, holding a golden crown above his head and continually whispering in his ear, "***respice***," or, "look behind." This ominous warning to watch his back was intended to remind the general that he was, in fact, mortal and not a god after all.

Triumphs ultimately went to the wayside in favor of building triumphal arches. These carved edifices—many placed prominently around the Forum—depict scenes commemorating someone's great political or military deeds. We're fortunate they made this switch since these are some of the best remaining architectural pieces from ancient Rome.

After their military conquered a new place, Rome's policies of self-governance held the empire together. Newly acquired provinces that paid Roman taxes and accepted military rule could continue their local customs and religion under the supervision of governors loyal to Rome. Eventually, in 212 CE, Rome would extend citizenship to free people in conquered lands as well—a major perk. Incorporating the cultures of the different lands they conquered was another key to Rome's prolonged success. It encouraged conquered peoples to accept Roman rule and live peaceably under it. It also didn't hurt that people benefited from Rome's substantial infrastructure upgrades, which helped their economy and improved their safety and general well-being.

Everyday Life

While country living remained relatively the same around the Roman world (perhaps with better roads), city life was taken to a whole new level, literally. With aqueducts that could supply unending fresh water and quick, safe trade routes that could bring food from near and far, Rome could support larger cities than the world had ever seen. At its height, Rome had a population of over 1,000,000—the first city to ever achieve these numbers!

Wealthy residents lived in villas outside the city or in a single-family home called a *domus*, usually built on Palatine Hill. For commoners, apartment buildings called *insulae* sprung up—very high, in fact. Some were seven stories tall! If you lived on the ground floor, life wasn't too bad. You probably had multiple rooms, running water, and even sewer access. However, if you lived on the upper floors, your family might share a single cramped and dark room. You must carry your water up in jugs from the public fountain and dump your refuse out the window into the street.

Insula

Roman Bathhouse

By 150 BCE, there were over 46,000 *insulae* in Rome, packing the narrow, filthy streets. However, conditions did improve after the Great Fire of Rome in 64 CE during Emperor Nero's reign that leveled two-thirds of the city. The Romans took this opportunity to rebuild wider roads, limit the heights of insulae, and build them with balconies so that the upper floors had more access to fresh air (and a way out in case of trouble).

With the limitations on in-home plumbing, public baths became all the rage and ultimately an essential part of a Roman city. More than just a place to get clean, public baths were a place to socialize and even conduct

179

business. All classes of society went to the baths. In 33 BCE, there were over 170 baths in Rome alone. Bathhouses had several different sections. There might be a **gymnasium** to exercise, an **apodyterium**, or a changing room. Then, you would enter the actual baths, which were more like pools. First, the **tepidarium**, or warm room, allowed you to get acclimated. Then, the **caldarium**, or hot room, gave more of a sauna experience. Finally, the **frigidarium**, or cold room, refreshed you for the evening ahead. Slaves maintained the temperatures at just the proper levels for the perfect bath experience.

Free time was important for everyone in urban Rome. Work was done between daybreak and noon. Then, the afternoons were for leisure. Rich and poor alike spent their afternoons taking in a spectacle at the theater or socializing at the baths. Sometimes shops would reopen in the evening.

While the father was head of the family, the home was the domain of the mother. In early Roman times, women did not appear in public, much like Greek women. But by the end of the Republic, she could attend dinner with her husband, go to the baths, attend spectacles, and work in different trades such as baking or pharmacy. Mothers might teach the children at home until a tutor was found or until boys were sent to school at about the age of seven. Boys and girls learned basic reading and writing, and girls learned domestic duties.

Wealthy Romans enjoyed food brought on Roman ships and roads from far and wide. They particularly loved a fermented fish sauce called **garum**, which was put into nearly every dish, including sweet ones. Ancient Roman food was not much like what we think of as Italian food today. There were no tomatoes at all, and seasoning like garlic and basil are only rarely mentioned in recipes. They did have olives and, of course, wine. Well-to-do Romans ate reclining on sofas as the Greeks did, and they usually ate with their hands, sometimes spoons. They loved seafood and exotic foods like roasted parrot, stork, or flamingo.

Food for the poor was **subsidized**, just like entertainment. Remember, "bread and circuses" were how the mass population was kept happy and under control. A city the size of Rome could not feed itself on its surrounding fields. They depended on imports from the fertile fields of Egypt and elsewhere to supply the monthly grain allotments that each commoner received. From this grain, families made the bread and porridge that made up the majority of their diet.

Styles of dress were, like so many other things, adapted from the Greeks. The everyday dress was a tunic, similar to the Greek **chiton**. A woman's version was called a **stola**. The most famous piece of Roman clothing was the **toga**. It

Toga

180

was an 18-foot-long piece of fabric wrapped and draped to cover the left arm and leave the right arm free.

One's social class could be determined by the different colors, patterns, and fabrics a person would wear. Upper-class women wore makeup and, sometimes, wigs. Like today, different styles were popular at different times. At one point, blond wigs made from the hair of captured Teutons (a Germanic people) were very popular.

Roman Time Periods

You might have already noticed that there were three major time periods of ancient Rome. The **Regal Period**, the time of kings, saw Rome's early character as a warrior nation form. The **Republican Period** was years of great ideals and cementing what it meant to be Roman. And the **Imperial Period** see-sawed between prosperity, peace, and glory; and division, destruction, and collapse. Let's look at all three, along with some of the major players and events of each.

Fasces

One symbol of authority throughout Rome's three periods was the **fasces**, which comes from the Latin word for "bundle." These ceremonial symbols were made of a single axe head projecting from a bundle of birch or elm rods bound with a leather strap. They represented order and strength through unity and were carried over the shoulder of **lictors**, attendants to the magistrates.

When a magistrate went out and about, his *lictors* walked before him carrying his *fasces* to let people know he was coming and remind them of his authority. A lower ranking magistrate would salute a higher ranking one by lowering his *fasces* when they met. When a magistrate died, he could have a picture of the *fasces* on his tomb. If he committed any wrongdoing, he resigned, and his *fasces* were broken in front of him as a gesture of humiliation. During the Republic, a ranking system was developed where higher ranking officials had a higher number of *fasces*. They also played a prominent role in ceremonies and triumphs.

Today, *fasces* are still a symbol of Republican values and strength. If you ever visit Washington, DC, look closely. You can find them all around, with and without their signature axe head. Abraham Lincoln rests his hands on them in the Lincoln Memorial. George Washington leans against them inside the Washington Monument. You can also find them in the House of Representatives and even the Oval Office.

The Regal Period — c. 753–508 BCE

Rome's regal period stretched across seven kingships that began with Romulus, the very founder of the city. In case you are interested in their names, they were, in order of succession:

Romulus, Numa Pompilius, Tullus Hostilius, Ancus Martius, Lucius Tarquinius Priscus (Tarquin the Elder), Servius Tullius, and **Tarquinius Superbus (Tarquin the Proud).**

Although they all went by the title "King," or **Rex** in Latin, they were not the typical hereditary king or grab-the-throne-by-force king we are used to. Each one, after Romulus, was elected to their position by the Senate. Despite this, they were kings nonetheless. They served for life, and they had absolute authority once elected.

Most of what we know about this time period was written well after, but legends do suggest that it wasn't always a simple and respectful election. There was likely some conniving, deceit, and violence involved, especially once we reach kings five, six, and seven. The inherent problems with the monarchy ultimately led the Romans to reject it altogether.

Tarquin the Proud (r. 534–510 BCE) would be the last king of Rome. He was responsible for enlarging Rome's territory but also ruled as an absolute tyrant. He killed senators who disagreed with him, and even his family members were a terror to the city. Finally, Tarquin and his family were run out of Rome and the Republic, governed by two consuls, was formed in 509 BCE.

Tarquin would leave such a bad royal taste in the mouth of Romans that they would go to great lengths to ensure no one person held all the power in Rome again. We'll come back to this point in the Imperial Period.

The Republican Period — c. 509–27 BCE

The Republican period stretched from the ousting of King Tarquin to the rise of Julius Caesar's adopted son Augustus, the first true emperor. With its Assemblies, Senate, and elected magistrates, the Roman Republic was one of the world's first representative democracies, even if it was a very flawed one.

The Republic's early years were characterized by the *plebeians'* struggle for representation. This fight began almost immediately upon Tarquin's exit and lasted well into the 300s BCE. By that time, power rested mostly in the Senate, which was made up of *patricians* and wealthy *plebeians*.

Another thing that characterized this period was expansion. Rome began to outgrow its city-state and became embroiled in wars with the Etruscan and Latin states on the Italian peninsula. By 264 BCE, Rome had control of the whole boot.

The Gauls Sack Rome

Another major event left a lasting impression on Rome during this time and charted their course for the future. In 390 BCE, a band of people called the **Gauls** (from modern-day France and Western Germany) came, raiding and plundering, down into Italy. They swiftly and easily defeated the Roman army and sacked and burned the city of Rome itself. Humiliated, Rome was forced to pay a large ransom in gold to get the Gauls to go home, a defeat they would learn from. Rome remade its army stronger and better than before. They built a better wall around their city. And they would not forget the Gauls, who would see them again later.

The Punic Wars

In the meantime, however, Rome had another problem. As they expanded throughout southern Italy and onto the island of Sicily, they were bumping up against what was, at the time, the Mediterranean's undisputed power—Carthage. This friction would lead to a series of wars, called the **Punic Wars**, that would end with the total destruction of the Phonecian colony of Carthage and cement Rome's reputation as a force to be reckoned with.

The **First Punic War (264–261 BCE)** was fought primarily for control of Sicily. This prosperous and strategically located island was already a point of contention between Carthage and Greece, who had the colony of Syracuse there. Now, Rome wanted a piece of it, too.

It was during this war that Rome learned to become a naval power. Until then, they had no great experience with ships or battles at sea. But, here, we see them bring to bear what they *were* good at—borrowing technology and making it better. First, Rome captured Carthaginian ships and copied them, training rowers on benches while the ships were being built. Then, they added their own unique modifications, bridges with spikes on the end that could be lowered and attached to enemy ships. This way, Roman boats could row up next to a Carthaginian boat, lower the bridge, and Roman infantry could cross and board the enemy boat. This essentially turned a naval battle into a land one, where the Romans excelled.

The war raged on with victories on both sides, but in the end, Sicily was conceded to Rome. However, much like Rome and the Gauls, Carthage did not forget this defeat, and they would be back.

Hannibal (247–183 BCE), son of a Carthaginian general, grew up with the stain of the First Punic War alive and well in his family. As a young boy, his father had him swear an oath to never be a friend of Rome. Hannibal took that seriously and would become one of Rome's most hated enemies.

When he was elected commander of Carthaginian troops in modern-day Spain at the age of 25, tensions were already rising again between the two superpowers. So when the Romans declared war for the second time in 218 BCE, Hannibal decided to take the fight directly to the city of Rome itself.

In the **Second Punic War (218–201 BCE)**, Hannibal crossed the Alps with his army, including many war elephants. Can you imagine? Elephants crossing the Alps! What a sight that must have been for the residents of Northern Italy, not to mention surprising for those in Rome who thought Hannibal was still in Spain.

Despite losing many men and elephants in the hazardous trek over the mountains, Hannibal's clever tricks and battle tactics allowed him to evade or defeat the Roman army in the north of the peninsula for a long time. The Romans, however, decided to take a trick from Hannibal's bag and send their army to attack Carthage on their home turf.

Roman general **Scipio Africanus** (236–183 BCE) sailed a fleet to Northern Africa and began to march toward Carthage. The plan worked, and Hannibal was recalled from Italy to defend his homeland. At last, Hannibal and Scipio faced off on the plains of Africa. But Scipio had studied Hannibal's tactics and was ready for him. When Hannibal's war elephants charged, the Romans simply broke ranks, stepped aside, and let them run past. Then, they killed the elephant's handlers and sent the animals in disarray back into the Carthaginian troops, followed by their own cavalry charge.

The Second Punic War ended with Rome the victor again. Carthage was allowed to keep their colonies, but they had to give up almost all of their warships and pay a hefty tax to Rome for the next 50 years. Rome now controlled the Western Mediterranean and what is now Spain.

Carthage actually did quite well for itself in the years that followed. Rome watched with wary suspicion as Carthage managed to pay its debts *and* regain its prosperity. Part of the peace treaty with Rome stipulated that Carthage was not supposed to go to war without Rome's permission. Well, after paying off their war debt, Carthage considered everything with Rome settled and done. They rebuilt their navy and decided to go to war with one of their neighbors, Numidia. But Rome was looking for an excuse to wipe Carthage off the map, and this was it. They said that Carthage had violated their treaty, declared war, and invaded—beginning the **Third** and final, **Punic War** (149–146 BCE). This time, there would be no peace treaty. Rome's complete destruction of the city of Carthage would spell the end of this civilization. The city would remain uninhabited for 100 years until it was refounded by Julius Caesar. Now, Rome controlled North Africa, and their domination of the Mediterranean was complete.

Rome Takes Over Greece

At the same time the Romans were battling the Carthaginians, they were also expanding east. As we saw in the Greek Hellenistic Period, during the First (214-205 BCE) and Second (200-197 BCE) Macedonian Wars, Rome allied with Greek city-states to take Macedonia from King Philip V. After that, Rome promptly annexed the entire Greek peninsula in 146 BCE, culminating with the sack of Athens by Roman general Sulla in 86 BCE.

Roman culture was growing and evolving throughout this time thanks to their contact with other cultures. Rome was becoming both a military superpower and a cultural mixing bowl.

They borrowed cultural elements from different civilizations, added their own flavor, and then spread them wherever they went.

Internal Struggles

The late Republic was marked by internal struggles in Rome's homeland. Until this time, a man had to own land to join the army. This meant that when a farmer went off to war, he usually left his farm in the hands of his wife and young children. This worked fine for short campaigns. But as Rome became involved in longer wars in more distant lands, farms began to go bankrupt without their owners there to manage them.

Rich, aristocratic landowners began buying the smaller farms and undercutting their prices, forcing even more farmers out of business. These unlanded families moved to the cities, where they struggled to find work. This created poverty and an overcrowding problem *and* widened the gap between the many poor and few rich in Roman society. Also, it was massively reducing the pool of available soldiers since so few people now owned land.

One insightful commander, **Tiberius Gracchus**, saw what this was causing. After his career in the army, he was elected tribune and attempted to enact many reforms that would restore land to the people and limit the ownership abilities of the aristocrats. This, of course, made him very popular among the *plebeian* masses and very unpopular with the Senate, whose members were the very aristocrats who owned all the land. After he attempted to run for an unprecedented second term as tribune, the Senate saw him as too much of a threat. In 133 BCE, Tiberius and 300 of his closest followers were murdered by a mob of Senators wielding wooden chairs.

His brother, **Gaius Gracchus**, tried to continue in his footsteps but met a similar end in 121 BCE, thanks to a mob under the Senate's control. This time, 3,000 followers were killed. These shocking acts of violence are seen as the beginning of the end of the Roman Republic, and a time of political turbulence followed.

The Dictatorship Changes

Rome was becoming increasingly divided politically. There were two main groups or factions, the **Optimates**, those who favored the powerful Senate, and the **Populares**, those who wanted power to remain in the hands of the common people.

In 83 BCE, when **Sulla** (138—78 BCE), an *optimate*, returned from conquering Greece and sacking Athens, this devolved into a full-scale civil war between his army and the *populares*. When Sulla reached the city of Rome, he had his enemies killed, erected a lovely statue of himself in the Forum, and "suggested" that they revive the practice of dictatorship, which hadn't been used in 120 years. Sulla didn't want to be a dictator for only six months, so he was named dictator for life. The Republic was firmly set on a course from which it would not recover.

Sulla expanded the number of senators to 600 and filled the positions with people loyal to him. He passed many reforms, too, aimed at strengthening the Republic but which really only strengthened the power of the Senate. Eventually, he retired to his country home to spend his remaining days writing his memoir.

Julius Caesar

Enter **Julius Caesar** (100-44 BCE). Caesar was a member of the *populares* faction. He rose to popularity as a successful soldier and orator. Even his enemies couldn't deny what talent he had for public speaking. From the beginning of his career, it seemed that Caesar could do anything he put his mind to and do it exceptionally well.

Modesty was not among his virtues, however. In 75 BCE, Caesar was kidnapped by pirates while sailing to Greece. When the pirates ransomed him for the price of twenty **talents**, Caesar protested that he was worth at least fifty! During his captivity, Caesar often told his kidnappers how he would hunt them down and kill them for this offense once he was free. The pirates took this as a joke. "Sure you will, Julius! Haha!" But Caesar was the last one laughing because he made good on his promise. This story shows both Caesar's high opinion of himself and his unceasing determination.

Caesar returned from travel to a Rome that was practically in chaos, and a collapse of the Republic seemed imminent. In 60 BCE, Caesar formed an alliance with two other influential players in Roman politics to stabilize the situation and achieve his personal goals. These two men were military leader **Gnaeus Pompeius Magnus** or **Pompey the Great** and **Marcus Licinius Crassus**, the wealthiest man in Roman history and the one responsible for putting down the Spartacus rebellion. They were called the **First Triumvirate** or the "Gang of Three." Together, they would pool their money, influence, and talent for mutual benefit.

Things worked fairly well at first. Relations were sometimes tense, but everyone managed to get along. This was helped by the marriage of Pompey to Caesar's daughter, Julia. All three men were enjoying political successes from the union.

After spending 59 BCE as *consul*, supported by Pompey and Crassus, Caesar decided there was fame and glory to be gained in Gaul. You see, the Romans had never forgotten the sacking of Rome way back in 390 BCE. So he marched an army westward, and—like everything else Caesar attempted—he was wildly successful. He conquered Gaul and became, essentially, ruler of that realm with all the wealth it contained. But meanwhile, there was trouble back in Rome.

The First Triumvirate had broken up. Crassus had been killed in battle, and Julia had died in childbirth, breaking Pompey's family bond to Caesar. Pompey was now in total control of

Rome and ordered Caesar to disband his army and return as a civilian. Caesar knew what that meant—Pompey had plans for him, and they were not good.

As Caesar marched with his army over the Alps, he had to consider what he would do—surrender his army at the **Rubicon River**, the traditional boundary of Italy proper, or continue forward toward Rome in a clear act of treason and try to take it from Pompey by force. It would be interesting to know how much thought Caesar actually gave this choice. At any rate, he chose the second option, and with the famous words *ālea iacta est*, "the die is cast," he marched his army to Rome in 49 BCE. Today, the phrase "crossing the Rubicon" refers to any decisive action that, once done, cannot be undone.

Pompey did not make the stand that you might anticipate. Instead, he left Rome, and Caesar pursued him, first to Greece, where they met in battle, and then to Egypt, where Pompey had contacts and hoped to find refuge. There, Pompey was killed immediately upon arrival by orders of the pharaoh, Ptolemy XIII. At this time, Egypt was a Roman province but retained the right to govern itself as long as it respected Rome's authority and continued to provide it with the grain Rome depended on.

Ptolemy, believing Caesar would be pleased with him for dispatching his enemy, was surprised when Caesar arrived and was outraged. Caesar, in no hurry to skip back to Rome, set up shop in the Egyptian palace. Here, he met and began a relationship with Cleopatra, the legendary final pharaoh of Egypt. Caesar would spend the next nine months there, helping Cleopatra regain her throne from her brother. Many historians believe that a major reason he went to this trouble was to punish Ptolemy for his role in Pompey's death.

Amazingly, during this time, Caesar found time to jump over to Asia Minor and engage in another brief war with the Kingdom of Pontus at the Battle of Zela. This is notable because it is where we get another one of Caesar's famous quotes. In a letter to the Senate describing the battle, he summarized it as follows: "*Veni, vidi, vici!*" (I came, I saw, I conquered!) More typical Caesar arrogance, yet also true.

Finally, Caesar returned to Rome with Cleopatra, giving her a lovely home where he would visit her frequently. The Senate strongly objected to this, seeing that Caesar was already married to someone else. But Caesar's charm continued to work in his favor, and, despite the senators' misgivings, in 44 BCE, Caesar was given the title dictator for life, just as Sulla had been.

Little did Caesar know, however, that this title's expiration date was almost up. He quickly pressed forward his political agenda. He passed many reforms, often in favor of the poor. This, of course, the Senate did not love. Neither did they love Caesar's method of dismissing their advice and simply telling them what was going to happen. The *optimates* felt he was becoming too powerful too fast, and they decided he had to be stopped.

On March 15, 44 BCE, the **Ides of March**, Caesar attended a meeting of the Senate despite warnings of bad fortune from a **soothsayer** and against the wishes of his wife, who had dreamed that something bad would happen to him. Upon arriving, he was assassinated—stabbed to death—by a group of senators, including his close friend, **Brutus**. In William Shakespeare's play *Julius Caesar*, Caesar's final words are quoted as, "*Et tu, Brute!*" (You, too, Brutus!) Ironically, Caesar fell dead at the foot of a statue of Pompey.

Unfortunately, in all their preparations for the assassination, the senators had failed to prepare for what would happen after Caesar was gone. Although Caesar had done many good things for the Republic, the chaos that followed would mark the transition from Republic to Empire. There were so many fascinating Romans whose stories we, unfortunately, don't have time to tell here. But one more political leader from this period needs to be mentioned. **Marcus Tullius Cicero** (106-43 BCE), more commonly known as just Cicero, was a successful politician, orator, and writer during the days of Caesar and Pompey.

Interestingly, Cicero is not known for his political work and largely stayed out of the turmoil that swirled around the end of the Republic. He declined friendly gestures from Caesar that might have included him in the First Triumvirate. He was away from Rome when civil war broke out between Caesar and Pompey.

Cicero *is* known for being the undisputed greatest orator that Rome had known at that time. He is also known for his writings. Over 900 of his personal letters survive, giving a unique insight into this influential man's time period and thought process. He is perhaps most famous for translating the philosophers of ancient Greece into Latin. His eloquent writing style and meticulous translation made his work a must-read into the modern age for anyone in the Western world who wanted to call themselves educated. Cicero is one more example of the rich cultural legacy that Rome has left to the world.

The Imperial Period — c. 27 BCE–476 CE

Caesar's adopted nephew, **Gaius Octavius Thurinus** (66 BCE-14 CE), better known as **Octavian**, strategically rose to power after Caesar's death. First, to connect himself with his uncle's legacy, he took his name, becoming Gaius Julius Caesar. The name Caesar eventually became synonymous with the title Emperor, even though Julius Caesar himself never actually held that title. The words "Kaiser," the title for German emperors, and "Czar," the title for Russian emperors, are derived from it.

In 43 BCE, Octavian formed the Second Triumvirate with one of Caesar's close friends, **Mark Antony**, and another supporter, **Marcus Aemilius Lepidus**. Together, they hunted down Caesar's rivals and assassins, clearing the way for their own agenda. At first, they split up the Roman territories between the three. But after a falling out between Octavian and Lepidus, Lepidus was kicked off the Triumvirate, and now it was down to two.

The deterioration of Antony and Octavian's relationship was a complicated one, but one of the main reasons for it was Cleopatra. Much like Caesar had done with Pompey, Octavian had cemented his alliance with Antony by marriage. Antony wed Octavian's sister, Octavia, even though he was already in a relationship with Cleopatra. Octavian, of course, didn't take kindly to Antony's subsequent disrespect and ignoring of his sister in favor of the Egyptian queen.

Tensions escalated until Octavian finally declared war against Antony. The future of Rome was decided in the Battle of Actium in 31 BCE when Antony's ships were outmaneuvered by Octavians and defeated. Antony and Cleopatra fled to Egypt, where they both famously committed suicide.

Octavian, now the sole power in all of Rome, was clever and intended to avoid the pitfalls that had gotten his uncle killed. For this reason, he was very careful to give the appearance of restoring the institutions of the Republic and doing everything for its benefit, while in reality, he kept all real power for himself.

In 27 BCE, in a show of goodwill, he resigned all of his powers to the Senate, which—surprise, surprise—gratefully gave the power right back to him and bestowed upon him the title of *Augustus*, "the illustrious one." He was, again, careful never to use that title in public, preferring to humbly call himself *Princeps*, or "First Citizen." In the Roman provinces, he was called *Imperator*, or commander-in-chief. This is where we get the word "emperor." **Augustus Caesar** was now the first emperor of Rome. It's interesting to wonder how many Roman citizens at that time even realized what a large page had just been turned in the history books.

Augustus Caesar

Augustus ruled for 56 years and brought much-needed stability to a Rome tired of violence and chaos. He instituted social reforms, encouraged culture and arts, and kept the peace in all but the fringes of Roman territory with a strong army. The next 200 years were so glorious and prosperous that they would be called the **Pax Romana** or **Roman Peace**.

This was Rome's "Golden Age." It was the time of Roman roads, unparalleled trade that spread wealth and culture far and wide, and law and order dispensed by Roman courts. However, it was also a time when the middle class had just about disappeared. Society was made up of the very rich and the very poor. The strong Roman values of family and religion were weakening as well. This was the age of "bread and circuses," meant to appease the masses.

Augustus was enormously popular and drew a large cult following. After his death in 14 CE, the Senate deified him. Thus began the long tradition in which the Senate declared popular emperors to be gods upon their death.

The Julio-Claudian Dynasty

Augustus was the first emperor of Rome's first dynasty—the **Julio-Claudian Dynasty**—so named because all five emperors were either born or adopted into one of these two families. They were, in order of succession: Augustus, **Tiberius** (r. 14-37 CE), **Caligula** (r. 37-41 CE), **Claudius** (r. 41-54 CE), and **Nero** (r. 54-68 CE).

Nero would go down in history as one of Rome's worst and most wicked emperors. He was a terror to his own family, conspiring to have several family members killed, including his mother. He spent Rome's money lavishly on games and spectacles, which the people were fine with at first. But, it soon became apparent that Nero wanted all the attention for himself.

Nero fancied himself a musical prodigy and—rather than working on the problems of Rome—preferred to spend all his time singing (badly) and playing the lyre. He would put on concerts for literally captive audiences. People were prohibited from leaving while the Emperor performed. It is said that women even gave birth during performances. Soon, Nero's spending, cruelty, and self-centeredness made him very unpopular, and then there was a fire.

The **Great Fire of Rome**, in 64 CE, lasted six days and burned ten of the city's 14 districts. What was left by the fire was destroyed by looters after the fact. Rumors abound that Nero callously played the lyre and sang as he watched his city burn, commenting on the beauty of the flames. Others blamed him for setting the fire to clear space for the expansive palace he built afterward. To deflect blame from himself, Nero decided to blame another group of people already growing in unpopularity, the Christians. This began the horrible persecution and execution of Christians under Roman rule.

Regardless of his role in the fire, by 68 CE, the Senate had had enough of Nero and appointed **Galba** the new emperor, ending the Julio-Claudian Dynasty. Nero committed suicide, and his last words were reportedly, "What an artist dies in me."

Nero's death was followed by a period of unrest called the **Year of the Four Emperors**, which was precisely that. Galba took the throne in 69 CE, proved awful, and met a violent death. He was followed by equally horrible **Otho** and **Vitellius**. One year to the day after Galba took the throne, **Vespasian** (r. 69-79 CE) took power. He would rule for the next ten years.

The Flavian Dynasty

Vespasian founded the Flavian Dynasty, characterized by a return to massive building projects and expanding the Empire's borders. Vespasian was followed by his son **Titus** (r.

79-81 CE) and then his other son **Domitian** (r. 81-96 CE), who—unpopular with the Senate—was assassinated, ending the Flavian Dynasty.

The Colosseum was built during this time, officially called the Flavian Amphitheater. And two other historic events also occurred in this dynastic period. One was a second enormous fire in Rome in the year 80. The other was the eruption of **Mt. Vesuvius** in 79 CE, which buried the cities of **Pompeii** and **Herculaneum** in volcanic ash.

The Nervan-Antonian Dynasty

Domitian was followed by his advisor, **Nerva** (r. 96-98 CE), who began the Nervan-Antonian Dynasty. This dynasty includes some very famous names, and the first five were referred to as The **Five Good Emperors**.

Trajan (r. 98-117 CE) was known as a kind emperor, famously erecting his column in the Forum that tells the story of his military campaigns.

Trajan's Column   Close-up of Trajan's Column

Monuments such as these replaced triumphs and, thankfully, provided us with much more information about Rome's conquests than the parades did.

Hadrian (r. 117-138 CE) came next. He went down in history for his wall that ran coast to coast across the island of Britain, separating Roman territory from the "barbarians" up north.

Map of Hadrian's Wall

Hadrian, with no sons, adopted the 51-year-old **Antoninus Pius** (r. 138-161 CE) to be his heir. He presided over a relatively peaceful and uneventful reign. Pius was followed by **Marcus Aurelius** (r. 161-180 CE). Marcus was known for being a follower of the Greek Stoic philosophy and authored a book entitled *Meditations*, which is still famous for its pithy wisdom today. He had a co-emperor—his adopted son, **Lucius Verus** (r. 161-169 CE).

Lucius would not survive Marcus. He fell victim to the **Antonine Plague**, a new and horrible disease that had arrived from the east around 165 CE. This disease is listed among the causes of the *Pax Romana* coming to an end. It decimated the Empire, killing, by some estimates, a quarter to a third of the entire population. This, naturally, affected both Rome's military might and its economy.

Unfortunately, the run of "good" emperors would end with Marcus. His natural-born son, **Commodus** (r. 180-192 CE), succeeded him and proved a disastrous choice. He was corrupt, inept, and conceited. He considered himself the reincarnation of Hercules and demanded to be treated accordingly. He dressed up in a lion's skin and carried a club. He put statues of himself everywhere. He renamed the city Rome Colonia Lucia Annia Commodiana and called its inhabitants Commodiani, after himself. He also loved participating in gladiatorial combat in the arena—always with some unfair advantage, of course. Eventually, the people around Commodus could take no more of his foolishness, and he was killed in his bathtub by his personal trainer.

The **Year of the Five Emperors** followed. In 193 CE, Pertinax, Didius Julianus, Pescennius Niger, Clodius Albinus, and Septimius Severus take the throne in short order.

The Severan Dynasty

Septimius Severus (r. 193-211 CE) began the Severan Dynasty with a period of civil war where several potential candidates for emperor vied for power. During his reign, he brought some measure of stability; however, he used a lot of Rome's money to do it.

His sons **Caracalla** (r. 211-212 CE) and **Geta** (r. 211-217 CE) followed him. During this time, Roman citizenship was extended to all free men in the Empire, but that was probably just so that there would be more people to tax.

Macrinus (r. 217-218 CE), who never set foot in Rome while emperor, a 14-year-old **Elagabalus** (r. 218-222 CE), controlled by his mother, and **Alexander Severus** (r. 222-224 CE), aged 13 and also controlled by *his* mother, were next in line. As you can see, things are becoming increasingly unstable and chaotic.

The Imperial Crisis

The chaos would reach its pinnacle of height after the death of Alexander Severus. The Roman Empire began a period called the **Crisis of the Third Century** or the **Imperial Crisis** (235-284 CE).

A variety of factors were in play here. The plague still lingered on, and the economy was in ruins. There was no clearly defined way to choose a new emperor. The military was taking more and more of a role in politics, putting emperors on the throne and then quickly assassinating them. Emperors chosen by the army came to be nicknamed **"Barracks Emperors."** Enemies were pressing in on all sides. More enemies meant the need for a bigger army, which meant fewer farmers and less food. Things were not going well. Violence prevailed. The Empire was near anarchy. Civil war took hold, and twenty "Barracks Emperors" would take the throne over the next fifty years.

This is where we see the first significant fractures in what was once the greatest empire in the world. In 260 CE, the governor of Germania, **Postumus**, decided he could manage his people much better than the utterly inept government back in Rome. He broke away and formed the **Gallic Empire**. In 270 CE, **Queen Zenobia** of Palmyra did the same thing in the east, creating the **Palmyrene Empire**. Roman emperors were too busy killing one another to pay much attention. Emperor **Aurelian** (r. 270-275 CE) briefly reunited the empire again, but the chaos continued until **Diocletian** took the throne in 284 CE.

The Eastern and Western Roman Empires

If you recall, we learned about Diocletian (r. 284-305 CE) before. He was responsible for the Great Persecution of Christians. Well, Diocletian understood that a big part of Rome's problem was its bigness. The vast empire was simply too large to rule and run efficiently. So, he made a monumental decision. He split the Empire between East and West, giving the Western half, led from Rome to his son-in-law, **Maximian** (r. 286-305 CE). Diocletian, who had never really liked the city of Rome, kept the Eastern half of the Empire for himself. He ruled from the city of **Byzantium** (modern-day Istanbul).

Diocletian also attempted to solve the problem of imperial succession. Under his plan, each of the two emperors, east and west, would choose their successor, who would serve as a Caesar under them. These emperors-in-training would, then, be available for a seamless transition to the throne, whereupon they would choose a new Caesar under themselves. This was known as the *tetrarchy* or **"rule of four."**

Constantine the Great

After Diocletian's death, though, the *tetrarchy* died as well. Various factions faced off for control of the whole empire. **Constantine I** (r. 306-337 CE), who we saw play a pivotal role in the spread of Christianity, emerged on top.

After defeating rival Maxentius at the Battle of the Milvian Bridge, Constantine was the sole contender left standing. In addition to advancing Christianity, Constantine stabilized the economy, reformed the military, and officially moved the capital from Rome to Byzantium, which he renamed **Constantinople** after himself. But despite Constantine's reforms, the western half of the empire would struggle and flounder, while the eastern half thrived and began developing a culture all its own.

Constantine began a dynasty that wavered back and forth between supporting Christianity and trying to revive Rome's pagan tradition. But by 380 CE, Christianity was firmly established. The Greek schools of philosophy, including Plato's Academy, were closed by order of the emperor. Pagan worship was outlawed, and temples were converted to churches.

Theodosius I (379-395 CE) was the last emperor to rule over the entire empire. After him, it was again divided between east and west. The Eastern Roman Empire was known as the **Byzantine Empire.** Everything from its language (which became Greek), to its form of Christianity, to its art started to diverge from that of the Western Roman Empire. The course of their history diverges from Rome's here as well, and we follow what happened in the west.

Decline and Fall

Between 376 and 382 CE, Rome fought a series of wars against Gothic invaders. They were beset from all sides by the Angles, Franks, Saxons, Huns, and Vandals as well. Then, in 410 CE, the city of Rome was sacked once more, this time by the Visigoths.

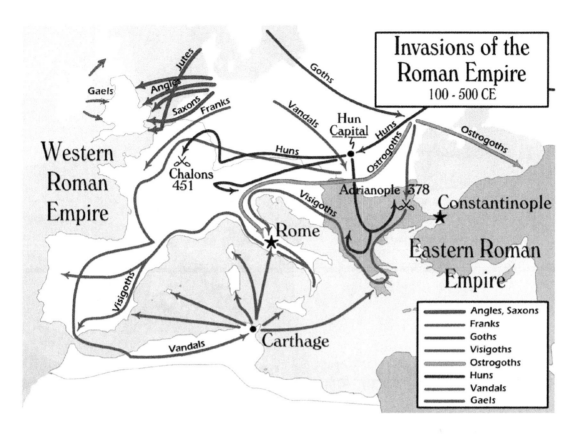

On September 4, 476 CE, the final emperor of the Western Roman Empire, **Romulus Augustulus**, was deposed by Germanic king **Odoacer**. The Roman Empire had officially ended. This is also the date when people usually draw a line between ancient history and the Middle Ages.

Thousands and thousands of pages have been written about the decline and fall of the Roman Empire. People love to list and debate the reasons why:
- instability from the Empire's enormous size,
- corruption within the government,
- barbaric invaders,
- the switch to an unloyal mercenary army,
- using too much slave labor rather than employing the lower class,
- a poor economy caused by loss of trade and devalued money.

Some even point the finger at Christianity, saying it weakened Rome's social cohesion by offering people a god interested in them individually rather than gods tied to the state. Others insist that Rome died a self-inflicted death by attempting to hold on to political and social structures that no longer worked. Whatever the cause or causes of Rome's fall, it was a long, slow descent.

Like the Greeks, the Romans have left such a lasting impression on Western culture that they almost seem to be with us still.

Historical Highlights

Here we are at our last Historical Highlights! So what made Rome the ancient powerhouse that we still can't get enough of today? Here are some important things to remember about them.

- The city of Rome was founded on seven hills along the Tiber River in 753 BCE by twin brothers Romulus and Remus, who were, according to legend, raised by a wolf.
- Beginning with Romulus and ending with Tarquin, Rome was ruled by a series of seven kings elected to office and advised by a group of men called the Senate.
- The central unit of Roman society was the family, and the father had absolute authority over family members. Society was also divided into aristocrats, called *patricians*, and commoners, called *plebeians.*
- The Romans adopted many things from Greek culture, including many of their gods, which they renamed. Jupiter was their chief god, the equivalent of Zeus. They also worshiped many of their emperors.
- In 509 BCE, Rome got rid of its kingship and formed a republic. They created a hierarchy of magistrates to govern, with two *consuls* who served one-year terms at the top of the hierarchy. Different Assemblies gave citizens a voice in their government by voting on various matters, but Rome was not a democracy in the strictest sense, meaning each person did not vote individually on each issue.
- During the Republic, the Senate gained more and more power, the *plebeians* won relatively equal rights and a voice in the government, and Rome expanded its territory.
- Rome had a large slave population, mostly prisoners of war. They relied on slave labor for many jobs, which created an unemployment problem for the lower class and led to slave revolts, such as the one led by Spartacus.

- Rome's military was a highly disciplined and trained fighting force that dominated the entire Mediterranean region during its height of power. They were organized into groups called *legions*. A major key to their success was the roads they built everywhere, allowing for quick movements and a reliable supply chain.
- In addition to roads, Rome improved life within its borders by building aqueducts to transport water to cities. Their infrastructure allowed cities to support more residents than ever before.
- Improvements in cement and concrete and the use of the arch allowed Rome to build massive structures like the Colosseum, where they held spectacles like gladiatorial combat.
- Romans spoke and wrote Latin with an alphabet adapted from the Greek alphabet. Latin is the basis for many modern languages today.
- The Republic fell apart when Rome became divided into two factions who constantly fought one another and when dictators, who were only supposed to rule for six months at a time, began to hold absolute power for life.
- Julius Caesar was the last dictator of Rome. After his assassination, his nephew, Octavian, became the first emperor of Rome in 27 BCE. He would be known by the honorary title Augustus.
- Rome's Imperial Period began with 200 years of peace and prosperity called the *Pax Romana*. After that, weak and inept emperors, a plague, and increasing violence and chaos within the government began to cause a decline in the empire.
- After years of near anarchy, the empire was split between the Western Roman Empire with its capital in Rome, and the Eastern Roman Empire, which became the Byzantine Empire, with its capital in Byzantium.
- Emperor Constantine laid the groundwork for Christianity to flourish and eventually become the state religion of Rome. He officially changed the name of Byzantium to Constantinople. Today, this is the city of Istanbul.
- After Constantine, the Western Roman Empire continued to decline, plagued by invasions from barbarian tribes, a poor economy, and continued chaos within the government.
- In 476 CE, the last emperor, Romulus Augustulus, was deposed, ending the Roman Empire and ushering in the Middle Ages.

Conclusion

Thank you for trekking with us through ancient times in Mesopotamia and the Mediterranean region! Hopefully, you've had fun learning new facts and definitions and trying a few activities. But we hope you've witnessed first-hand how fascinating and *alive* history really is.

We started this book by telling you a few reasons why it's important to study history. American novelist Pearl Buck once said, "If you want to understand today, you have to search yesterday." This is definitely one of those reasons! Now, we are more informed about the world around us and how it came to be what it is—like where so many of our words come from, how our planets got their names, and why purple is the color of kings, just to name a few things. So which throw-back to ancient history most surprised you?

We told you how studying history helps us foresee where our civilization might be headed and even possibly control that for the future good. History often repeats itself. The same causes tend to lead to the same effects. Now, we better understand the arch that civilizations take as they rise, flourish, and decline. We also see how civilizations can reverse course and prosper after a tough time, as the Romans did during the *Pax Romana.* Are there any elements of rise or decline that you see in the world around you today?

We told you how studying history could be personally inspiring by reading the real stories of real people. Then, we saw clever young Alexander tame his horse Bucephalus, Spartacus lead his fellow slaves to freedom, and Socrates condemned to death for daring to be different. Who was your favorite, and how will they inspire you?

We told you that history deepens our appreciation of diversity. We hope you've seen how drastically different people from different cultures, races, and time periods have contributed to our collective culture and knowledge. Which civilization most surprised you with its advanced technology, knowledge, and sophistication?

We also said that knowing our history lets us participate fully in our society because we are well-informed and educated citizens. As you reflect on the early days of Greek democracy and the Roman Republic, do you have a greater appreciation of what it means to vote and have a public voice?

Finally, and most importantly, we told you that history is *your* story. When you think about the unbroken chain of history that connects you with these people and their civilizations, do you feel a part of it all? You should! The history books never really end. New pages just get added. What will you write on yours?

"... [W]hat is the worth of human life unless it is woven into the life of our ancestors by the records of history?"

— Marcus Tullius Cicero, Roman Statesman

Index

Printed in Great Britain
by Amazon

20814498R00122